Julie C. Hulse
Cockermouth

LITERARY LONDON

A guide to

LITERARY LONDON

Eric Lane

DEDALUS/HIPPOCRENE BOOKS

Published in the U.K. by Dedalus Ltd.
Langford Lodge, St. Judith's Lane, Sawtry, Cambridgeshire
PE17 5XE.

Published in the USA by Hippocrene Books Inc, 171 Madison Avenue, New York NY10016

ISBN 0946626 34 0

Copyright © Eric Lane

Printed by The City Printing Works (Chester-le-Street) Ltd., Broadwood View, Chester-le-Street, Co. Durham DH3 3NJ.

This book is sold subject to the condition that it shall not, by way of trade or otherwise be lent, re-sold or hired out or otherwise circulated without the publishers prior consent in any form of binding or cover other than that in which it is published and without a similar condition including this condition being imposed on the subsequent purchaser.

British Library Cataloguing in Publication Data

Lane, Eric
A guide to Literary London
I. London. Literary Association. Visitors' guides
I. Title
914.2104 858

ISBN 0 946626 34 0

Acknowledgements

I would like to acknowledge the help I received from the staff of the British Museum's Reading Room, the London Library and the Guildhall Library and to say thank you to Katrine Prince, Oswald Clark, Marilyn Whensley and Helen Tozer of the London Tourist Board for shaping my view of London.

The sources I have used are acknowledged either in the text or in the bibliography, but I would like to express my gratitude to Christopher Hibbert whose many books dealing with London have been particularly useful and to Margaret Drabble for the timely arrival of her edition of the Oxford Companion to English Literature.

I would like to thank the following publishers for permission to use material still in copyright: The estate of the Late Sonia Brownell Orwell and Secker & Warburg Ltd, Hamish Hamilton, The Grove Press, Penguin Books Ltd, Jonathan Cape Ltd and Faber & Faber.

To Marie, Anthony and Timothy

T.S. Eliot (1888-1964)

LIST OF CONTENTS

		page
1.	Bloomsbury	1
2.	The British Museum	9
3.	The Inns of Court	40
4.	Gray's Inn and surrounding area	42
5.	Red Lion Square	54
6.	Lincoln's Inn Fields	64
7.	The Strand	75
8.	Middle Temple	82
9.	Inner Temple	94
10.	The City of London	100
11.	Fleet Street	101
12.	St Bride's and surrounding area	111
13.	The Public Records Office	123
14.	Lincoln's Inn and Holborn	126
15.	Clerkenwell	147
16.	The Barbican	157
17.	St Giles Without Cripplegate	159
18.	Charterhouse Square	161
19.	Smithfield	168
20.	Cheapside	194
21.	The Guildhall	202
22.	Moorgate	208
23.	The Theatre and Shoreditch	223
24.	The Tower	251
25.	The Great Fire	262
26.	London Bridge	264
27	Southwark	267
28.	St Paul's Cathedral	285
29.	Bibliography	295
30.	Index of authors	301

LIST OF ILLUSTRATIONS

The 28 portraits of famous authors are from The National Portrait Gallery — London, the pictures of The Death of Chatterton by Richard Wallis, Proserpine by Dante Gabriel Rossetti, Ophelia by Sir John Everett Millais and Elohim creating Adam by William Blake are from The Tate Gallery — London, John Stow's monument is from the Guildhall Library and the photos of London are by Marie Lane.

		page
1.	University College Hospital	3
2.	The frieze on the RADA building	4
3.	Bust of Sir Hans Sloane	11
4.	Thomas Hardy	12
5.	Senate House	17
6.	William Makepeace Thackeray	18
7.	Virginia Woolf	23
8.	Giles Lytton Strachey	24
9.	Woburn Walk	29
10.	Charles Dickens and his daughters	30
11.	Statue of Sir Francis Bacon in Gray's Inn	43
12.	Sir Francis Bacon	44
13.	Algernon Charles Swinburne	49
14.	The Death of Chatterton by Richard Wallis	50
15.	Bertrand Russell	55
16.	Bust of Bertrand Russell in Red Lion Square	56
17,	Proserpine by Dante Gabriel Rossetti	59
18.	Ophelia by Sir John Everett Millais	60
19.	Statue of Dr Samuel Johnson behind St Clement Danes in The Strand	71
20.	Dr Samuel Johnson	72
21.	The Royal Courts of Justice in The Strand	79
22.	James Boswell	80
23.	Sir Walter Ralegh and his son	87
24.	The Temple Church	88
25.	Samuel Pepys	107
26.	John Dryden	108
27.	Lincoln's Inn Chapel's Undercroft	127

28.	The Gateway of Lincoln's Inn	128
29.	The courtyard of Staple Inn	135
30.	Entrance to St Andrew's Holborn	136
31.	The Charterhouse	163
32.	A courtyard in the Charterhouse	164
33.	Entrance to St Bartholomew's Smithfield	171
34.	Period houses in Cloth Fair Smithfield	172
35.	Bust of Charles Lamb at Holy Sepulchre's Newgate	175
36.	Statue of gluttony at Cock Lane	176
37.	Oscar Wilde	187
38.	Samuel Taylor Coleridge	188
39.	John Donne	199
40.	John Milton	200
41.	Henry Howard, Earl of Surrey	203
42.	The Guildhall	204
43.	John Keats	209
44.	Leigh Hunt	210
45.	John Bunyan	215
46.	Elohim creating Adam by William Blake	216
47.	William Shakespeare	225
48.	Ben Jonson	226
49.	Alexander Pope	241
50.	The Bronte sisters	242
51.	The monument in St Andrew Undershaft Church of John Stow	245
52.	Geoffrey Chaucer	246
53.	Sir Philip Sidney	293
54.	Sir John Soane's Museum	299
55.	T.S. Eliot	*frontispiece*

BLOOMSBURY

Bloomsbury is the intellectual centre of London. Its once refined and fashionable squares are now dominated by the ever expanding needs of London University and the British Museum. There is still a cluster of publishers, including the country's newest publisher, the Bloomsbury Press, and a whole area of specialist bookshops around the British Museum.

Bloomsbury developed in the late 17th century on the lands of the Southampton family (descendants of Henry Wriothesley, Earl of Southampton, Shakespeare's patron) giving London its first open space to be called a square in 1660. London was expanding rapidly in the west and the gentry made fortunes as property speculators, building fine homes round private gardens for the upper classes. With the intermarriage of the Southampton and Bedford families, the squares of the two families merged to form what is now Bloomsbury.

Beginning in **GOWER STREET** (near Euston Square Tube Station) we have the classical facade of University College, built in the 1820s by Wilkins, the architect of the National Gallery. It was the first college to be founded of London University. Inspired by the utilitarian philosophy of Jeremy Bentham and James Mill it opened up university education to non Anglicans, unlike the existing universities of Oxford and Cambridge who debarred all except members of the Church of England. Its most famous exhibit is the fully clothed skeleton of Jeremy Bentham, which the philosopher bequeathed to the college at his death. It is kept in a brown cabinet, with the philosopher's name on, and will be opened on request. Former students include the novelist and critic, **David Lodge** (1935-) the author of **Changing Places** (1975) **How Far Can You Go** (1980) and the masterly, **Small World** (1984). His novels deal with university life and the problems of being a catholic in the modern world and are normally comic in tone.

In 1935 a postgraduate student at the Psychology

Department, Rosalind Obermeyer helped her lodger, George Orwell, give a party at her house in Parliament Hill and brought along a fellow student, Eileen O'Shaughnessy to help make up the numbers. Eileen and the young novelist took an instant liking to each other and married the following year. Eileen died in March 1945 and George Orwell remarried in the last few months of his life when he was a patient in University College Hospital, the red brick building across Gower Street. His doctor, Andrew Morland, who treated D.H. Lawrence during his last illness, was a consultant at the hospital. Orwell arrived on 3 September 1949 and paid £17 a week for a private room. He married Sonia Brownwell in a bedside ceremony on October 13 and was too ill to attend the wedding lunch at the Ritz. He was given the signed menu instead. It was decided that Orwell would benefit from treatment in a Swiss sanatorium and as part of his preparation for the journey made a new will on 18 January, making Sonia his sole beneficiary, and providing for Richard, his adopted son, still only a small boy. He also expressed a wish to be buried according to the rites of the Church of England. He died a few days later, 21 January 1950 from a lung haemorrhage. His funeral service took place in Christ Church, Albany Street (near Regents Park) and he was buried in the churchyard of All Saints, Sutton Courtenay. An obituary described Orwell as "the wintery conscience of a generation" a man "with the independence of Swift mixed up with the humility of Oliver Goldsmith." Orwell who was only 46 when he died spent most of his life in genteel poverty but as the author of **Animal Farm** (1945) and **1984** (1948) he bequeathed a fortune to his 31 year old widow, Sonia Brownwell, the Venus of Euston Road. (She was Cyril Connolly's secretary at Horizon, whose offices were in Euston Road).

Further up on the left a blue plaque commemorates the residence of **Charles Darwin** (1809-82) author of **The Origin of the Species,** whose writing had a profound effect on 19th century literature, especially Thomas Hardy. More recently it has given us the preface of Robert Irwin's novel, **The Limits of Vision.**

Dillon's University Bookshop, now owned by the Birmingham based bookshop chain of Pentos, dominates

University College Hospital in Gower Street

The frieze on the RADA building in Gower Street

the corner of Malet Street, and is one of London's best stocked bookshops. The frieze on the RADA building enlivens a very dull and grimy street, chock-a-block with one way traffic.

Senate House is visible further on at the bottom of Keppel Street. Built in the 1930s it houses the library and administration of London University. For the London of the 1930s it was a Manhattan skyscraper, with an imposing if sinister appearance. George Orwell in **1984** modelled the physical appearance of the ministries on Senate House, and made it the setting for his Ministry of Truth.

> *"The Ministry of Truth – Minitrue in Newspeak – was startingly different from any other object in sight. It was an enormous pyramidal structure of glittering white concrete, soaring up, terrace after terrace, three hundred metres in the air. It was too strong, it could not be stormed. A thousand rocket bombs would not batter it down."*

Graham Greene, worked in Senate House during World War II, when it served as the Ministry of Information. He nicknamed the building the 'Bloomsbury lighthouse' as it was illuminated at night while the rest of London was blacked out during the war.

KEPPEL STREET is where the novelist **Anthony Trollope** was born in 1815. His family moved shortly after to Harrow, where he attended the public school, and later when his father was in America, he was a pupil of Winchester School. Trollope's schooldays were unhappy because of his lack of money and shabby clothes which earned him the derision of his fellow pupils.

Further down we pass the splendour of **Bedford Square,** where the publishers Jonathan Cape, Bodley Head and Chatto share an office. They are now part of Random House, a large American publishing corporation. Jonathan Cape has established itself as the premier literary publishing house in England. Its authors include Salman Rushdie, Julian Barnes, Ian McEwan, Martin Amis and Clive James, the very best of the younger generation of British writers. Cape also publishes Marcia Marquez, Singer and John Fowles. What established Jonathan Cape was the success of T.E. Lawrence's **The Seven Pillars of Wisdom** (1935), which was an outstanding bestseller, as were for Cape Ian Flemings' James Bond novels in the 1950s and 60s. In 1945 Jonathan Cape made its most spectacular publishing error, turning down a novel from the already well established novelist, George Orwell, **Animal Farm**. In their rejection letter to Orwell's agent Cape wrote:

> *". . . My reading of the manuscript gave me considerable personal enjoyment and satisfaction, but I can see now that it might be regarded as something which it was highly ill-advised to publish at the present time. If the fable were addressed generally to dictators and dictatorship at large then publication would be all right, but the fable does follow, as I see now, so completely the progress and development of the Russian Soviets and their two dictators, that it can apply only to Russia, to the exclusion of other dictatorships. Another thing: it would be less offensive if the predominate caste in the fable were not pigs. I think the choice of pigs as the ruling caste will no doubt give offence to many people, and particularly to anyone who is a bit touchy, as undoubtedly the Russians are . . . I think it is best to send back to you the typescript of ANIMAL FARM and let the matter lie on the table as far as we are concerned."*

To the suggestion that he use some other animals rather than pigs Orwell commented in the margin of the letter, "balls."

Bodley Head's main author in recent years has been **Graham Greene** (1904-   ) the author of **Power and Glory** (1940), **The Heart of the Matter** (1948) and many successful entertainments and thrillers. Nearly all his novels have been filmed. Bodley Head was fortunate to be the publisher of James Joyce's **Ulysses** (1936) its most prestigious and lucrative publication.

The Cape group used to include the feminist publishers Virago, but they bought their freedom to avoid becoming part of Random House.

The London Office of Yale University Press is at no 17, their list includes biographies of Dryden and Pope. The Publishers Association is at no 19, and Hodder and Stoughton, Heinemann Educational and British Museum Publications have their offices in the square.

For a time the lawyer and novelist **Anthony Hope** (1863-1933) who wrote the **Prisoner of Zenda** lived at no 41. The square although no longer residential, still retains its Georgian style, with the garden in its centre still private. The London Review of Books was here until recently, but it is now lost in the gloom of Tavistock House.

At no 12 Gower Street **Ottoline Morrell** (1873-1938) used to live. From an aristocratic family and married to a Liberal MP she entertained a wide circle of politicians and writers at her soirées at Gower Street and at her country home of Garsington Manor. Her circle included at various times, Henry James, Lytton Strachey, Bertrand Russell, Virginia Woolf, T.S. Eliot, D.H. Lawrence and Aldous Huxley. She was tall with a rather startling appearance and extravagance of manner, which led to her being parodied by some of her protegées. In D.H. Lawrence's novel, **Women in Love,** she is easily recognisable as Hermione Roddice, with her sing song voice. She was deeply offended by this portrait and considered suing Lawrence for libel. She was equally unhappy with Aldous Huxley's portrait of her in **Crome Yellow.** Her generosity to her friends and protegées was remarkable. She sometimes overawed her guests, making them feel ill at ease. When Bertrand Russell introduced her to a young American poet and philosopher, T.S. Eliot, she found him "dull, dull, dull. He never moves his lips but speaks in a mandarin voice. I think he has lost all spontaneity and can only break through his conventionality by stimulants or violent emotion." Later Eliot was able to overcome his nervous stiffness with Ottoline Morrell, and they enjoyed a long and turbulent friendship.

Her **Memoirs** were published posthumously, in 1963 and the second volume in 1974.

The street changes its name to Bloomsbury Street, and at no 30-34 Thames and Hudson, the art book publishers, have their offices. Their list contains a good introductory series of Literary Lives. Left into **GREAT RUSSELL STREET,** where a blue plaque outside the Good Book Guide Bookshop records the residence of the novelist **George du Maurier** (1834-96) the grandfather of the more famous Daphne. He is best known for his novel **Trilby** (1894) which features the musician with hypnotic power, Svengali. Trilby O'Ferrall's hat, a soft felt one with an indented crown, gave rise to the term 'trilby'. Next door at No. 93 are the offices of Ben Weinreb's Architectural Book Company, with a bookshop in the nearby Museum Street. Ben Weinreb, along with Christopher Hibbert, is the editor of the **London Encyclopaedia** (1983), which is the best all purpose reference book on London, an indispensable companion for anyone fascinated with London past or present.

The iron railings on the left introduce us to the largest classical facade in Great Britain, that of the British Museum: the museum of antiquities.

THE BRITISH MUSEUM

An act of parliament in 1753 authorized the purchase of Sir Hans Sloane's collection of antiquities and the Harleian manuscripts; it provided that a building should be purchased to house them and the Cotton collection which the nation already owned. The money was raised by a public lottery, with the winning tickets being drawn in the Jerusalem Chamber of Westminster Abbey. The British Museum was opened on a limited basis to the public on the 15 of January 1759. Unlimited access to the museum was only permitted to the public in 1879. George II presented in 1757 the Royal Library's 10,500 volumes (built up by British Monarchs from Henry VIII to Charles II), a gift which brought with it the privilege of receiving a copy of every book registered at Stationers Hall. This privilege was enshrined in the Copyright Act of 1911.

The Lansdowne manuscripts containing State papers and the correspondence of prominent figures from the time of Henry VI until George III were added to the museum's treasures in 1807. The bequest in 1823 by George IV of his father's library of 12,800 volumes led to the British Museum being rebuilt, as it was by then far too small.

The present building, built in stages by Robert Smirke from 1823 to 1847 is the largest classical building in Great Britain. Even so more space was soon required and so the courtyard was converted into a domed Reading Room between 1852 and 1857, following the plan of the librarian Sir Arthur Panizzi, Sydney Smirke being the architect.

The Reading Room has been used by Thomas Carlyle, G.B. Shaw, Lenin and Karl Marx, with many like Charles Dickens having used it to supplement their meagre formal education. Thomas Hardy spent several years researching his last major work **The Dynasts** here. Another user George Gissing gives a very bleak description of the domed, circular Reading Room and the futility of making books out of other people's books in his novel **New Grub Street**. (Chapter 8.)

"... she (Marian Yule) looked up at the windows beneath the dome and saw that they were a dusky yellow. Then her eye discerned an official walking along the upper gallery, and in pursuance of her grotesque humour, her mocking misery, she likened him to a black, lost soul, doomed to wander in an eternity of vain research amongst endless shelves. Or again, the readers who sat here at these radiating lines of desks, what were they but helpless flies caught in a huge web, its nucleus the great circle of the Catalogue? Darker, darker. From the towering wall of volumes seemed to emanate visible motes, intensifying the obscurity; in a moment the book-lined circumference of the room would be but a featureless prison-limit."

A more lighthearted look is provided by David Lodge's 1961 novel, **The British Museum is Falling Down**. In Lodge's novel there is a masterly pastiche of the writing styles of novelists from Jane Austen to James Joyce.

In the 1950s, the novelist and short story writer **Angus Wilson** was the deputy-superintendent of the Reading Room. He had the practice of introducing readers to each other who were researching the same subject, not always with happy consequences. In 1954 he befriended a young man who was using the Reading Room to write a novel, **Ritual in the Dark**, based on Jack the Ripper. Wilson took the manuscript home to read over the Christmas holidays, promising to recommend it to his publisher if he liked it. While waiting for Angus Wilson's decision **Colin Wilson** began his study of alienation, **The Outsider**, which he wrote in the Reading Room. It was published by Gollancz, while Wilson was still only 24 and is dedicated to Angus Wilson. **Colin Wilson** (1931 -   ) has produced many non-fiction books and novels since, but only the **Occult**, has shared the success of his first book.

Angus Wilson (1913-   ) gave up his post at the Reading Room in 1955 to concentrate on his writing. One of his most interesting novels, **Anglo-Saxon Attitudes** appeared the next year. His most ambitious novel is, **No Laughing Matter** (1967) a family saga, covering fifty years in the life of the Mathews family. His most brilliant works are his first collections of short stories, **The Wrong Set** (1949) and **Such Darling Dodos** (1950). He has also written on **Zola** (1950), **Dickens**, (1970) and **Kipling**, (1977). In 1963 he began teaching at the then new univer-

Bust of Sir Hans Sloane in the British Museum

Thomas Hardy (1840-1928)

sity of East Anglia, becoming the Professor of English Literature in 1966. He now lives in France.

From 1875 to 1884, **Richard Garnett** (1835-1906) was the superintendent of the Reading Room, before becoming the editor of the library's first printed catalogue. His erudition became legendary within the British Museum. He was a poet, a translator and a biographer and edited many works, including **Relics of Shelley** (1862). His best known book, is a collection of pagan tales, **The Twilight of the Gods** (1888).

Garnett's father (another Richard) also worked in the British Museum, and was from 1838, the assistant keeper of printed books. He founded the Philologist Society and was an expert on Celtic subjects.

The poet, playwright and art critic **Laurence Binyon** (1869-1943) worked in the printed books department, and from 1913 to 1933 was in charge of Oriental prints and paintings. He left to become the Norton professor of poetry at Harvard. As a poet he is best known for his **Odes** (1901), and his much anthologised, **For the Fallen:**

> "They shall not grow old, as we that are left grow old:
> Age shall not weary them, nor the years condemn.
> At the going down of the sun and in the morning
> We will remember them".

It was set to music by Elgar, who also set his play, **Arthur** (1923) to music. **The Fallen,** was first published in the Times on 21 September 1914, and lines from it are carved on the wall at the entrance to the museum as a war memorial to the staff.

To use the Reading Room one needs a reader's ticket, but it is possible on the hour to be shown round in a group by a member of staff. In 1973 the Reading Room became part of the British Library and will be moving away from its domed splendour to a building near Kings Cross, which is currently being constructed, and is estimated should be ready in 1991. The library owns two and a half million volumes and periodicals and needs a further two miles of shelving each year to keep pace with the increase in its stock.

The Manuscript and Document Galleries of the British Museum contain the manuscript of **Beowulf** (1100), the **Winchester Psalter** (1060), the 11th century **Anglo-**

Saxon Chronicles, a 15th century manuscript of Malory's **Morte D'Arthur,** which predates Caxton's edition, and the **Canterbury Tales.** There is also a **First Folio** edition of Shakespeare's plays (1623). It was produced seven years after Shakespeare's death by two of his fellow actors, Condell and Hemmings, and contains a preface by his illustrious colleague Ben Jonson. Without this edition it is interesting to speculate how much of Shakespeare's work would have come down to us and in what form, as twenty years later the Puritans closed the theatres, and when the Restoration came Shakespeare went out of fashion until the 18th century and the revivals of David Garrick. It was Garrick who commissioned and paid for the **Roubiliac** statue of Shakespeare next to the **First Folio** in the gallery.

The exhibits in the British Museum have been a source of wonder and inspiration for countless artists, with the Elgin Marbles producing from Keats a sonnet, *"Mortality,/Weighs heavily on me like unwilling sleep"* and inspiring an "Ode on a Grecian Urn."

The poet **W.H. Davies** (1871-1940) lived at 14 Great Russell Street in 1916-22. As a young man he went to seek his fortune in America, and spent several years on the road. He recounted his experiences, in his best known book, **The Autobiography of a Super-Tramp** (1908) which had a preface by G.B. Shaw. His **Complete Poems,** with an introduction by O. Sitwell appeared in 1980, and his extraordinary courtship of a young girl, whom he married when he was 52, is told in **Young Emma** (1980).

At the end of the street is **BLOOMSBURY SQUARE.** Bloomsbury Square was London's first open space to be called a square (1660) and was originally called Southampton Square, after the landowners, the earls of Southampton, serving as a model for many of the fashionable Bloomsbury and West End squares. The diarist John Evelyn thought it, "noble." The Irish playwright and essayist, **Richard Steele** (1672-1729) lived here, while it was still at the height of fashion, from 1712 to 1715. He is best remembered for the two magazines he founded with Addison, **The Tatler** (1709-11), and **The Spectator** (1711-12). His best work was the social and moral essays he wrote for The Tatler. The 18th c was the period of the magazine and the newspaper with a great increase in literacy widening the potential readership. (The first newspaper, The Daily Courant, was printed in Fleet Street in 1702.) As a supporter of the Hanoverian succession Steele received a knighthood in 1715 and political office under George I. For a period he was a member of parliament.

In the 19th c the square was less fashionable when the literary historian **Isaac Disraeli** (1776-1848) lived here, with his family, from 1817 to 1829. He published the six volume, **Curiosities of Literature** (1791-1834). More interesting is his, **The Literary Character** (1795), in which he attempts to identify the qualities of temperament common to creative writers. Lord Byron admired this book greatly. He also wrote a five volume study of **The Life and Reign of Charles I** (1828-30). Disraeli is best remembered as the father of **Benjamin Disraeli** (1804-81), the author of popular novels and a Conservative Prime Minister.

The square is now dominated by the institutions of London University and in the garden there is a statue of the 18th century politician, Charles James Fox, by Westmacott. Fox a great orator was a member of Dr Johnson's Literary Club, but rarely had much to say in front of the formidable doctor. Gibbon remarked "that Mr Fox could not be afraid of Dr Johnson; yet he certainly was very shy of saying anything in Dr Johnson's presence." Fox was a politician at the time of the Gordon Riots (1780), the last major riots in Central London, which Dickens took as the subject matter of his much neglected historical novel, **Barnaby Rudge**. Its hero, the half-wit Barnaby Rudge was to be hanged in Bloomsbury Square for his part in the riots, in front of the house of Lord Chief Justice Mansfield, which was burnt and sacked by the rioters. Dickens achieves a happy ending with Barnaby being pardoned. Two of the ringleaders of the riot, Charles King and John Gray, were actually hung outside of what was left of the Lord Chief Justice's house.

Other writers to have lived in the square, were the Newcastle poet **Mark Akenside** in 1750-9, and the dramatist and friend of Dryden, **Charles Sedley** in 1691-1701.

From Great Russell Street, left into **BEDFORD PLACE**. Shortly after it was built in 1805, the playwright and novelist, **Richard Cumberland** (1732-1811) lived in the street. During his lifetime he was best known for his very successful sentimental comedies, **The Brothers** (1769), and **The West Indian**, which was produced by Garrick in 1771. Today he is best remembered as Sir Fretful Plagiary, his caricature in Sheridan's play, **The Critic** (1779).

Most of the street's remaining late Georgian houses are now hotels or hostels. When **T.S. Eliot** first arrived in London in August 1914, he had lodgings at no. 28. A postgraduate student from Harvard he went up to study briefly at Oxford. While in London he went and saw his fellow American poet, Ezra Pound in Holland Park. Pound thought Eliot's early verse, including **Prufrock**, was "as good as anything I've seen," and helped to champion his work in England and America.

Into **RUSSELL SQUARE**, one of London's largest squares, laid out in 1800 by Repton, and named after the landowners, the Russells, Dukes of Bedford. From the beginning it was much favoured by lawyers and professional men. The upper classes now favoured the more fashionable West End. These social differences are admirably reflected in Thackeray's novel of London society, **Vanity Fair** (1847-8). The prosperous City families of the Osbornes (at no 96) and the Sedleys (at no 62) lived in the square, while the aristocratic Miss Crawley had a house in Park Lane and the very rich resided in Gaunt Square (Berkeley Square). Becky Sharp came to visit Amelia Sedley and charmed her brother Jos during a visit to Vauxhall Gardens into almost proposing, but the bell for the fireworks and the strength of the rack punch thwarted Becky's schemes.

In 1925 the publishers Gwyer and Faber were founded (now Faber & Faber) and they had their offices at no 24. Geoffrey Faber was looking for a literary adviser, and when the journalist Charles Whibley introduced him to **T.S. Eliot** in 1925, he was so impressed and charmed by the poet that he made him a director of the new company. This job meant that Eliot could give up his job with Lloyd's Bank, for whom he had worked since 1917. At last

Senate House photographed from Russell Square

William Makepeace Thackcray (1811-63)

Eliot had a secure job which allowed him to concentrate on his writing. He published the work of writers he admired like James Joyce, Ezra Pound, Wyndham Lewis and later Auden, Spender, MacNeice, George Barker, Vernon Watkins, Ted Hughes and Thomas Gunn. With his very strong convictions Eliot was able to shape the literary tastes of a generation and turned Faber into the most important publisher of twentieth century poetry in England. A position it still has to a lesser degree today. One of his most felicitious publishing decisions was to offer an advance of £300 in July 1931 to publish James Joyce's **Finnegan's Wake**. Like all publishers Eliot had his share of turning down work which he ought to have published. He recognised the merit of George Orwell's first novel, **Down and Out in Paris and London**, but politely rejected it, as he did with less justification **Animal Farm**. Following on from Gollancz and Jonathan Cape, Eliot rejected Animal Farm in a letter of the 13 July 1944.

> *"We agree that it is a distinguished piece of writing; the fable is very skilfully handled, and that the narrative keeps one's interest on its own plane – and that is something very few authors have achieved since Gulliver.*
>
> *On the other hand, we have no conviction that this is the right point of view from which to criticize the political situation at the present time. It is certainly the duty of any publishing firm which pretends to other interests and motives than mere commercial prosperity, to publish books which go against the current of the moment; but in each instance that demands that at least one member of the firm should have the conviction that this is the thing that needs saying at the moment. I can't see any reason of prudence or caution to prevent anybody from publishing this book – if he believed in what it stands for."*

After stating that the book was too negative, only against and not pro anything Eliot expresses his regret, as he had high regard for Orwell's work, "because it is good writing of fundamental integrity."

Orwell, who was ready to publish the book himself as a 2 shilling pamphlet, tried the small publishing house of Secker and Warburg, nicknamed in those days, "the Trotskyite publisher", who published it in 1945.

Eliot also turned down the poems of a young musician, **Anthony Burgess**, but marked three poems as good.

Later as a novelist, Burgess interspersed his fiction with poems and wrote a trilogy about the unsuccessful poet Enderby, and a verse epic, **Moses**.

Much to the annoyance of Virginia Woolf, Eliot transferred his own work to Faber, and when they published an edition of his poetry, including **The Waste Land**, which she had published in the Hogarth Press, she called Eliot shifty.

Eliot separated from his first wife Vivien in 1931, and years later she would come in search of Eliot to the Russell Square offices, only to find that he was always out. Eliot would even disappear down the fire escape to avoid being confronted with Vivien. In 1948, the same year that he won the Nobel Prize for Literature, Valerie Fletcher started working for him as his secretary, eight years later Eliot proposed and they married in St Barnabas Church, Kensington. Eliot was 68, Valerie was only 30.

During the war Eliot lived outside London in Shamley Green. He would spend three days a week in London, staying in the flat above the Faber office, where as part of the war effort he would go up to the roof during the evenings on fire duty. Faber & Faber's offices are now on the other side of Bloomsbury in Queen's Square.

The lawyer and diarist **Henry Crabb Robinson** (1775-1867) lived at no 30 (gone), from 1839 until his death in 1867. It is from his letters and diaries that we get a lot of our information about the literary events of his day. He was a friend of Wordsworth, Coleridge, Lamb, Hazlitt and Carlyle. Robinson participated in the founding of the Athenaeum Club and London University College.

Mary Russell Mitford (1787-1855) lived at no 56. She turned to writing when forced to earn her own living by her father's extravagance and gambling. She had several successful plays, mainly on historical subjects such as **Rienzi** (1826) but they quickly went out of fashion and she is best remembered for her series of sketches of country life, grouped together in 1832 under the title of **Our Village**. Her letters to Lamb, Ruskin, Elizabeth Barrett, Browning, Landor and Haydon were published posthumously in 1870. In 1836 she writes of one of her literary dinner parties in Russell Square:

> *"Mr Wordsworth, Mr Landor and Mr White dined here. I like Mr Wordsworth, of all things, Mr Landor is very striking-looking and exceedingly clever. Also we had a Mr Browning, a young poet, . . . and quantities more of poets."*

The novelist, **Mrs Humphry Ward** (1851-1920) lived with her husband at no 61 from 1861 to 1891. She inherited the strong moral purpose of her grandfather, Thomas Arnold of Rugby School, and her father, Thomas Arnold, the schools inspector. She wrote a very succesful novel, **Robert Elsmere**, which combines a vivid evocation of the Oxford of Pater, Pattison and T.H. Green with a debate on all the many varieties of religious faith which flourished after the ferment of the Oxford Movement. The novel's hero gives up his holy orders to follow a life of social service in London's East End, much to the distress of his family. The Prime Minister Gladstone even reviewed the book. She wrote many other novels on similar social themes. **A Writer's Recollection** (1918) gives a fascinating picture of Oxford life (her husband was an Oxford don) and of the domestic influence of William Morris, Burne Jones, and Liberty prints; with portraits of Jowett, the legendary master of Balliol College, Pater, Henry James and other friends.

Before the square was laid out in its present form and was an exclusive residential area with an uninterrupted view of Hampstead Heath the poet **Thomas Gray** (1716-71) had lodgings here, where the Imperial Hotel now stands. He is best known for his **Elegy written in a Country Church-Yard** (1751). In a letter to Horace Walpole in February 1768 he gives encouragement to would-be authors. *"Any fool may write a most valuable book by chance, if he will only tell us what he heard and saw with veracity."*

William Cowper (1731-1800) while reading law had lodgings at no 62 in the 1750s. He is best known for his hymns and his long poem, **John Gilpin** (1785). This comic ballad tells of a linen draper's ride on an unruly horse from Cheapside to Edmonton, where the horse fails to stop at the Bell Inn and carries poor Gilpin on to Ware:

> *"John Gilpin was a citizen
> Of credit and renown,*

> *A train-band captain eke was he*
> *Of famous London town."*

Bedford Way leads from Russell Square to Gordon Square.

BEDFORD WAY. The physician and scholar **Dr Roget** lived at no 18 from 1843 until his death in 1869 (the street was then known as Upper Bedford Place). His **Thesaurus of English Words and Phrases** was published in 1852 and has been edited by the Roget family until 1953, when Dr Roget's grandson, Samuel Romilly Roget died. The present editor is Susan M. Lloyd. It has been an invaluable aide to writers and poets ever since. When the critic David Holbrook was studying Dylan Thomas' worksheets for **Poem on his birthday**, he was greatly dismayed to find that the scribbled numbers, 223, 161 and 424 alongside a list of synonyms referred to pages in Roget's Thesaurus.

Stewart Headlam lived at no 31 and on May 19 1897 he and More Adey met **Oscar Wilde** on his release from Pentonville Prison at 6.15 a.m. and took him by cab to Headlam's home. Wilde was visited by his friends here including Ada and Ernest Leverson, who tell how Wilde broke into tears when a letter arrived refusing him a place at a Retreat. In the afternoon Wilde went down to Newhaven where he took the night boat to Dieppe, where he took up residence at the Hotel Sandwich under the name of Sebastian Melmoth.

GORDON SQUARE.

This late Georgian square is now dominated by the institutions of London University. In the south east corner there is the university church of Christ the King, a most attractive 19th c Gothic Revival church. Adjacent is Dr Williams Library (at no 41). This religious library has over 130,000 volumes, and was formed when Daniel Williams, a prominent Presbyterian minister, left his library and his estate to a charitable trust in 1716. It has been housed in the Unitarian University Hall in Gordon Square since 1890. It contains 2,000 items from the library of G. Lewes and George Eliot, which Lewes' son presented in 1882.

Across the square at no 46, **Virginia Woolf** (1882-

Virginia Woolf (1882-1941)

Giles Lytton Strachey (1880-1932)

1941) lived from 1905. She was the daughter of **Sir Leslie Stephen** (1832-1904) and his second wife, Julia Duckworth. His first wife, Minny, was one of Thackeray's daughters, and he succeeded the novelist as the editor of the Cornhill Magazine, and was regarded as one of the leading intellectuals of his day. He was a very perceptive editor, and many writers, especially Thomas Hardy benefitted from his editing skills. He was the editor of the **Dictionary of National Biography** and an important critic. Virginia Woolf gives a good account of her father and their summers spent in Cornwall in her novel, **To the Lighthouse** (1927), another interesting portrait is in Meredith's novel, **The Egoist** where he is "a Phoebus Apollo turned fasting friar." Virginia was born at her parents house at 22 Hyde Park Gate in Kensington (blue plaque) in 1882. When her father died in 1904 (her mother had already died in 1895) she moved with her brothers and sister to Gordon Square, which was then an unfashionable and not very respectable part of middle class London. The Stephen family and their friends became the nucleus of what became known as the Bloomsbury Group. Most of the group had been up at Cambridge at the same time and were greatly influenced by the Cambridge don, G.E. Moore's philosophy, which put the emphasis on "the pleasures of human intercourse and the enjoyment of beautiful objects", expounded in his book **Principia Ethica** (1903). The circle of the Stephen family included, **Leonard Woolf** (who married Virginia in 1912), **Clive Bell,** (who married Vanessa Stephen in 1907), **Lytton Strachey, Maynard Keynes, Duncan Grant** and **E.M. Forster,** and with fringe members like **T.S. Eliot.** There was a regular, "Thursday evening" at the house, and by 1907 there were regular Friday evenings of readings from the work of Shakespeare, the Restoration dramatists, Swinburne and Ibsen amongst others. When Vanessa and Clive Bell married in 1907, Virginia and her brother Adrian left them the Gordon Square house and went to live at 39 Fitzroy Square (plaque), in the same house that George Bernard Shaw lived in from 1887 to 1898, not very far away in Soho (even a less reputable area than Bloomsbury).

The Bloomsbury Group's influence on twentieth

century thought has been immense, especially in literature, with Virginia Woolf regarded as one of the great novelists of the century. After early realistic novels her mature work moved to indirect narration and poetic impressionism in **Jacob's Room** (1922), whose hero's life and death in World War I relate very closely to the tragic premature death of her elder brother Toby in 1906. Followed by **Mrs Dalloway** (1925), **To the Lighthouse** (1927), **The Waves** (1931). She and Leonard Woolf made a major contribution to English literary life with the founding of their publishing house The Hogarth Press in 1917. The name comes from the house where they were living at the time in Richmond. Its first publication was **Two Stories**, one written by Virginia, the other by Leonard. Their policy was to publish new and experimental work, and they published the early work of T.S. Eliot and Katherine Mansfield, and introduced the work of Jeffers, J.C. Ransom and E.A. Robinson to England. Translation of leading foreign writers like Gorky, Chekov, Tolstoy, Dostoevsky, Bunin, Rilke, Freud and Svevo were prominent in their list, as well as pamphlets on psychoanalysis, politics, aesthetics, economics and disarmament. At its height it had a truly outstanding list. For the first six years the press operated on a subscription basis only. When the Woolfs moved to Tavistock Square in 1924, the press expanded and J. Lehman, the poet, became an assistant and later part owner. Since 1947 the Hogarth Press has been an allied company of Chatto and Windus, now part of the Jonathan Cape group of companies which were bought in 1987 by Random House.

In art Clive and Vanessa Bell organized the first ever exhibition of Impressionist Art in England, and in their painting and criticism championed the Impressionist cause. In biography Lytton Strachey's debunking of "the great and important people" in his book, **Eminent Victorians**, helped to make biography a serious literary form, rather than a mere exercise in praise. E.M. Forster's novels, especially **Howard's End** and **A Passage to India**, though not modernistic or stream of consciousness like the novels of Virginia Woolf will survive as amongst the best of the period. Culturally the Bloomsbury Group were in the forefront in rebelling against the values of Victorian art and morality, and it is often the bohemian life style of the Bloomsbury set which attracts the interest of the curious rather than their work. Virginia Woolf's affair with Vita Sackville-West and Lytton Strachey's menage à trois with Dora Carrington and Ralph Partridge led to the description of the Bloomsbury Group as couples living in squares who had triangular relationships. One can only surmise what would have happened if the brief engagement in 1909 of Lytton Strachey and Virginia Woolf had ended in marriage. We would no doubt have finished up with the equation of couples living in squares and having quadrangular relationships.

From 1909 the Strachey family lived at no 51 (plaque) which **Lytton Strachey** (1880-1932) made his London base, and it was here he wrote **Queen Victoria** (1821). The house is now the London University's Publishing Department.

The most scandalous love life of the Bloomsbury Group was that of **E.M. Forster** (1879-1970) because not only did he break the sexual taboos, but did the unpardonable and loved beneath his social class, having a long affair with a married policeman. Forster wrote a novel with a homosexual hero, **Maurice**, and it was considered that its publication would damage his reputation during his lifetime so it was published posthumously. Though he wrote little criticism, his **Aspect of the Novel** (1927), from his Clark lectures at Cambridge, is an important critical study of the novel.

Leave the square via **ENDSLEIGH STREET**. The novelist **Dorothy Richardson** (1873-1957) lived in the top floor room of no 7 between 1896-1906, and in her 4 volume autobiographical novel, **Pilgrimage** (1915/67) she calls it Transley Street. A pioneer of the stream of consciousness technique, she narrates the action through the mind of her heroine Miriam. Her work came back into fashion with the growth of feminism and was reissued by Virago in 1979, and has been admired by critics as diverse as Virginia Woolf, Angus Wilson and Anthony Burgess.

If we turn left into Woburn Place and walk a few yards before crossing over the road we come to the delightful, **WOBURN WALK**, where **Dorothy Richardson** moved to in 1906. Designed by Thomas Cubitt as a small shopping centre, its bow fronted shops are beautifully preserved, and it is one of the prettiest little streets in London. Across the street the Anglo-Irish poet **Yeats** (1865-1930) had lodgings from 1895 to 1919 at **no 5 Woburn Walk** (plaque). The son of a distinguished artist he was educated in London and Dublin and became an art student. At 21 he gave up art for literature and frequented the literary salons of London. Speranza Wilde, Oscar Wilde's mother, introduced him to many of the major writers of the day, and helped him to make a name for himself as a poet in London. It was Yeats who gathered testimonials in support of Oscar Wilde from Irish men of letters during his trials in 1895, while most of the English intelligentsia disowned him. In 1891 Yeats formed the Rhymers Club which would meet at the Cheshire Cheese pub off Fleet Street. Other members included Ernest Rhys, Dowson, L. Johnson, Arthur Symons and J. Davidson. It published two collections of verse, in 1892 and 1894. At his rooms in Woburn Walk he held literary gatherings on Monday evenings, where he distributed cigarettes, Chianti and laid down the law about poetry. Later when Yeats befriended the young American poet **Ezra Pound**, (1885-1972) Yeats was happy to see him distributing the cigarettes, Chianti and laying down the law on poetry. His early verse in the 1890s is in the elaborate style of the pre-Raphaelites but he slowly moved to a spare colloquial lyricism and produced some of his best verse in the 1920s and 30s, and won the Nobel Prize for Literature in 1923. There is an excellent study of Yeats in Richard Ellman's, **The Man and the Masks**.

Next to Woburn Walk is the impressive Greek Revival church of St Pancras New Church, modelled on the smaller of the two temples on the Acropolis in Athens, the Erechtheion. When it was built in 1819-22 it was the most expensive church of its time.

Retracing our footsteps we soon come into **TAVISTOCK SQUARE.** There is a plaque on the British Medical Association buildings commemorating Dickens residence in Old Tavistock House between 1851-1860. The building was demolished in 1901. It was here that Dickens wrote **Bleak House, Little Dorrit, Hard**

Woburn Walk

Charles Dickens with his daughters

Times, **A Tale of Two Cities** and part of **Great Expectations**. He also built his own little theatre in the garden where he put on plays for his friends. At this time Dickens produced and acted in plays in private performances for Queen Victoria, including his friend Wilkie Collins', **Frozen Deep**. Dickens left his big mansion in the square when he decided to part from his wife. In his magazine Household Words on June 12 1858 Dickens explained on the front page why he had separated from Catherine. Punch's editor Mark Lemon refused to publish Dickens' public explanation of his differences with Catherine. The proprietors of Punch, Bradbury and Evans, were also the publishers of his novels and quarter owner of Household Words, Dickens' magazine. A furious Dickens went back to Chapman & Hall as his book publisher, stopped editing Household Words, and forced the sale of the magazine which he bought, and incorporated it in his new magazine All the Year Round. The magazine was a great success and continued up to 1895, 25 years after the death of Dickens. Dickens wrote **A Tale of Two Cities** as a weekly serial to launch the new magazine, which was followed by Wilkie Collins', **The Woman in White**, which was a best seller and launched Collins' career. So great was Dickens enmity to his former publisher he did not attend his eldest son, Charley's marriage with Evan's daughter in 1860. The financial settlement was that Dickens' wife was to have her own house and £600 a year. Dickens sold Old Tavistock House in 1860 to Mrs. Davis, a jew, who shocked Dickens by telling him that Fagin had made the jewish community think him hostile to it. He made amends by the creation of Riah, the good orthodox jew in **Our Mutual Friend**. Dickens left London for the country, buying a house in Gads Hill. He was never to live in London again, but would rent houses in London from time to time so that his daughter, Mamey, who loved society could indulge her taste, but more frequently he would use the rooms he had furnished above his magazine office as his London base. He now wrote less fiction and his amateur philanthropy and theatricals gave way to a new professional activity — the reading of his own work in public for his own financial benefit. Of the £93,000 he left at his death almost half came from the profits of these performances.

One of the reasons for Dickens' separation was his infatuation with Ellen Ternan, a young actress whom he met during the tour of **Frozen Deep** in 1857. She probably became Dickens' mistress later, and was certainly a frequent visitor to Gads Hill. The elegant squares of Bloomsbury were on Dickens' walk to work as a small boy when he worked at Warren Blacking Factory at Hungerford Stairs (now Charing Cross). From his lodgings in Bayham Street, Camden Town, the twelve year old boy would walk with his lunch tied in his handkerchief ready for his 10 hours of menial drudgery at the factory. And on Sunday he would walk to Southwark to visit his family in the Marshalsea prison for debt. These experiences provided the darker side of Dickens' work.

Virginia and Leonard Woolf lived at no 52 from 1924 to 1939.

The London Review of Books now has its offices in the labyrinthine British Medical Association House. Founded in 1979 by Karl Miller, professor of Modern English Literature at University College London, in a conscious effort to emulate the New York Review of Books in both design and editorial approach. A literary heavyweight it has published articles and essays by the most prominent critics and scholars of the day, including Christopher Ricks, John Bayley, Frank Kermode, A.J.P. Taylor and David Lodge.

Tavistock Square changes to Woburn Place, and the turning off to the left is **CORAM STREET**. Named after Captain Coram the founder of the Foundlings Hospital, it is where the novelist **William Makepeace Thackeray** (1811-1863) lived between 1837-1843. He had married Isabella Shaw in Paris in 1836, where he worked as a journalist on his father-in-law's paper. When the paper failed he returned to London, and his first child Anne was born in Coram Street in 1837. A second daughter born in 1839 did not live long, and after the birth of Harriet Marian (later Sir Leslie Stephen's first wife) in 1840 Isabella Thackeray suffered a mental breakdown which proved permanent. Thackeray placed her in a private home and sent his two daughters to live with his mother in Paris. Mr. Todd, the junior partner in Osborne and Todd lived in Coram Street (then known as Great Coram

Street.) **Vanity Fair** which appeared in instalments during 1847, was his first major novel and the best book he was to write, established him as an important writer and not just a journalist and illustrator. A lot of the anecdotes we have of Thackeray come from the memoirs of his daughter Anne, a very lively and witty personality, who later became a novelist in her own right. She and her sister rejoined their father in 1846.

The next street along on the left is **BERNARD STREET** which we follow to Coram Fields. **Dr Roget** lived here between 1808-43 while he was a medical practitioner. On his retirement he compiled his **Thesaurus** while living in Bedford Way. **Roger Fry**, the artist and art critic, and a member of the Bloomsbury Group lived here in 1927-34.

In 1959 the novelist **Anthony Burgess** (1917-) on his return from the Far East had a room in a private hotel in Bernard Street, while he was having treatment at the Hospital for Tropical Diseases and then at the Neurological Institute in Bloomsbury. While a patient in the Neurological Institute Burgess would sneak out of the hospital to go to an illegal drinking club in Coram Street with his wife after the pubs were closed. His experiences are related in a comic novel **The Doctor is Sick**. Told that he had a brain tumour and only had a year to live Burgess set himself to work with frantic effort and produced five novels in a year, one of which was **The Clockwork Orange**. His publisher Heinemann told him that it was impossible to publish five novels by the same author in only twelve months, so two appeared under the pseudonym of **Joseph Kell**. Despite his "brain tumour" Anthony Burgess is still with us, twenty nine years later.

We come to the largest open space in London outside of the parks, comprising the garden squares of Brunswick, Mecklenburgh and Coram Fields, often called Children's London as it was formerly the site of the Foundling's Hospital. Despite being centrally located it is a pleasant and generally quiet and uncrowded part of London to stroll.

BRUNSWICK SQUARE

A pleasant backwater spoilt by the intrusive Brunswick

Centre Development, without it Isabella's words in Jane Austen's **Emma** (1816) would still ring true:

> *"Our part of London is so very superior to most others. You must not confound us with London in general, my dear sir. The neighbourhood of Brunswick Square is very different from all the rest. We are so very airy, I should be unwilling, I own, to live in any other part of town; there is hardly any other that I could be satisfied to have my children in; but we are so remarkably airy. Mr Wingfield thinks the vicinity of Brunswick Square decidedly the most favourable as to air."*

In **Vanity Fair,** Lady Southdown's London home was in the square, and she was sent for by Miss Crawley to conclude Jane and Pitt's marriage, disinheriting Rawdon and the villainous Becky.

When the lease on their house in Fitzroy Square ran out **Virginia Stephen (Woolf)** and her brother Adrian moved into no 38 (gone) a four storey house they shared with J.M. Keynes, Duncan Grant and Leonard Woolf. Virginia and Leonard Woolf left the house in 1912 when they married. Another Bloomsbury Group member **E.M. Forster** (1879-1970) lived in the square in 1929-39.

At no 40 are the headquarters of the Thomas Coram Foundation for Children, which contains many of the treasures of the Foundling Hospital which used to stand in Coram Fields before its demolition in 1926. The beautiful Court Room was re-erected here with its original woodwork, ceiling, and plaster decoration and part of the oak staircase. There are paintings by Hogarth, Kneller, Gainsborough, a cartoon by Raphael and sculptures by Rysbrack and Roubiliac. There is also the manuscript of Handel's Messiah. The house is open to the public Monday - Friday, 10 - 12, 2 - 4 and is well worth visiting. The staff are particularly friendly.

CORAM FIELDS is on the site of Captain Coram's Foundling Hospital, founded in 1742 to house the infants abandoned by their parents in the streets of London. The hospital was moved to Berkhampstead in 1926 and the Coram Fields' building was demolished, apart from the impressive entrance arcades. The site was bought as a children's playground, and adults are not allowed inside unless accompanied by a child.

Hogarth was a great admirer and friend of Captain

Coram and became a governor of the Hospital and got other distinguished painters to give portraits to decorate the Governors Court Room. This attracted the public to see the children and the pictures and to contribute to the upkeep of the Foundation. So successful was this scheme that there was an annual exhibition of the artists' work. This was the first great stepping stone to the establishment of the Royal Acadamy of Art. The Foundation's other great benefactor was the musician Handel, who presented the chapel with an organ in 1750, on which he used to play at the chapel's service. He taught the hospital choir and made the Foundling Hospital a fashionable place of worship; people rented pews and came from all over London to hear well known preachers. Dickens was a regular member of the congregation. In his novel **Little Dorrit** (1855-57) Tattycoram was a child from the Foundlings. It was to raise money for the nearby Great Ormond Street Children's Hospital that Dickens gave his first public reading. The success of his reading of **A Christmas Carol** in 1858 led Dickens onto a career as a public performer of his own work.

The affluent City Family of the Osbornes in Thackeray's **Vanity Fair** "had the best pew at the Foundlings." Thackeray sings the chapel's praises in his **Ballad of Eliza Davis:**

> "P'raps you know the foundling Chapel,
> Where the little children sing
> Lord I like to hear on Sunday,
> Them there pretty little things."

MECKLENBURGH SQUARE. No. 37 was Virginia and Leonard Woolf's last London address from where they ran the Hogarth Press from 1939 until the bombings in September 1940 necessitated its evacuation to Letchworth. It was there during a fit of depression that Virginia Woolf committed suicide in 1941. One of the reasons The Hogarth Press was founded was to help counter Virginia's bouts of depression with activity.

The socialist historian, **R.H. Tawney** (1880-1962), who was the professor of economic history at the London School of Economics from 1931, lived at no 21. He was the author of **Religion and the Rise of Capitalism** (1926), **The Acquisitive Society** (1921) and **Land and Labour** in China (1932).

Into **DOUGHTY STREET** where **Sydney Smith** (1771-1845) lived at no 14, in 1803-6. He founded the Edinburgh Review, to provide a Whig voice to balance the Tory Quarterly. In 1803 he came down to London and lectured with great success on moral philosophy at the Royal Institution and was a popular member of the Whig circle at Holland House, where the most cultured members of the establishment were entertained. A great conversationalist, his superb wit can be seen in his humorous letters, reviews and essays. In 1831 he became a canon of St Pauls.

No 48 is where **Charles Dickens** lived from March 1837 until October 1839. Dickens had married Catherine Hogarth, the daughter of the editor of the Evening Chronicle, the paper for which Dickens wrote sketches under the pseudonym of Boz, in April 1836 at St Luke's, Sidney Street, Chelsea. They began their married life with Dickens brother Fred and Catherine's sister, Mary in the cramped bachelor quarters at Furnival's Inn. Their first son Charley was born in January 1837, so Dickens decided to move to a larger house. He was now famous, with Pickwick appearing in monthly instalments. At Doughty Street he finished **Pickwick Papers** while writing **Oliver Twist** at the same time for a new magazine, Bentley's Miscellanies, of which he was the editor, as well as doing various hack jobs, like the biography of the clown Grimaldi. What was undoubtedly the happiest time in Dickens' life soon came to an end with the death of his young sister-in-law, Mary Hogarth, to whom Dickens was greatly attached. The seventeen year old girl died in Dickens' arms after returning from an outing with Dickens and his wife at the theatre. Mary Hogarth was buried in Kensal Green cemetery in a plot bought and owned by Dickens. The novelist wanted to be buried with her, but when George Hogarth, Mary's brother died in 1841, he was buried there instead. There has been a lot of speculation about Dickens "love" for his sister-in-law, all of it based on little substance. At this time Dickens and Catherine got along well, and Mary, like Dickens' brother Fred, was an integral part of a happy family. Mary's death interrupted his writing and made **Oliver Twist** an exceedingly difficult book for Dickens to write. It was the birth of Dickens' third child in 1839 that led Dickens to seek a larger house, and the family moved to **1, Devonshire Terrace** (gone), where Dickens is commemorated by a frieze on the side of the office block now on the site. It was at Doughty Street, that Dickens, always a convivial man, began to entertain. There was almost no one in high society and in London's artistic circles who didn't want to meet him. The novelist Harrison Ainsworth, John Forster (who was to be Dickens' lifelong friend and his first biographer) and Leigh Hunt came to dinner. Dickens frequented the literary salons, gaining the favour of Lady Holland, who ruled the Whig world from Holland House, the friendship of Lady Blessington and Count D'Orsay at Gore House, and an invitation to the Regency wit and poet, Samuel Rogers' famous breakfasts, in their last years. He liked the company of artists and actors especially, and became very good friends with Macready. The up and coming people like Thackeray, Browning and later Tennyson, would come to seek him out, as did the young millionaire philanthropist Angela Burdett-Coutts. Dickens revelled in company and took a great delight in entertaining and being entertained. His tremendous energy was just as discernible in his social life as in his vocation as a writer. In his meteoric rise from shorthand reporter, to journalist, to bestselling author, to famous and important public figure, he left Catherine behind, his wife never quite able to adapt to the world which became Dickens. She married a young and successful journalist and almost overnight had an internationally famous public figure courted by the rich, the famous and the brilliant, as her husband. It was a difficult transformation to adapt to, and Catherine never quite managed it.

Doughty House is the only house Dickens lived in London which is left. The Dickens Fellowship founded in 1902 bought it, and has opened it as a museum to the public. Amongst the Dickens memorabilia are holograph letters, parts of the manuscripts of **Pickwick Papers** and **Nicholas Nickelby**, the desk that Dickens as a young clerk in Grays Inn used at the offices of Ellis and Blackmore, objects from the school in Bowes, which was the model for the horrendous school in Nicholas Nickelby, Dotheboys

Hall, the wooden figure of a Midshipman outside Solomon Gills' shop in Dombey and Son. Of particular interest is the portable desk Dickens designed for himself from which he gave public readings. The basement has a replica of the Dingley Dell kitchen in Pickwick Papers. There is an extensive Dickens library. The three storey house, complete with basement and attic, is very narrow and must have been very cramped for a growing family and their servants. It gives a good idea of what living in a Georgian terrace house was like. It is open Mon - Sat, 10 - 5 (fee).

Dickens wrote **Nicholas Nickelby** here in 1838/9, and began **Barnaby Rudge** before moving to the Marylebone house. The rent at 48 Doughty Street was £80 a year. At 56 there are the offices of the Spectator magazine. Founded in 1828 as an organ of "educated radicalism" it adopted the name of Addison & Steele's 1714 periodical. It campaigned vigorously for Lord John Russell's Reform Bill of 1831, demanding, "the Bill, the whole Bill and nothing but the Bill." At one stage it was owned by **John St Loe Strachey** (1898-1925) during which time his cousin Lytton Strachey was a frequent contributor. It has enjoyed an impressive list of contributors, including Graham Greene, Evelyne Waugh, P. Quennel, Kingsley Amis, Bernard Levin, Katharine Whitehorn and Oberon Waugh. The novelist and biographer of Milton, **A.N. Wilson**, was the literary editor during the 1980s, now succeeded by Mark Armory. It has recently been bought by The Daily Telegraph.

Doughty Street changes its name to John Street before it leads into **THEOBALDS ROAD.** This was once part of the route to Kings James I' house in Hertfordshire, and gets its name from the house, Theobalds. It was heavily bombed during World War II and is now dominated by modern office blocks. Some of the 18th century houses built for City merchants and professional men have however survived including the house where **Benjamin Disraeli** was born in 1804, no 22. It has a brown plaque. His first short story was published when he was only 15, in Leigh Hunt's magazine, The Indicator. Although he kept terms in Lincoln's Inn he never got called to the Bar and followed in the footsteps of his father, Isaac, as a man of letters. A writer of epics, verse tragedies and satire he finally settled on being a novelist when his first novel, **Vivian Grey** was a bestseller. A political pot boiler written while he was 22, so great was its success he added a further four books in 1827. One can discern Disraeli's father, Isaac as the scholarly Mr Grey, Byron (a friend of the family) as Lord Alhambra, and Lockhart as Cleveland. His partner in a failed newspaper venture, John Murray was much to his annoyance only too apparent in the character of the Marquis of Carabas, while Mrs Lorraine recalls Lady Caroline Lamb. Disraeli later disowned the book, which he called puerile, but was unable to suppress it, so great was its fame.

He went on to write political novels of merit, which used the novel as a vehicle for social change, **Coningsby** (1844), **Sybil** (1845), and **Tancred** (1847). Disraeli's last novel, **Endymion** (1880) earned the former prime minister an advance of £10,000, which is more than most novelists earn in 1988. In **Endymion** Disraeli settles his scores with Thackeray for his satire, **Codlingsby**, by making fun of him in his character St Barbe. A popular novelist, he received little critical appreciation, Wordsworth thought his novels, "trashy" and Trollope termed them, "spurious".

The house is a few doors down from the junction with John Street. If we cross over the road we can visit one of the four Inns of Court, Gray's Inn.

THE INNS OF COURT

The Inns of Court developed at the end of the thirteenth century when Edward I in 1292 created a monopoly of practice in the courts to persons selected by the judges. As judges were all serjeants at law (senior barristers) this led to the barristers becoming our court room lawyers, a privilege they still have today. As English Common Law, made by the judges, was not studied at the universities, where students studied Roman Law in Latin, it was necessary to create a series of hostels for students and the people they were to learn from, the practising barristers. The Inns developed in this way. There were the four Inns of Court and eight or more Inns of Chancery, which initially trained court officials but became junior inns of court, affiliated to the four major Inns, and the students they trained were called to the Bar by the four Inns of Court. When the number of students declined the Inns of Chancery began to disappear, some surviving in name only as social clubs for attorneys and solicitors. The seven to eight years of study, with lectures from senior barristers, followed by discussion, with music, dancing and social skills also being learnt, gave way to almost no education at all by the 18th century. To be a barrister one would have a master, and learn by assisting him in his work and discussing cases with him over dinner. Thus dining became of paramount importance, and even today one can not be called to the Bar without having dined 24 times in ones Inn, during the prescribed dining terms. Twelve dinners later, one has the right to practice. The education of barristers has got more demanding and exams were made compulsory in 1872, and it is now a totally graduate intake into the Inns of Court, where more money is still spent subsidizing the dining requirements than in furnishing the more formal parts of a barrister's education. There are about 5,000 barristers practising with each year another thousand being called to the Bar, most of whom never get to practise. As the lawyers put it, "many are called, but few are chosen."

Serjeants-at-law, the highest rank of barrister was

necessary before you could become a judge, and the serjeants were appointed by the King's Writ. In Chaucer's Prologue one is mentioned. Few in number, they were each allocated a pillar at St Pauls Cathedral where they would meet their clients. On becoming a serjeant the barrister would leave his Inn with great ceremony and transfer to the Serjeant's Inn, none of which survive. The last serjeant to be created was in 1875, Lord Lindley. The modern day equivalent would be a Queens Counsel, from whom judges are drawn for the High Court. A Queens Counsel must always appear with another barrister, his junior counsel, so they are an expensive luxury and only do the more difficult cases. As you can only employ a barrister through a solicitor, you will have at least three lawyers everytime a Queens Counsel appears.

Dickens immortalized the rank of serjeant-at-law in **Pickwick Papers,** when the noble Pickwick was dragged before the courts by Mrs Bardell for breach of promise at the Guildhall and Serjeant Buzfuz and Serjeant Snubbin did battle. It is Dickens who is the lawyers' novelist, almost the pied piper of the Inns of Court, and is greatly loved by the legal profession even though he had nothing good to say about it. How they would have loved it if he had become a lawyer as he once proposed, and even went as far as dining, when he was unsure whether literature would provide sufficient financial support. We will find him everywhere while we go round the four Inns of Court; Middle Temple, Inner Temple, Lincoln's Inn and Gray's Inn.

GRAY'S INN

Sir Reginald Grey, Chief Justice of Chester, who died in 1308 had his London house here, and it is his name that the hostel for lawyers that grew up later that century was called after. It was in the most delightful rural setting with an uninterrupted view of the hills of Hampstead. One of the first developments licenced to take place outside the City of London was at the nearby fields, where the disinterred bodies of the three regicides, Oliver Cromwell, Ireton and Bradshaw had lain, the night before their desecration at Tyburn (now Marble Arch.) The mettlesome lawyers of Gray's Inn downed their papers and attacked the workmen, trying to stop the development, but the workers led by the developer Nicholas Barbon won, and the seventeen acre paddock became Red Lion Square in 1684. Fittingly the crest of the Inn is a golden griffin rampant on a black field.

The most impressive thing about Gray's Inn is its superb gardens, the only garden of the four Inns of Court open to the public. They were laid out by Sir Francis Bacon in 1606 and quickly became a fashionable place for walks. Samuel Pepys in his **Diary** frequently talks of taking the air here. More dangerously they became notorious for duelling. Legend has it that the old catalpa tree which faces the rear of 4 Raymond Buildings, was planted by Bacon personally from slips brought back by Ralegh from the New World. Charles Lamb called them, "the best gardens of any in the Inns of Court, my beloved Temple not forgotten."

Verulam Buildings, in the N.E. of Gray's Inn Square, is on the site of Bacon's former chambers, and were named after Sir Francis Bacon, later Lord Verulam. **Bacon** (1561-1626) entered Gray's Inn as a student in 1576, became a Bencher in 1586, and treasurer in 1608. He was the son of Sir Nicholas Bacon, a major official in Queen Elizabeth's reign (Lord Keeper) and Francis was born in York House in The Strand in 1561. He became a Member of Parliament in 1584, and was very energetic furthering

Statue of Sir Francis Bacon in Gray's Inn

Sir Francis Bacon (1561-1626)

his career and seeking advancement, not always by very honourable means. He rewarded the Queen's favourite, Essex for his patronage, by his vigorous efforts in securing his conviction and execution after the 1601 rebellion. It was in the reign of James I that his career progressed rapidly, and by 1618 he was Lord Chancellor. When his career was at its height, and he had just been made a viscount he was charged with taking bribes as a judge. Bacon admitted the charges made in the House of Commons to his great shame and was tried by his peers in the House of Lords, and the country's most senior judge was imprisoned in the Tower, made to pay a large fine, disqualified from parliament and excluded from the court. He only spent a few days in the Tower and his fine was remitted, but his career was over. He spent the last five years of his life in energetic study and writing. He attempted a systematic classification of all the known branches of knowledge, **The Great Instauration**, a work he never completed. The work is a mixture of philosophy, science and natural history.

The most readable of all his writing is his Utopia, **New Atlantis**, published the year after he died, in 1627. Written in Latin it is available in a collection of Utopias called **Ideal Commonwealths**. His **Essays**, which appeared in various editions during his own lifetime, deal mainly with advice on how to lead a successful life and how to govern other men, contain the delightful essay, **The Gardens**, showing his love of nature. He also wrote copiously on the law, and produced a biography of **Henry VII**, which is perhaps the first biography that tries to understand and explain the subject's life and not merely relate it as a chronicle. Bacon died, it was said, from the after effects of one of his scientific experiments. He caught a cold while stuffing a fowl with snow near Highgate, in order to observe the effect of cold on the preservation of flesh. The cold proved to be fatal and he was buried in St Michael's church, St Albans. Obsequious to the extreme he would change his decisions in the Court of Chancery if the king's favourite Buckingham expressed suprise at his decision. His patron Buckingham took advantage of his downfall to obtain Bacon's London mansion, York House, but gained little pleasure from it, being stabbed to death in

1628. Bacon is seen as Gray's Inn's most distinguished former member and his statue adorns South Square. In **South Square**, the smaller of the Inn's two squares, is **The Hall** which was built in 1556-60. It was badly bombed in 1941 but was rebuilt in its original style in 1951. It was here that the first performance of Shakespeare's **Comedy Of Errors**, took place in 1594, when Shakespeare's patron, the Earl of Southampton, was a member of the Inn. It is said that the Hall's wooden screen was made from the wood of a captured Spanish Galleon. The portraits of Nicholas and Francis Bacon hang in the Hall. The library and chapel were both destroyed in the war, but happily the chapel's stained glass windows were removed before the bombings of May 1941. The east window is particularly interesting (1895) commemorating the 4 archbishops of Canterbury associated with the Inn, John Whitgift, William Juxon, William Laud and William Wake.

Charles Dickens worked in South Square (then called Holborn Court) as a clerk in 1827-8, and earned at 15 years of age 13s 6d. His desk at Ellis and Blackmore, a firm of attorneys, is now in the Dickens house in Doughty Street. Mr Phunky, Pickwick's junior counsel in Bardell v Pickwick had chambers in the square. Amongst the Inns famous members are, **Sir Philip Sidney** (1554-86), the author of the **Arcadia**, a prose romance, which includes poems and pastoral eclogues in a wide variety of verse forms. There are two versions of this work, the first finished in 1581, the second a radical revision in 1583-4 was never completed. This was once a highly successful book but which went out of favour after the seventeenth century. T.S. Eliot called it, "a monument of dullness." It is however on most English literature syllabi for A level and higher, and critics like C.S. Lewis have tried to bring it back into favour.

Sidney's dashing reputation as a soldier owes more to later embellishment than actuality. There is a lovely story by Greville of how Sidney was wounded during an attack on a Spanish convoy, and as he was being carried from the field he saw a dying soldier gazing at his water bottle, and gave it to him, with the words, "Thy necessity is yet greater than mine." Unfortunately for veracity Greville was not present to witness the scene. Sidney died in Spain and was buried in great pomp in St Paul's Cathedral.

William Camden (1551-1623) antiquarian and historian, was the legendary headmaster of Westminster school where his pupils included Ben Jonson.

Thomas Campion (1567-1620), poet, musician and doctor was educated here but did not practise. **George Gascoigne** (1534-77), was a soldier and a poet. His poems and plays published in his lifetime as a **Hundred Sundrie Flowres**, were popular until they became overshadowed by later Elizabethan poets, like Marlow, Spenser and Sidney. To modern taste his most interesting work is a novel of sexual intrigues, **The Adventures of Master P.J.**

Thomas Middleton (1570-1627), who collaborated with Webster, Dekker and Rowley is best known for the tragedies of **The Changeling** (1622), **Women beware Women** (1620-7) and **The Revengers Tragedy** (1607) all of which have been successfully revived in recent years on the stage. During his lifetime, his comedy, **A game of Chesse**, caused a public furore, and was taken off after nine nights at the Globe. This satire of the projected marriage of Prince Charles, (later Charles I) to a Spanish princess, reflected the public aversion to the match and led to Middleton and the cast being summoned before a furious Privy Council. T.S. Eliot called the play "a perfect piece of literary political art."

James Shirley (1596-1666), was the author of about 40 plays, and masques for entertainments at Gray Inns. He had a considerable reputation during his lifetime and died a rich man. His and his wife's death was caused by shock and exposure fleeing their house during the Great Fire of London in 1666. **The Lady of Pleasure,** (1635) is his best comedy, while his tragedy, **The Cardinal** (1641), he considered the best of his flock.

Robert Southey (1774-1843) entered in 1797 but finding the law, a "laborious indulgence" soon gave up his studies. He settled in the Lake District and is very much a Lake Poet. He was made poet laureate in 1813, a post he came to dislike. A writer of long narrative poems and ballads, biographies and histories, almost nothing of his work is read today. He is best known for his quarrel with Byron, resulting in his **A Vision of Judgement** attack, which Byron replied by parodying in, **The Vision of Judgement**. **Don Juan** has also frequent mocking references to Southey.

The historian, **Lord Macaulay** (1800-59) was called to the bar, but the success of his essay on Milton in the Edinburgh Review in 1825, led him to give up law for a literary career. Almost everything he published was a great success in his lifetime, beginning with the **Lays of Ancient Rome** (1842). His **History of England** (1855) was one of the century's bestselling books, and has remained in print ever since. It brought him great wealth and a peerage. His style is impressive and history is packaged to look glamorous, and very different from most academic history books. He lived at 8 South Square.

One feature you will notice when walking round the Inns of Court is that the accommodation is grouped in chambers on staircases, with the list of tenants, as barristers in chambers are called, outside. The head of chambers appears at the top of the list and the names descend, reflecting who was called to the bar last.

Leaving Gray's Inn by Theobald Road we proceed up Holborn, passing Great James Street on the right. At no 3 **GREAT JAMES STREET**, the poet **Algernon Swinburn** (1837-1909) lived in 1872-75, and again in 1877-78. Swinburne was educated at Eton where he was termed, "mad", as Shelley had been before him, and Balliol College, Oxford, where his brilliant but irregular behaviour led him to leave without taking his degree. It is believed that he was persuaded to go, as the Master of Balliol, Benjamin Jowett who had made his college pre-eminent intellectually at Oxford did not want the scandal and the ridicule which would result if Swinburne was sent down as Shelley was before him. At Oxford Swinburne met the painter Dante Gabriel Rossetti, and the designers William Morris and Burne-Jones, when they came to decorate the Union Building in 1857. Later Swinburne shared a house with the widowed Rossetti and the novelist Meredith at Cheyne Walk in Chelsea in 1862. Swinburne would get exceedingly drunk and slide down the bannisters in the nude and his debaucheries soon got Meredith to leave, and even got the bohemian Rossetti to ask Swinburne to leave. Swinburne changed house frequently,

Algernon Charles Swinburne (1837-1909)

"The Death of Chatterton" by Richard Wallis

partly to escape the attention of his family who were worried about his fragile health and dissolute life-style. He was rescued from his excesses by his friend Watts-Dunton, who took him off to live in Putney, and turned the wild poet into a mild suburban dweller. It is the earlier pagan and decadent work which is his best, written in a lush evocative style which was greatly admired by his contemporary aesthetes. His **Atlanta in Calydon,** (1865), a classical verse drama made his name, while his first collection of **Poems and Ballads** (1866) made him notorious, for his repudiation of Christianity, obsession with masochism and femmes fatales. Perhaps his most notorious poem, is **Dolores, Our Lady of Pain**, which contains his best known lines.

> *"Changes in a trice,*
> *The lilies and languours of virtue*
> *For the rapture and roses of vice. (ix)*

★ ★ ★

> *"What ailed us, Oh Gods, to desert you*
> *For creeds that refuse and restrain?*
> *Come down and redeem us from virtue*
> *Our lady of pain"*   (xxxv)

On a lighter note Swinburne gave some very good advice to publishers and the literati who felt the need to hype their product and the works of their friends.

> *"There was a poor poet named Clough,*
> *Whom his friends all united to puff,*
>   *But the public, though dull,*
>   *had not such a skull*
> *As belonged to believers in Clough."*

The novelist and poet, **George Meredith** (1828-1909) lived at 26 with his father in the 1840s. He married the daughter of Thomas Love Peacock Mary, a young widow, in 1849. Meredith published his early poems at his own expense in 1851. His series of eastern fantasies, subtitled, An Arabian Entertainment, were published in 1856 under the title **The Shavings of Shagpat**. It was well received by the critics and George Eliot went as far as to call it, "a work of genius", commercially however it was a flop and was soon remaindered. In 1856 he sat as the painter Richard Wallis' model for The death of Chatterton: It was painted in Chatterton's room in Brooke Street, where he committed suicide aged only 17. The picture hangs in the Tate Gallery in Pimlico. The following year Meredith's wife left him for Wallis. An interesting picture of these events can be found in Peter Ackroyd's recent novel, **Chatterton** (1987), a novel which will fascinate anyone with the slightest interest in literary London. Meredith's first novel, **The Ordeal of Richard Feverel**, published in 1859, received critical praise, created a scandal and sold badly. A steady stream of published poems and novels established his reputation, and he became the president of the Society of Authors and a revered literary figure. Although he considered himself as a poet first and a novelist second, his poems soon lost their appeal while his novels, especially, **The Egoist** (1879) have survived. His great reputation has not stood the test of time, and he is seen as a minor novelist, whose prose style is little to contemporary taste, and his major novels go in and out of print.

As a reader for Chapman and Hall, Meredith was given Thomas Hardy's first novel, **The Poor Man and the Lady** to read and publication was recommended if Hardy would pay. The terms were beyond Hardy's means so he refused. He was invited to meet the publisher's reader, and Meredith (whose poems Hardy admired and copied) advised the Dorset writer to produce a novel with less social comment and more art, and with plenty of plot. Hardy followed his advice and produced, **Desperate Remedies**, which was very much in the style of Wilkie Collins and Harrison Ainsworth, and was eventually published in 1871 by Tinsley, with Thomas Hardy paying £75 towards the cost. The book flopped, and Hardy received only £15 in royalties, so losing £60 on his first published novel, which was most of his savings.

Dorothy Sayers (1893-1957), one of our best known crime writers of recent years, lived at no 24. Her amateur detective Lord Peter Wimsey still has great popularity, and her novels lend themselves to radio where they appear frequently. Her religious plays were written mainly for radio and have recently been revived by the BBC. Perhaps her best novel is **Murder Must Advertise** (1933) which uses her experience as an advertising copywriter to good effect. She was working on a translation of Dante's Divina Commedia at her death, and produced two thirds of what was the standard Penguin edition. It has now been superceded by a more recent translation.

Francis and Vera Meynell ran the Nonesuch Press from here in 1924-36. The press aimed at producing books of high quality, both in content and presentation, at a moderate price, a most laudable aim. It produced over 100 in its 12 years existence.

Theobald Road sweeps round into Red Lion Square.

RED LION SQUARE

One of the first developments licensed to take place outside of the City, and part of London's rapid development westwards, linking the City and Westminster. It is a garden square which is no longer residential and is now a mixture of institutional and commercial buildings, and is a quiet oasis in the evenings and on weekends. In the garden there is a statue to Fenner Brockway, an ardent socialist and campaigner still going strong although over ninety. It was Brockway, a leading member of the Independent Labour Party who gave George Orwell letters of introduction to socialists in Spain in 1936, so facilitating his acceptance into the socialist militia, the P.O.U.M. Orwell and Brockway met in France while Orwell was escaping from Spain and Brockway was about to go there. Orwell's book, **Hommage to Catalonia,** gives a very lucid account of a very complex situation and is considered by many to be his best work. It is a model of clear and lucid prose.

There is also a bust of the philosopher **Bertrand Russell** (1872-1970), a brilliant logician. He was a fellow at Trinity College, Cambridge where his pupils included Wittgenstein, and colleagues, G.E. Moore, with whom he collaborated. He lost his fellowship and was sent to prison in World War I for his pacificism. This experience turned the philosopher into a controversialist, who made a living by lecturing and journalism. A believer in free love, he married four times and had numerous affairs, including the wives of his friends. He knew all the major figures of his day in literature and politics, including Ottoline Morrell, D.H. Lawrence, G. Murray, and the Bloomsbury Group. He befriended the then young philosopher T.S. Eliot, recently married, putting the Eliots up in his Bury Street flat and finding reviewing work for Eliot with the New Statesman and other periodicals, and introducing him to Ottoline Morrell and the literati of Bloomsbury. The friendship was shaken but survived Vivien Eliot sleeping with Russell in the autumn of 1917.

There was until recently, a statue of Pocohontas, the

Bertrand Russell (1872-1970)

Bust of Bertrand Russell in Red Lion Square

Indian princess that Captain John Smith brought back from America, and who caused such a sensation in London at the Court of King James I.

Walking round the square we pass Hanway House on the site where **Jonas Hanway**, (1712-1786), philanthropist, traveller and writer lived. He was the first Englishman to carry an umbrella, and so excited the scorn of the little children of Holborn they would pelt him with mud and stones. The umbrella however took off, and by the beginning of the 19th c the Duke of Wellington had to forbid officers in the British Army from going into battle carrying their umbrellas. His seventy four books are of no interest today, and he is remembered for his famous controversy over tea with Dr Samuel Johnson. Hanway wrote an essay on Tea, which Dr Johnson reviewed, causing the normally mild Hanway to write an angry response, to which Boswell tells us, the great Doctor, "after a full and deliberate pause, made a reply to", the Doctor entering into the matter, "con amore". We will leave the final word on the subject with Samuel Johnson, in his review in the Literary Magazine in 1757 he says:

> "*A hardened and shameless tea-drinker, who has for twenty years diluted his meals with only the infusion of this fascinating plant; whose kettle has scarcely time to cool; who with tea amuses the evening, with tea solaces the midnight, and with tea welcomes the morning.*"

A little further along is Conway Hall, the home of the South Place Ethical Society founded in 1839. The society became agnostic in 1869 and organizes meetings and concerts. Speakers at its meetings have included Bertrand Russell, Fenner Brockway, Michael Foot and George Orwell. Orwell who was a poor speaker, with a weak voice after being shot in the throat in Spain, dutifully addressed meetings here, as a member of the society.

Around the square is the house where **Dante Gabriel Rossetti** (1828-82) lived, and later William Morris and Burne-Jones. No 17 has a plaque. Dante Gabriel Rossetti grew up in a cultured and very political home. His father was a member of the Italian Independence Movement, the Carbonari, and lived in exile in London where he was the professor of Italian at the then new University of London.

He studied painting at the Antique School of the Royal Academy with Millais and Holman Hunt, and formed with them and four other artists the Pre-Raphaelite Brotherhood in 1848. The Brotherhood wanted to combat the influence of contemporary painting by returning to pre-Renaissance art, with vivid colour and details. The views of the movement were set out in the four issues of their magazine, The Germ, which was edited by Rossetti's brother, William. Some of Rossetti's early poetry appeared in The Germ, including, **The Blessed Damozel**. The Germ appeared in 1850 the year Rossetti met Lizzie Siddal, who worked in a hat shop off Leicester Square, and became his model and mistress, and later under the promptings of the very moral Ruskin, his wife. Lizzie Siddal, was the model also for Millais in his haunting picture of the drowned Ophelia, which can be seen with many of Rossetti's pictures at the Tate Gallery in Pimlico. The tempestuous relationship of Rossetti and Lizzie ended in disaster; she had a still-born child, and after a violent argument with her husband she took an overdose of laudanum. The distraught husband on his return home got six doctors in an effort to revive her but to no avail. Overcome with grief he buried his poems with Lizzie in Highgate Cemetery, and left their flat in Blackfriars to live in Chelsea with Meredith and Swinburne in 1862. He later triumphed over his grief and in 1870 he got special permission for Lizzie's coffin to be exhumed, so that he could publish his poems. It is said they had to chop off the still gorgeous auburn hair of Lizzie, to disentangle his poems. These poems and others were published later that year. They were well reviewed, with most of the reviews coming from Rossetti's friends. Now inspired by Jane Morris, another of his models, he produced a flurry of poems and pictures, and set up a menage à trois, with Jane and her husband William Morris at Kelmscot Manor. Shortly after in October 1871 Buchanan's attack of his poems appeared in The Contemporary Review, entitled, The Fleshly School of Poetry, accusing Rossetti and his associates of impurity and obscenity, particularly objecting to the sonnet, **Nuptial Sleep**. Rossetti replied the next year with, **The Stealthy School of Criticism** in the Athenaeum. The bitter controversy ended with the pre-

Proserpine by Dante Gabriel Rossetti

Ophelia by Sir John Everett Millais

Raphaelites victorious. In 1861, **Poems and Ballads and Sonnets** appeared. His work was taken up by the younger generation of aesthetes including Pater and Wilde. Rossetti's last years were marred by his addiction to chloral and ill health but he still continued to write and paint. His brother William edited his collected works in 1911, but his poems with their lofty Victorian generalizations about Life and Death and Love are not to modern taste despite the powerful erotic and emotional details. His letters are fascinating and his translations from Italian, especially of the dolce stil novo poets are still worth reading. For us Rossetti will remain a colourful pre-Raphaelite painter with few, if any, turning to his writing. Dante Gabriel Rossetti's sister **Christina Rossetti** (1830-94) was a religious poet of merit whose work was also edited by their brother William, an Inland Revenue official.

Rossetti lived in Red Lion Square in 1851, and one of the terms of the lease was, "that models are kept under some gentlemanly restraint as some artists sacrifice the dignity of art to the baseness of passion." Rossetti's friends William Morris and Edward Burne-Jones shared the house in 1856-9. The firm of Morris and Co was set up at no 8.

William Morris (1834-96) trained as an architect with G.E. Street, and decorated the Oxford Union with frescoes in 1858 with Burne-Jones and Rossetti. He was one of the originators of the Oxford and Cambridge Magazine in 1856, of which 12 monthly numbers appeared. In 1858 he produced **The Defence of Guenevre**, a collection of poems with medieval settings, unusual for their striking mixture of brutality and beauty. In 1859 he married the exceedingly beautiful Jane Burden, and as they could not find furniture suitable for their home, the Red House at Bexley he founded the firm of Morris, Marshall, Faulkener & Co, the famous Morris & Co. It revolutionized public taste with its furniture, printed textiles, tapestries, wallpapers and stained-glass, leading the movement away from mass production back to the artisan. The publication of the **Earthly Paradise** in 1868-70, established Morris as one of the most popular poets of his day. It is a poem with a prologue and twenty four tales in Chaucerian metres. This Norse epic, no longer appreciated by the critics, stimulated his and the public's interest in the heroic themes of Icelandic Literature, and Morris visited Iceland, producing the epic, **Sigurd the Volsung** in 1876. From founding the Society for the Protection of Ancient Buildings in 1877 he turned increasingly towards political activity, becoming a socialist. He produced several prose socialist fantasies, the Utopian, **News from Nowhere** (1891) and a historical fantasy set in the days of the Peasant Revolt of 1381, **A Dream of John Ball** (1889). Morris found the time to found his own press in 1890, the Kelmscott Press, named after the manor house where he had lived with Rossetti and his wife Jane in a menage à trois. He published his own later works as well as reprints of the English classics, including Caxton's **The Golden Legend** and the works of Chaucer, and other smaller books by contemporary authors, including the poems of **Wilfred Scawen Blunt**. William Morris in all his various activities remains a profound influence on our times. **Edward Burne-Jones** (1833-1898) was a painter and a designer of renown, and designed tapestries and stained-glass windows for Morris & Co. He was also the uncle of **Rudyard Kipling**, the first English writer to win the Nobel Prize for Literature in 1907.

From Red Lion Square Theobalds Road loops round until it joins Holborn (underground station) which is a good spot to stop, or have lunch before continuing down **HOLBORN KINGSWAY**, a wide Victorian Improvement Scheme Road finished in 1905 when Edward VII was king. On the west side of the street there is the church of the **Holy Trinity** built in 1909 in the Renaissance style of St Maria della Pace in Rome. It is the second church on that site. The previous church had to be demolished in 1909 as it had been undermined by the building of the Piccadilly underground line. The spot has had a most unhappy history, as it was here that **Charles Lamb** (1775-1834) lived with his father, mother and sister Mary in 1796, when tragedy struck. It was in no 7 Little Queen's Street (as the street was then known) that Mary Lamb during a fit of insanity killed her mother. Mary was committed to an asylum, but was let out by the authorities into the guardianship of her brother. Charles Lamb spent the rest of his life looking after his sister, who remained liable to periodic breakdowns, and renounced his engagement and all thoughts of marriage. Lamb wrote verse, plays, childrens stories, essays and articles. His **Tales from Shakespeare** (1807), written with Mary sets out to make Shakespeare familiar to children and was successful and is still in print, while most of his work is permanently out of print. It is his letters and his amiability which endeared him to his contemporaries, and he is without doubt the best loved man of letters England has produced. A friend to all of the major literary figures of his day, he is much quoted still, if little read.

At the traffic lights turn to the left down Remnant Street to enter Lincoln Inn Fields.

LINCOLN'S INN FIELDS

Originally fields where the students of the nearby Lincoln's Inn used to play. It was also used for executions, with the catholic conspirator, Anthony Babington and thirteen others, being hung, drawn and quartered here for plotting to murder Queen Elizabeth in 1586 and replace her with Mary Queen of Scots. The plot also led to Queen Mary's execution at Fotheringay Castle in 1587. Other executions of catholic martyrs followed in the fields. Developers wanted to develop the site in the 17th c, but the lawyers of Lincoln's Inn successfully blocked the scheme, and petitioned King Charles I to turn the fields into an area of public walks like Moorfields. This idea was accepted but came to nothing, and another developer came forward with a scheme to build 32 houses, which Lincoln's Inn opposed. This time the scheme was accepted, although the developer agreed with the members of Lincoln's Inn that the main part of the fields should, "for ever and hereafter be open and unbuilt", so what was in effect a garden square was created in the 1640s. It was a fashionable place to live, but the large open space covered with grass in the square was often the scene of fights, robberies and still used for executions. In his **Trivia** (1716) Gay wrote:

> "Where Lincoln's Inn, wide space, is rail'd around,
>   Cross not with venturous step; there oft is found
> The lurking thief, who, while the daylight shone,
> Made the walls echo with his begging tone,
>   That crutch, which late compassion moved, shall wound
> Thy bleeding heart, and fell thee to the ground.
> Though thou art tempted by the linkman's call,
>   Yet trust him not along the lonely wall,
> In the mid way he'll quench the flaming brand
> And share the booty with the pilfering band."

Lady Dorothy Sidney, who the poet **Edmund Waller** (1606-87) courted unsuccessfully in the 1630's, and commemorated in verse as Sacharissa lived in the square, in 1660-65. Now the Royal College of Surgeons stands on this spot. An example of Edmund Waller's polished simplicity, which Dryden termed his "sweetness", which he lavished on the objects of his affection, especially his Sacharissima, can be found in his poem, **On a Girdle:**

> *"That which her slender waist confin'd*
> *Shall now my joyful temples bind;*
> *No monarch but would give his crown*
> *His arms might do what this had done."*

The great jurist and legal thinker, **Sir William Blackstone** (1723-80), whose annual lectures in English law at Oxford became the basis of his **Commentaries on the Laws of England** (4 volumes 1755-9), lived at the site of no 55/56.

The poet **Thomas Campbell** (1777-1844) lived at no 61 from 1828 to 1832. Immensely popular in his day he is now chiefly remembered for his war-songs and ballads.

John Forster (1812-76), biographer and critic lived in chambers at no 58 in 1832. He had a career in journalism before studying law and being called to the Bar in 1843. He did not pursue a legal career for long, writing instead biographies of Goldsmith, Landor, Dickens and the first volume of a biography on Swift. He was Charles Dickens' best friend for most of the novelist's life, and read everything Dickens wrote in manuscript from 1837 onwards. Most of what we know about Dickens' early life comes from Forster, and few have disputed the accuracy of his **Life of Dickens** (1872-4), although it is clear he always had Dickens' best interests at heart, colouring his narrative accordingly. In his middle age, the young novelist, Wilkie Collins replaced Forster in Dickens' affection to a great extent. On the 3rd of December 1844 Dickens read his Christmas book, **The Chimes**, at Forster's chambers to a distinguished circle, including Douglas Jerrold, Carlyle, Fred Dickens, Stanfield and Forster, while the artist Maclise sketched the scene. Dickens had returned expressly from Genoa, leaving his family there, so he could supervise the publication of this Christmas book.

In **Bleak House** (1852-53) Dickens gives Sir Leicester Dedlock's lawyer, Mr. Tulkinghorn, "a large house, formerly a house of state . . . let off in sets of chambers now; and in those shrunken fragments of greatness lawyers lie like maggots in nuts". This is based on no 58, Forster's house.

Only one original house is left in the square, Lindsey House, no 59-60, believed to be by Inigo Jones. There are some later houses from the 18th c left in the square, including the house of the architect, **Sir John Soane** (1753-1837). This is now open to the public as a museum and should definitely be visited, as it is a veritable Aladdin's cave of curiosities. There are pictures and a bust of Shakespeare, and a picture of the blind Milton being read to by his three daughters. Its greatest treasure is Hogarth's collection of pictures entitled the Rake's Progress (1735). It was to protect the engravings he made from being pirated that Hogarth promoted and got through parliament the 1735 Copyright Act, often called The Hogarth Act, protecting engravers' copyright in their work. As a pictorial dramatist Hogarth's work is the nearest we have to literature in paint; his series of pictures telling a story in the most dramatic form have inspired a whole generation of writers from Lamb and Hazlitt to Dickens and Thackeray. He was the first English artist of any importance and can be seen as the founding father of the British School of Painting. More of his paintings can be seen in the Tate Gallery in Pimlico, the principal collection of British painters in England, with Marriage à la Mode hanging in the National Gallery. His theories on art can be read in his book, **Analysis of Beauty** (1753). Sir John Soane's house can be visited from Tuesday to Saturday, from 10 - 5, closed on Bank Holidays and in August. While there try and see the sarcophagus of Seti I in the basement.

Walking round the square we leave it by Portugal Street, which will take us back into Kingsway. **PORTUGAL STREET** was named after Charles II's Portuguese wife, Catherine of Bragazanza. The George pub at no 28, is a successor to the Magpie and Stump which Mr Pickwick visits in **Pickwick Papers**. The street also boasts the oldest retail shop in England, a souvenir shop built in about 1567, and is now a listed building. During the 19th c the shop changed its name to The Old Curiosity Shop, hoping to increase trade by being associated with the home of Little Nell, in the Dickens novel. The original for Dickens' novel was almost certainly in Orange Street, behind where the National Gallery now is. It is no longer there.

Lincoln's Inn Theatre once stood in the street, and the poet **John Wilmot, Earl of Rochester's** (1647-1680) house was next door. He was one of the court wits surrounding Charles II, and was banished from the court for his satire, in which he describes Charles, as "A merry monarch, scandalous and poor". He later provided the king with the much quoted epitaph:

> *"Here lies our sovereign lord the King,*
> *Whose promise none relies on;*
> *He never said a foolish thing,*
> *Nor ever did a wise one."*

Charles II's reply to Rochester's epitaph for him was:

> *"This is very true: for my words are my own, and my actions are my ministers."*

As a young man he was very dashing and handsome, and when only 18 he eloped with the young heiress Elizabeth Malet in a coach-and-six, and despite the resistance of her family she married him eighteen months later on his return from the Dutch wars. Rochester divided his time between living quietly in the country with his wife and four children and the fashionable life of a roué in London, where he had many mistresses including the actress, Elizabeth Barry, and was the friend of the dissolute Duke of Buckingham and the Earl of Dorset, Charles Sackville. Many of his letters to his friends in London survive, giving a vivid picture of life at the court of Charles II. As a poet Rochester is often considered to be the last important Metaphysical poet of the 17th c, while his verse satires leads on to the Augustan age of Pope, Swift, Addison and Steele:

> *"Ancient person, for whom I*
> *All the flattering youth defy,*
> *Long be it ere thou grow old,*
> *Aching, shaking, crazy, cold;*
> *But still continue as thou art,*
> *Ancient person of my heart."*

(*A Song of a Young Lady to her Ancient Lover*)

His writing is more frank about sex than almost any writer before the 20th c, and his small output of verse still shows him as one of our wittiest poets. He was a great influence on the next generation of poets and was admired in his lifetime by such distinguished contemporaries as Andrew Marvell and Dryden. Having "blazed out his youth and health in lavish voluptuousness" (Dr Johnson) he became ill in his thirties and engaged in correspondence with a number of theologians including the royal chaplain, G. Burnet, who converted the poet on his death bed to Christianity. He is the villain in Harrison Ainsworth's **Old St Pauls** (1841) and in more recent times Graham Greene has written, **Lord Rochester's Monkey** (1974).

At the end of Kingsway stands **Bush House**, the overseas service of BBC Radio. The voice of English Culture, through its book programmes and plays for ex-patriates and Anglophiles abroad. The News Broadcast normally ends with the formula, That is the end of the World News, and **Anthony Burgess**, the novelist and critic, took this for the title of one of his best novels, **The End of the World News** (1982), which offers three stories for the price of one, in a kind of literary triptych.

Kingsway meets the Aldwych which swings round Bush House to join the Strand. We pass on the left Hughton Street and the London School of Economics, part of London University. It was founded in 1895 by Sidney Webb, and other members of the Fabian Society. G.B. Shaw took an active part in the plans for this new school. It is perhaps the most influential of any university school in politics and social administration, and has a world wide reputation for excellence. The rock star Mick Jagger, of the Rolling Stones, was a student here in the 1960s.

Where the Aldwych and The Strand meet there is the beautiful Wren church of **St Clement Danes**, with its magnificent spire. It was built in 1679, when the previous church, which had survived the Great Fire, was pronounced unsafe. The tower was raised a further 25ft in 1719 following the designs of James Gibbs. The church which has a strong association with **Dr Johnson** was bombed in 1941, with the interior gutted, although the splendid spire survived almost unscathed. It was rebuilt in 1958, with the RAF contributing £150,000 to the rebuilding costs and the church is now dedicated to the RAF, and most of its commemoration services and marriages take place in the church.

In the pre-Wren church, the dramatist **Charles Sedley** was baptised in 1639. His tragedies and comedies are no longer performed and he is chiefly remembered for his extravagant and colourful life, and as the Lisideius of Dryden's, **Of Dramatick Poesie**, who defends the imitation of French drama in English, something that Sedley did in **The Mulberry Garden** (1668). The Elizabethan courtier, humanist and dramatist **John Lyly** (1554-1606) was married here in 1583. His prose romance in two parts, **Euphues** (1578-80) made his name, but is now only remembered for its peculiar style, which gave us the word euphemism. His allegorical prose plays **Midas** and **Endimion**, are considered his best work, although dramatically slight, they are ingenuous with some nice songs.

John Donne's wife Ann was buried in the churchyard in 1617, shortly after giving birth to her twelfth child. Her splendid tomb by Nicholas Stone was lost when the church was rebuilt, and the churchyard is now the site of King's College. Ann was 33 when she died. It was Donne's secret marriage to Ann in 1601, the neice of the poet's employer, Sir Thomas Egerton, that led to him losing his position and being imprisoned briefly in the Fleet Prison, where he wrote, "John Donne, Ann Donne, Un-done," in a letter to his wife. He endeared himself to his children by promising not to remarry so as not to inflict upon them the scourge of a step-mother. Also buried here were **Marchamont Needham** (1620-78) the journalist and editor of **Mercurius Politicus**, whose anonymous pamphlets were often thought to be the work of the greatest controversialist of the age, John Milton, so great is their power; **Thomas Otway** (1652-85) the playwright, the author of the tragedies, **Don Carlos** (1676), **The Orphan** (1680) and **Venice Preserv'd,** (1682). His play, **Alcibiades** gave the beautiful Elizabeth Barry her first successful part and Otway fell in love with her and remained so for the rest of his life. Unfortunately for Otway his love was not reciprocated by Mrs Barry who preferred the attentions of her lover and patron, the Earl of Rochester, John Wilmott. Was it Mrs Barry he was thinking of in **Venice preserv'd** when he wrote:

> *"Oh woman! lovely woman! Nature made thee*
> *To temper man: we had been brutes without you;*
> *Angels are painted fair, to look like you;*
> *There's in you all that we believe of Heaven,*
>   *Amazing brightness, purity, and truth,*
>   *Eternal joy, and everlasting love. (Act I).*

In the Wren church Dr Johnson was a regular member of the congregation in the 18th c. His seat was no 18 in the north gallery close to the pulpit. In his **Life of Johnson**, Boswell tells of he and the doctor attending service at the church on Good Friday 1773:

> *"His behaviour was, as I had imagined to myself, solemnly devout. I never shall forget the tremendous earnestness with which he pronounced the awful petition in the Litany: 'In the hour of death, and at the day of judgement, Good Lord deliver us."*

And after a serious illness in 1784, Johnson wrote to Mrs Thrales:

> *"After a long confinement of 129 days, more than the third part of a year, and no inconsiderable part of human life, I returned this day thanks to God in St Clement's Church for my recovery."*

Behind the church there is a bronze statue of Samuel Johnson, a gift from the sculptor Percy Fitgerald in 1910. On the front pedestal is a bronze plaque of James Boswell, and on the side another of Mrs Thrales. We can compare the likeness with Boswell's first impressions of Dr Johnson, after he had met him at Davies Bookshop in Covent Garden on the 16 May 1763:

> *"Mr J is a man of most dreadful appearance. He is a very big man, is troubled with sore eyes, the palsy, and the King's Evil. He is very slovenly in his dress and speaks with a most uncouth voice. Yet his great knowledge and strength of expression command vast respect and render him very excellent company. He has great humour and is a worthy man. But his dogmatic roughness of manners is disagreeable. I shall remark what I remember of his conversation."*

Happily for us and posterity Boswell did remark a lot of

The statue of Dr Samuel Johnson behind St Clement Danes in the Strand

Dr Samuel Johnson (1709-84)

Dr Johnson's conversation, and his biography, which was a long time in coming soon superceded the glut of Dr Johnson books which appeared after his death, and gave us one of the most remarkable biographies in our language. It tells of the titanic intellect, the great humanity and humour of the irrascible doctor, who so dominated the London of his day. The wit and wisdom of Johnson fill up the Anthologies of Quotations, and he remained London's greatest champion, proclaiming:

> "Why, Sir, you find no man, at all intellectual, who is willing to leave London. No, Sir, when a man is tired of London, he is tired of life; for there is in London all that life can afford."

St Clement Danes each year, usually at the end of February or in March has an Orange and Lemon service attended by the St Clement Danes primary school, in which oranges and lemons are presented to the pupils. The new peel of ten bells hung in 1957 replacing the ones cracked in the war plays the tune traditionally associated with the nursery rhyme, Oranges and Lemons. The nursery rhyme which imitates the sounds of "the bells of old churches of London Town" goes:

> *"Bull's eyes and targets,*
> *Say the bells of St Margaret's*
>
> *Brickbats and tiles,*
> *Say the bells of St Giles'*
>
> *Oranges and lemons,*
> *Say the bells of St Clement's*
>
> *Pancake and fritters,*
> *Say the bells of St Peter's*
>
> *Two sticks and an apple,*
> *Say the bells of Whitechapel.*
>
> *Old father Baldpate,*
> *Say the bells at Aldgate.*
>
> *Maids in white aprons,*
> *Say the bells at St Catherine's*
>
> *Pokers and tongs,*
> *Say the bells at St John's*

Kettles and pans,
Say the bells at St Anne's

You owe me five farthings,
Say the bells of St Martin's

When will you pay me,
Say the bells of Old Bailey.

When I grow rich,
Say the bells at Shoreditch.

Pray, when shall that be?
Say the bells at Stepney.

I'm sure I don't know,
Says the great bell at Bow.

Here comes a candle to light you to bed,
Here comes a chopper to chop off your head."

St Clement Danes has successfully commandeered the nursery rhyme as its own, even without its famous bells, and even though most people think that the St Clement's of the rhyme, is St Clement's Eastcheap, another Wren church.

We proceed down the bottom end of The Strand to the Temple Bar and Fleet Street.

THE STRAND

The word means a beach (and still does in the Irish English of James Joyce) and the road was at one time the beach on the river Thames. In 1860 the Thames was embanked, becoming a lot narrower and deeper, and the street is now a mixture of shops, offices and theatres, connecting Westminster and the City of London. The bottom end of The Strand near St Clement's Dane became well known for its coffee-houses and chop-houses, such as the New Church chop-house, where the young **James Boswell** (1740-85) often had his shilling dinner, and the Somerset Coffee House where he sometimes had breakfast. The **Grecian Coffee-House** stood in Devereux Court, Essex Street and was frequented by Addison, Steele and Goldsmith and by fellows of the Royal Society, including Sir Isaac Newton and Dr Halley (of Halley's comet fame), giving it a reputation for learning. It was first mentioned in The Tatler's first issue, which said that all the learned articles would proceed from the Grecian Coffee-House. It was the Athenaeum of its day, where learning was taken seriously, and an argument over the accent of a Greek word ended in a duel outside with one of the protagonists being killed. From being the haunt of literary men in the 18th c it became a lawyers' meeting place in the 19th c. There were many others, including Toms in the nearby area of Covent Garden. The Strand and its alleyways were a favourite haunt of prostitutes and pickpockets. Once **Dr Johnson** out walking with Boswell after their supper at the Turk's Head Coffee-House was accosted by a woman in the usual enticing manner, "No, no, my girl (said Johnson) it won't do." When **Boswell** was not in the company of Johnson it would do very nicely, and he would spend his 6d freely here.

    ESSEX STREET is on the site of the Earl of Leicester's great Tudor house, where **Edmund Spenser** (1552-99) was one of the household before he left for Ireland in 1580. He met Leicester's nephew here, Sir Philip Sidney and they formed the Areopagus Club with others. He dedicated his, **Shepheardes Calendar** (1579) to Sidney, and while still in Essex House he began to write, **The Faerie Queen**. In 1580 Spenser went to Ireland as the secretary of Lord Grey, appointed Lord Deputy of Ireland and finished the first three books of his major work here. The success of the **Faerie Queen** led the publisher, Ponsonby to issue Spenser's minor verse and juvenilia under the title of **Complaints, Containing sundrie small Poemes of the Worlds Vanitie** (1591). Spenser married Elizabeth Boyle in 1594 and celebrated his marriage in his joyful **Epithalamion**, a hymn in 24 stanzas. Visiting London in 1596 he stayed at Essex House and supervised the publication of the next three books of the **Faerie Queen**, and wrote verses celebrating the double marriage of the earl of Worcester's 2 daughters, the **Prothalamion**. In it he pays tribute to London the city of his birth and childhood:

> "mery London my most kyndly Nurse,
> That to me gaue this Lifes first natiue sourse" (stanza 8)

Insurrections in Ireland dispossessed him of the estates he had acquired and he returned to London with his wife and three children. He died in penury at his lodgings in King Street, Westminster in 1599. He was buried in Westminster Abbey at the expense of the Earl of Essex near the poet he so admired, Geoffrey Chaucer. There is a tradition that at his funeral all the notable poets of his day, including Shakespeare, cast their elegies into his coffin, honouring, "the prince of poets in his tyme". Twenty-one years after his death Lady Anne Clifford commissioned a monument for his tomb from Nicholas Stone. It was the burial of Spenser near Chaucer, who was at one time the clerk of the works at Westminster Abbey, that began the practice of burying poets in that part of the Abbey, now called Poets Corner.

Spenser's **Faerie Queen**, modelled on Castiglione's, **The Courtier**, is still read and is an integral part of any English Literature syllabus at A level or university, although most students are only expected to 'dip' into it. It is worth going to the bottom of Essex Street to view the red brick arch and steps, formerly the watergate to Essex House, and the only part of the house to survive, where one can imagine, "the gentle knights," of the **Prothalamion**, receiving their "fair brides".

Essex Hall housed the Cottonian Library in 1712-13, now part of the British Library at the British Museum. Coming back to The Strand end, New Essex Hall, the headquarters of the Unitarian Movement, has a plaque commemorating the novelist **Fielding** (1707-54) and his brief residence in the street. As a young man he settled in London and made a precarious living writing farces and satires. His most renowned is **Tom Thumb** (1730) a mock heroic farce full of exuberance, which even made the great Dean Swift burst into laughter. Hogarth designed the frontispiece when it was published and the two men became great friends. He married in 1734, Charlotte Cradock, and enjoyed ten happy years of marriage. His political satire, **The Historical Register for 1736**, offended Walpole's government and their Licensing Act of 1737 introduced censorship with theatrical works to be submitted to the Lord Chamberlain for approval. The need to be licensed by the Lord Chamberlain amazingly survived until The Theatres Act of 1968 abolished it.

Fielding decided that this meant the end of his career as a dramatist and enroled as a student of the Middle Temple and was called in 1740, the year in which his health began to fail and his gout became acute. His health interfered with his legal career, but did not prevent him writing satiric novels like **Jonathan Wild** and the parody of Richardson's Pamela, **Joseph Andrews**. He was shattered by the death of his wife in 1744 and almost ceased writing. His second marriage in 1747, to his wife's maid, Mary Daniel, caused a great stir. Becoming a Justice of the Peace for Westminster in 1748 he had a house in Bow Street and the financial security to survey the corruptions of English Society. An innovatory, honest and reforming magistrate he and his blind half-brother, Sir John Fielding set new standards of probity and efficiency for the bench and did much to combat crime and corruption in London, influence sentencing and penal reform and create an effective police force, the Bow Street Runners. His novel, **Tom Jones** (1749) was a great success. It is a comic epic in prose, an innovatory work which is in essence the first modern novel, and from it spring the novels of Dickens and Thackeray. A classic work which continues to appeal. Fielding's bad health led him first to retire to Barnes and then to Lisbon where he died in 1754. His **The Journal of a Voyage to Lisbon** was published posthumously in 1755.

Dr Johnson disliked the works of Fielding prefering the epistolary novels of his friend Samuel Richardson. "There is more knowledge of the heart in one letter of Richardson's than in all Tom Jones". And it was at the **Essex Head**, late in life, that Dr Johnson founded another club, the rules stating that they should meet thrice a week. Eight years after the death of Johnson, Boswell records that the club was still meeting there. The pub was kept by a former servant of the Thrales, the brewer who provided a second home for Dr Johnson at his houses in London and at his country villa in Streatham, now an inner London suburb.

At the beginning of the 20th c it was a street of publishers, with Methuen and Chapman and Hall still here in the 1950s. Macmillan are at no 4 Little Essex Street.

Crossing The Strand we come to the **Royal Courts of Justice** the massive Victorian Gothic Revival Building which replaced Westminster Hall as the civic law courts. Built by G.E. Street they were finished in 1882. There are 19 courts in the building and the public can enter and listen in the spectator's gallery. A judge sits without a jury, and in the Court of Appeal (no 3 court), three judges sit together to decide on appeal decisions, with often more than a dozen barristers present. During the time of **Lord Denning**, who retired aged 83 in 1983, the Court of Appeal became high entertainment as Denning turned it into a round the table discussion between the barristers and the judges, which despite the complexities of the law, gained an ever growing audience. Lord Denning's books on popular law and his autobiography, have enjoyed phenomenal commercial success. The English Civil Law Courts became the Palace of Justice in George Orwell's **1984**.

Orwell worked nearby as the Literary Editor of the Tribune, whose offices were in The Strand. For eighteen months he wrote his, "As I Please" column, establishing himself in the last two years of World War II as the Dr Johnson of the Tribune left.

The Temple Bar in the middle of the street marks the

The Royal Courts of Justice in The Strand

James Boswell (1740-95)

beginning of Fleet Street and the City, but before we enter we should first visit The Temple. There are two entrances, one for Middle Temple and, slightly further down, for Inner Temple. Above the Inner Temple Gateway there is the beautiful Jacobean half timbered building called **Prince Henry's Room**. Finished in 1611 it is, according to Pevsner, the finest half-timbered building in London. It can be visited Monday to Saturday from 1.45 to 5.00 for 10p and contains a magnificent ceiling. The room is done out as Samuel Pepys' Study and is maintained by the Samuel Pepys Society.

We enter The Temple by Middle Temple Lane.

MIDDLE TEMPLE

The Temple is shared by two Inns of Court, Middle and Inner Temple. The name comes from the Knights Templar, who built a church and a monastery on this site in the 12th c. So rich and powerful did this crusading order become that it was suppressed and their property passed in 1312 to the other crusading order the Knights Hospitalers, who leased part of the land to the lawyers for use as a hostel. The Knights Hospitalers were suppressed in their turn in 1539 during the reign of Henry VIII and their property passed to the Crown. In 1609 James I granted the ownership of the Temple to the Benchers of the two Inns, placing on them at the same time the obligation to maintain the church and the Master's House. The land of the Temple was formally divided between the two Inns in 1732.

The crest of Middle Temple depicts the Pascal Lamb with the flag of innocence. Proceeding down Middle Temple Lane we come to, on the right, **BRICK COURT**. **Oliver Goldsmith** (1730-74) lived at no 2 from 1765 until his death in 1774. Born in Ireland, the son of a clergyman, he studied at Trinity College Dublin, Edinburgh and Leyden. After wandering round Europe he arrived in London penniless and struggled to make a living as a physician in Southwark, supplementing his earnings by working as an usher in Peckham, and by hack journalism for the Monthly Review. Soon he was employed full time in writing for a great variety of magazines, making translations and producing scholarly works, such as **An Enquiry into the Present State of Polite Learning** (1759). He blamed the decline of learning in England on the writer's low status in society, "we keep him poor, and yet revile his poverty". His own periodical the Bee appeared for two months in 1759. He wrote various children's stories for the publisher John Newberry, and the nursery tale, **Goody Two Shoes** (1761) is thought to be by Goldsmith. In 1761 he met Dr Johnson and became one of the original members of Johnson's Literary Club. It was the doctor who saved Goldsmith from imprisonment by selling the manuscript of **The Vicar of Wakefield** to Francis Newberry. The formidable Johnson said of Goldsmith: "No man was more foolish when he had not a pen in his hand, or wise when he had" and advised that "Goldsmith should not be for ever attempting to shine in conversation: he has not the temper for it, he is so much mortified when he fails". Goldsmith for his part said of the doctor: "Johnson, to be sure, has a roughness in his manner, but no man alive has a more tender heart. He has nothing of the bear but the skin".

It was his poem, **The Traveller** in 1764, which achieved for Goldsmith literary distinction and the patronage of Lord Clare:

> *"In every government, though terrors reign,*
> *Though tyrant kings, or tyrant laws restrain,*
> *How small, of all that human hearts endure,*
> *That part which laws or kings can cause or cure!"*

In the same year, **The Vicar of Wakefield** was published, which although slow to find an audience has been the most enduring of his work, and is firmly established as a classic work of fiction. His comedies brought him a wider public, with **She Stoops to Conquer**, put on by Garrick in 1773, a huge success. He was quite prosperous in the last few years of his life, and furnished his chambers lavishly, and left debts at his death in 1744 of £2,000. He was buried in the churchyard of the nearby Temple church, and the Literary Club erected a monument to him in Westminster Abbey. His best epitaph comes from Dr Johnson:

> *"To Oliver Goldsmith, A Poet, Naturalist, and Historian, who left scarcely any style of writing untouched, and touched none that he did not adorn."*

In the chambers below Goldsmith lived **Sir William Blackstone** (1723-80), jurist and Professor of English Law at Oxford, who complained about Goldsmith's goings on and noise.

At no 3 **William Makepeace Thackeray** (1811-63) had chambers briefly. He entered Middle Temple as a student in 1831, but showed no enthusiasm for the law and soon gave it up in favour of journalism and studying art. He did however acquire a feeling for the Temple and its literary associations, and sang its praises in his novel, **Pendennis:**

> *"I don't know whether the student of law permits himself the refreshment of enthusiasm, or indulges in poetical reminiscences as he passes by historical chambers . . . but the man of letters can't but love the place which has been inhabited by so many of his brethren, or peopled by their creation as real to us at this day as many authors whose children they were – and Sir Roger Coverley walking in the Temple Gardens, and discoursing with Mr Spectator about the beauties in hoops and patches who are sauntering over the grass, is just as lively a figure to me as old Samuel Johnson rolling through the fog with the Scotch gentleman at his heels on their their way to Dr Goldsmith's chambers in Brick Court; or Harry Fielding with inked ruffles and a wet towel round his head, dashing off articles at Midnight for the Covent Garden Journal, while the printer's boy is asleep in the passage."* (Chapter 29)

Anthony Hope Hawkins (Anthony Hope), the author of **The Prisoner of Zenda** had chambers at no 1 in the 1880s. He was called to the bar in 1887, and practised until the great success of **The Prisoner of Zenda** (1894), allowed him to concentrate on a literary career. He wrote a sequel, **Rupert of Hentzau** (1896) and several other novels and plays. There was a film made of his first novel, starring Ronald Coleman. He was knighted in 1918.

John Buchan (1875-1949) had lodgings at no 4 in 1900. He was the author of popular thrillers, like **The Thirty Nine Steps** (1915), filmed by Alfred Hitchcock, and **Greenmantle** (1916). A government official, his knowledge of how government and the secret service worked, helped to glamorise the spy novel, and spawn a whole new genre.

Brick Court was badly bombed in the war and no 2 and 3 are now the site of the car-park.

The next courtyard down is **FOUNTAIN COURT**, where Tom and Ruth Pinch used to meet, and one day when Tom was late the ardent John Westlock wooed Ruth by the single jet fountain in Dickens' novel, **Martin Chuzzlewit**. Here is situated the most impressive of all the Halls of the Inns of Court, **MIDDLE TEMPLE HALL**. The present hall was completed in 1573 and has a magnificent oak double hammerbeam roof and an impressive screen of oak. The Bench Table is 29 feet long and made from a single oak. It is said that it was a gift from Queen Elizabeth I, and the Cupboard (the small table) was made from the hatch of the Golden Hind, Sir Francis Drake's ship. There are portraits of various monarchs, including Charles I hanging over the Bench Table. The Hall used to be used for lavish entertainments, including revels, masques and plays, and on February 2nd 1601, Shakespeare's **Twelfth Night** had its first performance here. Today it is used for the barristers' lunch and the dining terms of the students, and the various functions of the Inn, including calling students to the Bar. This ceremony comprises of the students, lined up in long rows in their (normally hired) wig and gown being called by name to the Bar, where they nod to the bencher, trying not to lose their wig in the process, and then signing their name in the book of members as a barrister.

Fountain Court leads via a short staircase down to **GARDEN COURT,** where **Oliver Goldsmith** lived for a while at no 2, and the splendid gardens, unfortunately not open to the public, which stretch down to the Embankment, and before 1860 to the river Thames itself. By tradition Middle Temple Garden was where the Lancastrian and Yorkist factions in the royal family plucked the white and red roses, so beginning the dynastic struggles of the War of the Roses, dramatized by Shakespeare in **Henry VI** and **Richard III.**

Retrace your steps to Middle Temple Lane and close to the Hall turn into **Pump Court** where **Henry Fielding** lived at no 4. Before proceeding into the Inner Temple, (to the visitor the two Inns seem like one,) we must mention other famous members or residents of the Middle Temple.

Sir Walter Ralegh (1552-1618) poet, historian, statesman and explorer. **Sir John Davies** (1596-1626), a Lord Chief Justice and poet, the author of satirical verse, **Epigrammes and Gullinge Sonnets,** and the philosophical, **Nosce Teipsum:**

> "*Skill comes so slow, and life so fast dost fly*
> *We learn so little and forget so much*"

His best known lines are on the subject of marriage:

> "Wedlock, indeed, hath oft compared been
> To public feasts where meet a public rout,
> Where they that are without would fain go in
> And they that are within would fain go out."
> (A Contention Betwixt a Wife, a Widow, and a Maid for
> Precedence I.193)

John Ford (1586-1640), the dramatist who wrote, we believe now, 18 plays, some with the collaboration of **Dekker** (1570-1641), **Rowley** (1585-1625), and **Webster** (1580-1625). He was greatly influenced by **The Anatomy of Melancholy** (1621) by Richard Burton, and his plays concentrate on portraying melancholy, torture, incest and delusion in "the distinct personal rhythm in blank verse which could be no one's but his alone" (T.S. Eliot). He was admitted to Middle Temple in 1602, but expelled soon after for debt. He was later readmitted, and though he styled himself, "Master John Ford of the Middle Temple", he was never called. His chief plays are, **The Lover's Melancholy** (1629), **Love's Sacrifice** (1633), **The Broken Heart** (1633) and **'Tis a Pity She's a Whore** (1633):

> "Why, I hold fate
> Clasp'd in my fist, and could command the course
> Of time's eternal motion, hadst thou been
> One thought more steady than an ebbing sea." (V.iv)

Also his historical play, **Perkin Warbeck** (1638), done as a study of delusion, with the hero genuinely believing he is the rightful King of England. A contemporary description of John Ford appeared in an **Elegy on Randolph's Finger:**

> "Deep in a dump Jack Ford alone was got
> With folded arms and melancholy hat."

Thomas Carew (1598-1693), the poet and court official for Charles I, was admitted in 1612. His masque **Coelum Britannicum** was performed before the King in 1634, and his poems published in 1640, including his elegy on John Donne. Like many poets before and after his time Carew reminds his love she is nothing without his praises:

> "Know, Celia (since thou art so proud,)
> 'Twas I that gave thee thy renown.

Sir Walter Ralegh and his son

The Temple Church

> *Thou had'st in the forgotten crowd*
> *Of common beauties liv'd unknown,*
> *Had not my verse extoll'd thy name,*
> *And with it imped the wings of fame."*
> *(Ingrateful Beauty Threatened)*

John Evelyn (1620-76), the diarist, whose **Memoirs** give an invaluable record of the period, although without the sparkle and spontaneity of Pepys. They show even a dramatist with the greatness of Shakespeare can go out of fashion:

> *"I saw Hamlet Prince of Denmark played, but now the old plays began to disgust this refined age." (26 Nov. 1661).*

Evelyn's view according with that of his fellow diarist Samuel Pepys.

John Aubrey (1626-97), the antiquarian and biographer, entered in 1646 but was not called. His **Lives** were published posthumously in 1813 in **Letters by Eminent Persons**. A lively mixture of anecdotes, observation and erudition they are still in print while more accurate and scholarly accounts have long since disappeared from the bookshelves. He has enlivened the lives of the great to such an extent that his legends are more appealing than any reality could ever be. From Aubrey we learn of the young John Milton:

> *"He was so fair that they called him the lady of Christ's College."*

and that young Walter Ralegh was such a good son, that he might sleep with his father's mistress but would not return his father's blows:

> *"Sir Walter, being strangely surprised and put out of his countenance at so great a table, gives his son a damned blow over the face. His son, as rude as he was, would not strike his father, but strikes over the the face the gentleman that sat next to him and said 'Box about: 'twill come to my father anon''.*

In his **Life of Venetia Digby**, Aubrey provides his own preface, "How these curiosities would be quite forgot, did not such idle fellows as I put them down".

Thomas Shadwell (1642-1692), the dramatist, who wrote comedies and operas, adapting Shakespeare's The Tempest into the opera, **The Enchanted Island** (1674).

He succeeded Dryden as poet laureate, when he was removed from office after the Glorious Revolution of 1689. He is now remembered, not for his plays, but for his quarrel with Dryden. Shadwell's many attacks on Dryden were counted by **MacFlecknoe**, in which the True-Blue Protestant Poet is the heir to the kingdom of poetic dullness, and in the second part of Dryden's **Absalom and Achitophel,** Shadwell is mercilessly satirised as Og:

> *"There rest to some faint meaning make pretence,*
> *But Shadwell never deviates into sense.*
>
> *Some beams of wit on other souls may fall,*
> *Strike through and make a lucid interval;*
> *But Shadwell's genuine night admits no ray,*
> *His rising fogs prevail upon the day.*
>
> *Thy genius calls thee not to purchase fame*
> *In keen iambics, but mild anagram;*
> *Leave writing plays, and choose for thy command*
> *Some peaceful province in Acrostic Land.*
> *There thou mayest wings display and altars raise,*
> *And torture one poor word ten thousand ways."*
> *(Dryden's - MacFlecknoe)*

Thomas Southerne (1659-1746), the Irish dramatist who turned Aphra Benn's novels, **The Fatal Marriage** (1694) and **Oroonoko** (1695) into successful tragedies.

William Wycherley, (1640-1716), the Restoration dramatist who had an eventful and turbulent life, was a student at Middle Temple after leaving Oxford without a degree. A lawsuit over his first wife's fortune impoverished him and led to him being committed to the Fleet Prison for debt. It was the King, James II, who paid his debts and got him out of prison and granted him a pension after seeing a performance of his play, **The Plain Dealer**. He argued with the young Alexander Pope, about his revision of his verses and remarried when he was 75 so that his nephew would not inherit his money. Eleven days later he died leaving a young widow. His last plays, **The Plain Dealer** (1677) and **The Country Wife** (1675) have kept their appeal and are frequently revived. They are frank social commentaries, critical of sexual morality and the marriage conventions of his day, with a dexterous handling of plot and character. In **The Country Wife** he advises:

> *"A mistress should be like a little country retreat near the town, not to dwell in constantly, but only for a night and away."* (Act I)
>
> and
>
> *"Go to your business, I say, pleasure, whilst I go to my pleasure, business."* (Act 2)

William Congreve (1670-1729), a fellow student of Jonathan Swift at Trinity College Dublin, entered Middle Temple in 1691, and after three years he got nearer to being called to the Bar of Will's Coffee House in Covent Garden than that of his Inn. His comedy **The Old Bachelor** (1693) made him famous. Others followed, **The Double Dealer** (1694), **Love for Love** (1695), and **The Way of the World** (1700), masterly exercises in the Restoration manner of the social pressures on love and marriage. His wit and subtlety far overshadow those of Wycherley, his contemporary dramatist. In the last years of his life he wrote little, with his eyesight failing, but owing to his support of the Whig party, he lived very comfortably from his sinecures, including that of being commissioner for wine licenses. He had an affair with the Duchess of Marlborough, by whom he had a daughter. It was the Duchess who paid for his funeral and monument in Westminster Abbey.

His brilliance made up for any lack of stagecraft, and his barbs are reminiscent of a later dramatist, Oscar Wilde, and are much quoted. From Congreve we learn, "I am always of the opinion with the learned, if they speak first" (**Incognita** 1692) and, "'tis well enough for a servant to be bred at a University. But the education is a little too pedantic for a gentleman", (**Love for Love** 1695) and to the jilted lover he offers the balm, "Say what you will, 'tis better to be left than never to have loved (**The Way of the World,** 1700).

His comedies are still regularly performed and he is generally considered to be the best dramatist of his time, the master of Restoration comedy, while his tragedy **The Mourning Bride** (1697), though long since forgotten, produced his best known lines. "Music has charms to sooth a savage breast" (Act I) and "Heav'n has no rage, like love to hatred turn'd. Nor hell a fury, like a woman scorn'd". (Act III)

Nicholas Rowe (1674-1718), who gave up his legal career to write for the stage. His play **Tamerlane** (1701) has William III as its hero, and was revived for more than 100 years, annually on November 5, the date William III arrived in England from Holland to displace the catholic James II, as King of England. **The Fair Penitent** (1703) was greatly praised by Dr Johnson, "there is scarcely any work of any poet at once so interesting by the fable, and so delightful by the language". The character of Lothario gave Garrick one of his favourite roles and was the model on which Richardson's Lovelace is drawn. Calista was one of Mrs Siddons great roles, as was the heroine in another of his tragedies, **Jane Shore**. His reputation as a dramatist has not endured, and he is only remembered for "that haughty, gallant gay Lothario".

Edmund Burke (1729-97) gave up the law for a career in politics and as a man of letters. A great orator, with Fox he championed the great liberal causes of the 18th c and he was one of the great figures of his century. Matthew Arnold said of him, "he brings thought to bear upon politics, he saturates politics with thought". His political and philosophical writings fill 16 volumes. He was an original member of Dr Johnson's Literary Club in 1764. Oliver Goldsmith, in his unfinished poem **Retaliation** (1774) settling old scores for the jibes he has suffered from his friends in the Club, said of Burke:

> *"Who, too deep for his hearers, still went on refining,*
> *And thought of convincing, while they thought of dining;*
> *Though equal to all things, for all things unfit,*
> *Too nice for a statesman, too proud for a wit."*

William Cowper (1731-1800), poet and hymn writer was called in 1754, but found life in London too much of a strain and retired to the country. For him, "God made the country, and man made the Town" (**The Task**). His sympathetic feeling for nature presages the Romanticism of Wordsworth and Coleridge.

William Hayley (1745-1820) entered in 1766 but was never called. His poetry was prolific and popular, and although not in the first rank he was offered the poet laureateship in 1790, but he declined the post. He wrote several biographies including that of his friend, **William Cowper** (1803). Ridiculed by Byron as, "Forever feeble and forever tame" his poems even got his friend Southey to remark, "Everything about the man is good except his poetry". His animal ballads were illustrated by his friend and protégé William Blake.

Thomas Moore (1779-1852) the son of an Irish grocer, studied at Trinity College Dublin before entering Middle Temple as a student in 1799. His **Irish Melodies** (1801-34) established him as the national bard of Ireland. He acquired a European reputation with the publication of **Lalla Rookh** (1817), a series of oriental tales in verse connected by a prose story. His satirical poem on the English flocking to France after the Napoleonic war, **The Fudge Family in Paris** (1818) was a great success, as was his **Loves of the Angels** (1823) about three fallen angels and their loves for mortal women. He wrote various biographies, including that of his friend **Byron**, but today his work is unread and he is remembered as the man who was entrusted by Byron with his **Memoirs** and who was persuaded to have them burnt to protect the poet's reputation.

Charles Dickens (1812-70) was, for a while, a student and kept a few dining terms.

INNER TEMPLE

The crest of the Inner Temple is the winged horse Pegasus. From Pump Court proceed via the cloisters to Tanfield Court and to **Inner Temple Hall**. The Hall is modern, built in 1955 to replace the bombed 19th c Gothic Building of Sydney Smirke. Close by is the **Temple Church**, one of the only surviving six round churches in England. The Knights Templars built it in the 12th c, modelling it, as with all their churches, on the Dome of the Rock in Jerusalem. Architecturally the round churches are interesting as a half way house between the Norman (romanesque) and Gothic styles, and are often referred to as Transitional. The church has been 'beautified' in its long history by various architects, including Sir Christopher Wren and Sydney Smirke, but all their work was destroyed in the bombings of World War II. The effigies of the Crusaders were also damaged in the bombing, but they and the fabric of the church have been skilfully restored. It is a very plain interior but well worth visiting.

The dramatist and divine, **John Marston** (1575-1634) was buried next to his father's grave in the church. His gravestone has since disappeared. Of the plays Marston wrote on his own, **The Malcontent** (1604) is considered his best. It is a satiric tragi-comedy reflecting "the poet's own ambitions and dissatisfied intelligence". It is dedicated to Ben Jonson, who Marston spent most of his life arguing and being reconciled with. He and Dekker are satirised as Crispinus & Demetrius, in Jonson's comedy, **Poetaster** (1601) and they replied with, **Satiromastix** (1602), where Jonson is Horace, whose peculiarities of dress and appearance, his vanity and bitterness are ridiculed; he is finally untrussed and crowned with nettles. Jonson wrote a play with Marston and Chapman, **Eastward Ho** (1605), which put the three playwrights in prison for a passage derogatory to Scots (not a diplomatic subject with a Scottish King of England, James I). Their friends got them out by influence at court. The play is of great interest for its picture of life in London.

John Selden (1584-1654), was a successful lawyer, historian and antiquarian. He was imprisoned during the reigns of James I and Charles I for opposing royal authority during his career as a member of parliament and as a jurist. His treatise, **De Diis Syris** (1617), an erudite work on the Syrian gods established his fame as an orientalist, and his valuable collection of oriental manuscripts is now in the Bodleian Library. His grave in the church can be seen through a glass panel on the floor, to the left of the entrance.

The essayist **Charles Lamb** was baptised in the church. Next to the west porch of the church used to stand the music shop of John Playford, Clerk of the Temple Church, and Pepys in his **Diary** tells of hurrying off there to buy the latest music.

Outside the church is Oliver Goldsmith's gravestone, which is no longer on the site of his grave. The exact location of his grave is not known but is in the general vicinity of his stone. He is commemorated by the nearby Goldsmith Buildings.

Proceed to **Mitre Court Buildings** where the legal writer and jurist, **Sir Edward Coke** (1552-1634) lived in the previous buildings on this site. A Lord Chief Justice, and a Speaker of the House of Commons, his rigour in the prosecution of Essex, Ralegh and Guy Fawkes and his fellow conspirators marr his reputation as the upholder of English liberty. He alone of the judges of his day opposed James I and Charles I in their use of the royal prerogative to erode the authority of parliament. Removed from the bench in 1617, imprisoned for nine months in 1621-2, he continued his opposition to royal policies and was largely responsible for rediscovering the Magna Carta and the Petition of Rights in 1628. His career in public life was as upright as his adversary's, Sir Francis Bacon's, was base. His eleven volumes of **Law Reports** (1600-1615), are a stepping stone for the legal profession, and have created the system, in which the law reports are all important, the common law of this country being contained in the judges' decisions reported. His four volume, **Institutes** (1628-44) is an important discussion of English Common Law and of great historical value.

Charles and **Mary Lamb** lived at no 16.

Descending towards the gardens there are the terraces of **Kings Bench Walk**, most of which are in the delightful redbrick style of Christopher Wren and were built in 1677-8, London's first terrace. **Oliver Goldsmith** lived at no 3 before he moved to Brick Court. **Henry Crabb Robinson** (1775-1867) also lived in no 3 in 1822-9, an author of a famous diary and a friend of the great literary figures of his day.

Sir Harold Nicholson (1886-1968), diplomat, critic and biographer lived with his wife **Vita Sackville-West** at no 4 in 1930-45. They used it as their pied-à-terre in London. **Vita Sackville-West** (1892-1962), daughter of the 3rd Baron Sackville was born at Knole House, Kent and wrote a book about her family and its history, **Knole and the Sackvilles** (1922). She was a poet and a novelist, but is best remembered today for her book on gardening and her love affair with Virginia Woolf. Virginia Woolf wrote **Orlando** (1928) for her, and their letters to each other inspire great interest. Her unorthodox marriage is described by her son in **Portrait of a Marriage** (1973).

George Moore (1852-1933), the Irish novelist lived at no 8 from 1886 to 1896. He studied painting in Paris where he came under the influence of the realist writers, Zola, Balzac and the Goncourts brothers, and it is this influence which gives the style of his novels. His best novel, **Esther Walters** (1894) is a naturalist novel of quality, which is still in print. His poetry and five volumes of autobiography are not. His opposition to the Boer War led to his self-imposed exile in Ireland until the beginning of the century, when he returned to London and lived at 121 Ebury Street in Victoria, which he called, "that long, lack-lustre street".

Rider Haggard (1856-1925) was the author of 34 adventure novels, set in exotic locations. He is best known for **King Solomon's Mines** (1886) and **She** (1887). Amongst his admirers was Jung, who referred to **She** in his writings as a good example of the anima concept. He lived at no 13.

Across from King's Bench Walk are **Paper Buildings**, so called as they are made of plaster and lathe and not brick. Sir John Chester, the villain of the piece in Dickens' **Barnaby Rudge** had his chambers here as did the lawyer, Stryer in Dickens' other historical novel, **A Tale of Two**

Cities, where Sydney Carton used to visit him late at night to prepare his cases for him.

Samuel Rogers (1763-1855), poet and famous host lived here in 1800-3. **John Galsworthy** (1867-1933), had chambers at no 3 in the 1890s before giving up the law for his writing. A novelist and a playwright he is best known for his long family saga on the **Forsyths**, which is still much read. Honours were heaped on him including the Nobel Prize for Literature in 1932, but he has never been highly acclaimed by the critics.

The beautiful gardens of the Inner Temple, where the Chelsea Flower Show was held until World War I and its removal to the Royal Hospital in Chelsea, is not open to the public. There is a statue of a little boy in the garden, with the inscription, "lawyers were children once" from an essay by Charles Lamb.

Lamb was born in the adjacent **Crown Office Row** (plaque) in 1775. His father was a clerk to Samuel Salt, a bencher of the Inner Temple, and the family lived at no 2, "the place of my kindly engendure in cheerful Crown Office Row" and grew up with his sister Mary and, "tumbled into a spacious closet of good old English reading, and browsed at will on that fair and wholesome pasturage". On Mr Salt's death they moved to no 7 Little Queen Street, where the disaster struck which changed irreparably the family's life.

Thackeray lived at no 19 in 1848-50. The present buildings were rebuilt, after war damage, in 1953-55.

Turning right one enters Elm Court and the connecting **Fig Tree Court**. The poet **William Cowper** (1731-1800) tried to hang himself here in 1763 during a mental crisis brought on by his examination for a clerkship at the House of Lords, and the refusal of his cousin Theodora Cowper to marry him. Happily for him his garter "which had held me till the bitterness of temporal death was past, broke before eternal death had taken place upon me". A servant hearing the noise, rushed into the room and resuscitated him. Cowper retired to Huntingdon, and later Olney, with no wish ever to return to the London of his trials and tribulations.

One proceeds up to Hare Court, where Farrar's Building is on the site where **James Boswell** (1740-95) had his chambers to be close to his friend Samuel Johnson who lived at no 1 Inner Temple Lane, now thé site of Dr Johnson's Buildings. Before leaving the Temple via Inner Temple Lane, we must mention other famous people associated with the Inner Temple.

Francis Beaumont (1584-1616), entered in 1600. He collaborated with Fletcher between 1606-1613, and they were amongst the most popular playwrights of their day, and until Beaumont's marriage in 1613, the two men shared their work, their lodgings and even their clothes.

William Browne (1591-1643) entered in 1611, the writer of pastoral poetry and masques, he is best known for his epitaph on the Countess of Pembroke:

> *"Underneath this sable hearse,*
> *Lies the subject of all verse,*
> *Sidney's sister, Pembroke's mother;*
> *Death! ere thou hast slain another,*
> *Fair and learn'd, and good as she,*
> *Time shall throw a dart at thee."*

John Forster (1812-76), Dickens' friend and biographer, was called in 1843 but gave up law for literature.

Thomas Hughes (1822-96), who had a successful career as a barrister and politician is best remembered as the author of **Tom Brown's Schooldays** (1857), an affectionate look at the Rugby of his youth and its headmaster, Thomas Arnold.

Sir Compton Mackenzie (1883-1971) a prolific author of novels, travel, biography, essays and poems, who is best known for his novels, including his long saga of the Ogilvie family, **The Four Winds of Love** (1937-45).

John Mortimer (1923 -   ), a rarity, a successful barrister and author. He is well known for his stand against censorship. He was the counsel for the defence in **R v. Calder and Boyars**, when the publishers were prosecuted under the Obscene Publications Act for publishing, **Last Exit to Brooklyn** by Herbert Selby Junior, a novel about drug abuse and homosexual prostitution in the slums of New York.

He once boasted that he was the best playwright to have defended a murderer at the Old Bailey, and had the temerity to congratulate a jury for having sat through the most boring case of the year and smile while the judge commented during his summing up, "The sole purpose of the criminal law is not to amuse Mr Mortimer".

He is best known for his **Rumpole** novels, about the irrascible, quirky advocate modelled on his father, his brilliant autobiographical play, **A Voyage Round My Father** (1975), and his autobiography, **Clinging to the Wreckage** (1982). He has adapted many plays for television including most of the plays of Shakespeare, and recently returned to novel writing, producing the splendid, **Paradise Postponed** (1986).

When he told his father that he wanted to be a writer he was given the following advice:

> *"My dear boy, have some sort of consideration for your unfortunate wife. You'll be sitting around the house all day wearing a dressing-gown, brewing tea and stumped for words. You'll be far better off in the law. That's the great thing about the law, it gets you out of the house."*

With that good advice we leave the Temple via Inner Temple Lane and enter Fleet Street and the City of London.

THE CITY OF LONDON

The Temple Bar marks the entrance into the City of London, which was all of London until the 17th c, and is still independent from the rest of London, a city within a city, comprising a single square mile.

The Romans built their city, Londinium, on the river Thames around the point they were able to ford the river, near the site of the present London Bridge. They encircled their city with a stone wall, with fortresses and six gates. The area of the City has only expanded once outside of the Roman City, that was to include Fleet Street during the Middle Ages. It was the sixth and most important trading centre in the Roman Empire, and the end of the trade route which began at Istanbul in the east and finished in the west at England. Its history is one of commercial and trading power, and to hold London is to hold the prosperity of England for a king or political faction. By the beginning of the 19th c the City dominated the commerce of the world, and as the century progressed it developed the service industries which are the source of its present wealth — banking, shipping, insurance, commodity dealing and finance. As means of transport improved people moved out of the City and commuted to work, by horse and carriage in the 18th c, by railway in the 19th c and by car in the 20th c. The progression from a place to live to a place just to work was completed by the bombings of World War II. Today three quarters of a million people work in the City while only 5,000 people officially live here. There are more than 400 foreign banks, including 242 American banks, (more American banks than in the whole of New York), keeping company with the major financial institutions like the Stock Exchange, the Bank of England, Lloyds and the commodity and currency dealers. It is the largest financial market in the world.

The best time to visit the City is in the week when it is alive with activity and people, unlike the weekend when it is quiet and empty and restaurants, pubs and even churches closed. We begin in Fleet Street.

FLEET STREET

Named after one of London's lost rivers, the Fleet which passes nearby, and is now part of London's sewer system. It is our street of newspapers and printing, its history stretching back five hundred years. By 1500, **Wynkyn de Worde**, had set up the second printing press in England, at the sign of the sun in Fleet Street. The first English press was set up by Caxton, Wynkyn de Worde's master, in the precincts of Westminster Abbey. Wynkyn de Worde printed over 800 different titles, his last book published in 1535 was the **Complaint of the too soon maryed. Richard Pynson** had premises at the sign of St George, and was by 1508 the king's printer. Other printers set up in Fleet Street in close proximity to St. Paul's Churchyard, the area of the booksellers in London. In the 17th and 18th centuries many writers lived in the vicinity to be near the printing presses and the booksellers. The first newspaper in the world was printed in Fleet Street on 11 March 1702, The Daily Courant. At the moment all the newspapers are relocating from Fleet Street to have new plant and equipment elsewhere, especially to the Docklands. By the end of 1989 there will not be one newspaper left, and the only link with its long history of printing and newspapers will be the crypt of **St. Brides Church**, and its Museum of Printing and Fleet Street.

The best way to visit Fleet Street is to walk down the road from the Temple and cross over and walk back on the opposite side of the road until Chancery Lane. No 1 has a blue plaque commemorating the **Devil Tavern**, a haunt of **Ben Jonson** and his cronies, where they established the Apollo Club, engraving the rules on the marble over the chimney piece. The poet and playwright **Thomas Randolph** (1605-35) met Ben Jonson here after writing some verses about having no money, and had the good fortune to have his verses accepted in payment. It is now the site of Child's Bank. This is the bank Dickens modelled Telson's Bank on in his novel, **A Tale of Two Cities:**

"Telson's Bank by Temple Bar was an old-fashioned place,

even in the year one thousand seven hundred and eighty. It was very small, very dark, very ugly, very incommodious. It was an old-fashioned place, moreover, in the moral attribute that the partners in the House were proud of its smallness, proud of its darkness, proud of its ugliness, proud of its incommodiousness. They were even boastful of its eminence in those particulars, and were fired by an express conviction that, less objectionable, it would be less respectable. This was no passing belief, but an active weapon which they flashed at more convenient places of business."

The bank is almost the main character of the novel, with its kindly manager, Mr. Jarvis Lorry, and its grotesque porter Jerry Cruncher, who supplemented his earnings from Telson's by his midnight occupation of grave robber. He would survey the world from his stool outside the bank:

"To the eyes of Mr Jeremiah Cruncher, sitting on his stool in Fleet Street with his grisly urchin beside him, a vast number and variety of objects in movement were every day presented. Who could sit upon anything in Fleet Street during the busy hours of the day, and not be dazed and deafened by two immense processions one ever tending westwards with the sun, the other ever tending eastwards from the sun."

We can contrast this view of the street with a more poetical and meditative one given by **Wordsworth** in a letter to Sir George Beaumont. It is Sunday morning in 1808 and the poet is "in a very thoughtful and melancholy state of mind" about his friend and fellow poet **Coleridge** from whom he had just parted:

"I had passed through Temple Bar and by St Dunstan's, noticing nothing and entirely preoccupied with my own thoughts, when, looking up, I saw before me the avenue of Fleet Street, silent, empty, and pure white, with a sprinkling of newly-fallen snow, not a cart or carriage to obstruct the view, only a few soundless and dusky-foot passengers here and there. You remember the elegant line of the curve of Ludgate Hill in which this avenue would terminate, and beyond, towering above it, was the huge and majestic form of St Paul's, solemnised by a thin veil of falling snow. I can not say how much I was affected at this unthought-of imagination. My sorrow was controlled, and my uneasiness of mind – not quieted and relieved altogether – seemed at once to receive the gift of an anchor or security."

No 10 is where **Richard Tottel** set up his printing press at the sign of The Hand and Star in 1553, and occupied the premises for over 41 years, becoming the leading publisher of legal books. He was the publisher of Thomas More's **Dialogue of Comfort** (1553), and his own poetry anthology, called **Tottel's Miscellany**, containing in its first edition in 1557, poems by **Henry Howard, Earl of Surrey** and **Thomas Wyatt**. Later the rooms above became Dicks Coffee House. Opened in 1680, it became the haunt of Addison and Steele, and they refer to it in The Tatler.

No 22 is the **Cock Tavern**, built in 1887 to replace a 16th c Alehouse of the same name which was across the street. To the former tavern **Samuel Pepys** came with the actress Mrs Knipp on April 23rd 1668 to drink, eat lobster and be merry. Later he "did tocar her corps all over and and besar sans fin her, but did not offer algo mas; and so back led her home". Dickens used to frequent it and later Alfred Lord Tennyson wrote his, **Will Waterproof's Lyrical Monologue** here.

Falcon Court on the right was no 32 where **John Murray** (1776-1843) had the offices of his publishing company and founded the Quarterly Review in 1809. His most important author was **Byron** and he published most of his work, although fear of the public reception of **Don Juan** led him to only publish the first few cantos, John and Leigh Hunt publishing the rest. He bought Byron's memoirs of 1818-21 from Tom Moore and consented reluctantly to having them burned in his house in Albermarle Street off Piccadilly. His other authors included Jane Austen, Coleridge, Leigh Hunt and George Borrows. During the publishing slump in the 1820s and 1830s Murray observed, "the taste for literature is ebbing" and sold his copyright of the Jane Austen novels.

His publishing house became a social meeting-place for many of the literary figures of his day, and the plans for founding a club for writers, the Athenaeum, was devised in his rooms. The publishing house is still going strong as an independent publisher.

Next to the corner of Old Mitre Court and Fleet Street stood the famous **Mitre Tavern**, where Dr Johnson and his friends used to meet. Here the good Doctor would drink a bottle of port wine during the evening, not an excessive amount for a gentleman in 18th c London. Charles James Fox would drink three bottles of port a day, while the Prime Minister, Pitt the Younger, was a six bottles a day man. **Dr Johnson** commented: "No sir, there is nothing which has yet been contrived by man, by which so much happiness is produced as by a good tavern or inn". On another occasion he said, "a tavern chair was the throne of human felicity".

It was in **Bouverie Street** at the Sussex Hotel in 1840 that **Harrison Ainsworth**, wrote most of his historical novel, **The Tower of London**, which was immensely successful at the time and has recently been re-issued by Dedalus, with the original illustrations by Cruikshank. **Harrison Ainsworth** (1805-82) wrote 39 novels, his most interesting are his two London Novels, **The Tower of London** and **Old St Paul's**. He has a very fluent and vivid style, and his language is too Victorian for many readers, but with the recent revival of interest in the 19th c his novels should come back into fashion, with a critical re-assessment of his work. A friend of Dickens, he succeeded him in the editorship of Bentley's Miscellany, going on to edit his own magazine and the New Monthly Magazine.

At no 6, the essayist and critic, **William Hazlitt** (1778-1830) lived in 1829 with his son, having separated from his wife. He gave up training for the ministry to become a painter, but then under the powerful influence of Coleridge he decided on a literary career. Charles Lamb befriended him in London, introducing him to other literary figures and helped him to get started on his long career as a prolific journalist, parliamentary reporter, drama and literary critic, essayist and lecturer. His first marriage in 1808 to Sarah Stoddart ended in divorce in 1822, during the period he was infatuated with Sarah Walker. His account of his love for this simple girl appears in his memoir, **Liber Amoris**, which de Quincey described as, "an explosion of frenzy", and whose publication led to his public ridicule. It was at this time he was arrested for debt. In 1824 he married again, Isabella Bridgewater. It was a short and unsuccessful marriage and his wife left him in 1827.

His reputation rests on the large body of literary criticism he left. Hazlitt did not believe in literary theories, taking the view that the critic should "feel what was good". He made his name with his essays, **Characters of Shakespeare's Plays** (1817), **Lectures on the English Poets** (1818), **Lectures on English Comic Writers** (1819) and his essays on his contemporary writers, Coleridge, Wordsworth and Lamb, in his collection, **The Spirit of the Age** (1825). Opinions today differ on how important a critic Hazlitt was, but he gave criticism a historical foundation that later critics profited from, and established literary criticism as a means of making a living.

The offices of Punch were at no 10 until their removal to Tudor Street in 1969. Founded in 1841 as an illustrated weekly comic periodical, initially strongly Radical, it became progressively less political and its satire blander. Dickens' friend Douglas Jerrold was on the original staff which soon included Thackeray, Thomas Hood, John Leech and John Tenniel.

At no 11, Bradbury and Evans had their offices, the publishers of some of Dickens' novels and Thackeray's **Vanity Fair.**

The Daily News began at no 19-22 in 1845 with Charles Dickens as its editor, Douglas Jerrold, as assistant editor, John Dickens (Dickens' father) as manager, and his father-in-law, George Hogarth as the music critic. His friend and adviser John Forster was a member of the staff. The newspaper was owned by his then publishers Bradbury and Evans and Dickens, annoyed by his subordinate position to the owners, resigned 19 days after the first issue, leaving the paper on February 9th, with John Forster taking over as its editor. Dickens did however continue to make regular contributions to it. The paper was begun as a Liberal rival to the Morning Chronicle. Its name was changed to the News Chronicle in 1930 and it continued until 1960.

The Sun and the News of the World were at no 30 before their move to Wapping. Bouverie Street joins Tudor Street, a very dingy road which was formerly crammed with newspapers. It still has for the moment at Northcliffe House, the Daily Mail, whose literary page is edited by John Bryant and the Mail on Sunday, whose literary editor Paula Johnson has a commendable interest in first novels, and does periodic roundups of new first novels. Both newspapers are moving to the Docklands in the near future. Punch is also in Tudor Street with its sister periodicals and provincial newspapers.

By turning left up either Primrose Hill or Dorset Rise we will arrive at **SALISBURY SQUARE**.

Partly on the site of the Bishop of Salisbury's London Palace, which was destroyed in the Great Fire of 1666, it was until the late 19th c known as Salisbury Court. It was here that the diarist **Samuel Pepys** (1633-1703) was born, the son of John Pepys, a tailor. Educated at St Paul's School and Magdalene College Cambridge he gained advancement by entering the household of his father's first cousin, Sir Edward Montague, later the first Earl of Sandwich, in 1656. He began his famous diary on January 1 1660 while he was living in Axe Yard, Westminster and was very poor. His career soon took off and in the ten years his **Diary** covers we have a fascinating picture of the major events and personages of his day, and one of the fullest, most honest portraits of a human being we have in literature. Pepys was not writing to be read, and wrote in legal shorthand so his servants could not read his Diary, the naughty bits he puts in French, the exceedingly naughty bits, of which there are many, are in Spanish. His Diary ends on 31 May 1669 as Pepys feared wrongly that his eyesight was failing. Later that year his wife died. His career in the Admiralty survived the various political vicissitudes of the times, until the Glorious Revolution deprived him of his appointment and he retired to Clapham. He left his large collection of books, including his Diary, to his old college in Cambridge. It was only in 1825, 122 years after his death that it was deciphered by John Smith and published. What made its deciphering difficult is the same symbol stood for more than one word. The Victorian editions of Pepys were without the naughty bits, it is only the edition of R. Latham and W. Mathews (1970-83) which has permitted us to enjoy the full uncensored Pepys. The same editors have produced a **Shorter Pepys** (now a Penguin paperback) and an **Illustrated Pepys**, which is perfect for the beginner to dip into. On his death his friend and fellow diarist, John Evelyn said of him, "a very worthy, industrious and curious person, none in England exceed-

Samuel Pepys (1633-1703)

John Dryden (1631-1700)

ing him in knowledge of the navy, universally beloved, hospitable, generous, learned in many things, skilled in music, a very great cherisher of learned men".

Salisbury Court Theatre was built here in 1629. It was one of the first theatres to be reopened at the Restoration and Pepys went to see a performance here on the 9 September 1661: "And thence," he tells us, "to the Salisbury Court Playhouse where was acted for the first time **'Tis Pity She's a Whore** a simple play and ill acted, only, it was my fortune to sit by a most pretty and most ingenious lady, which pleased me much". The theatre was destroyed by the Great Fire.

John Dryden (1631-1700) lived in the square between 1673 and 1682. Educated at Westminster School and Trinity College Cambridge, he supported himself by his writing. He excelled at almost everything he did, and was the major poet, playwright, critic and satirist of the second half of the 17th c. He is best known today for his satire on the succession problem, **Absalom and Achitophel** (1681), his plays, **Don Sebastian** (1689) and **Amphitryon** (1690), and his translations, including **Fables Ancient and Modern** (1700).

He was made poet laureate in 1668 and historiographer royal in 1670, both positions he lost when James II was deposed. As a critic and a dramatist he showed great flexibility and range and was not frightened to change his mind and contradict his earlier judgements. He was buried in Westminster Abbey.

In 1722 Samuel Richardson set up as a printer here. **Richardson** (1689-1761) was apprenticed to a printer in 1706 as his father could not afford to enter him for the church and in 1715 he was admitted as a freeman to the Stationers Company. He set up in business on his own and his business prospered because of his great industry. During the 1720s and 1730s he suffered the early deaths of his six children and in 1731 of his wife, Martha Wilde. He married again in 1733 and four of his daughters by Elizabeth Leake survived. He wrote his first novel, **Pamela** in two months, and it was a considerable success when published in 1740, and he was persuaded to continue the story into **Pamela II** (1741). Fielding's bitter parody, **An Apology for the Life of Mrs Shamela Andrews** appeared in the same year. Richardson never forgave Fielding for writing it. Richardson became the printer for the House of Commons and its Journals in 1742. He began writing his second novel, another letter novel, **Clarissa**, in 1744, which ran to eight volumes and over a million words. It was published in 1747 and 1748, and was again a success, but its length and doubts about its impropriety stopped it achieving the popularity of **Pamela**. **Sir Charles Grandison** followed in 1754, a novel about a "good man" to counter his previous two books. It was again successful although much criticised for its length and morality. By 1755 he was the master of the Stationer's Company and "took a range of old houses, eight in number, which he pulled down and built a commodious and extensive range of warehouse and printing offices" in Salisbury Court. He was a friend of Dr Johnson, and printed the fourth volume of The Rambler, and employed Oliver Goldsmith as a proof reader in 1757. It was in Richardson's house that Dr Johnson first met the painter Hogarth, and Boswell relates:

> (Hogarth) *"perceived a person standing at a window in the room, shaking his head, and rolling himself about in a strange, ridiculous manner. He concluded that he was an idiot, whom his relations had put under the care of Richardson. To his great surprise however, this figure stalked forward . . . and all at once took up the argument . . . He displayed such a power of eloquence that Hogarth looked at him in astonishment and actually imagined that this idiot had been at the moment inspired."*

Richardson is seen as one of the founders with Fielding of the modern novel. His epistolary novels are dramatic and analytical but extremely wordy, and Dr Johnson's predeliction for Richardson's "letters" over Fielding's **Tom Jones** is not the view of the 20th c century. **Dr Johnson's** dictionary contains ninety-seven citations from **Clarissa**, almost double that of any other work, high praise indeed.

From Salisbury Square we approach the truly magnificent Wren Church of St. Bride.

ST BRIDE

The church is built on the site of a Roman house and there were seven different churches built here between the 6th and 17th c, traces of their foundations were found during excavations after the bombings of 1940. In the 15th c Gothic Perpendicular church **Wynkyn de Worde** was buried in 1535.

Also buried in the church were **Thomas Sackville** (1536-1608) who wrote part of **Gorboduc**, completing Thomas Morton's play. It was one of the first English tragedies and was acted in Inner Temple Hall on Twelfth Night 1561. Sackville was a member of Inner Temple. Sidney praised the play as being, "full of stately speeches and well-sounding phrases". Sackville was made Earl of Dorset in 1567 and is an ancestor of Vita Sackville-West and appears in her book on her family, **Knole and the Sackvilles** (1922).

The poet **Richard Lovelace** (1618-57) died in the nearby Gunpowder Alley; now called Shoe Lane, which is off the other side of Fleet Street and was buried here. A Cavalier poet he was twice imprisoned during the English Civil War, the first time was in 1642, after he had presented the Kentish Petition to the House of Commons. While in prison in the Westminster Abbey Gatehouse, he wrote the lyrics, **To Althea, from Prison:**

> "*Stone walls do not a prison make*
> *Nor iron bars a cage;*
> *Minds innocent and quiet take*
> *that for an hermitage;*
> *If I have freedom in my love,*
> *And in my soul am free;*
> *Angels alone, that soar above,*
> *Enjoy such liberty*"

During his second imprisonment in 1648 he prepared his poems for the press, and they were published in 1649, and contain the lyric, **To Lucasta on going to the wars**:

> "*Tell me not (Sweet) I am unkind,*
> *That from the nunnery*

> *Of thy chaste breast, and quiet mind,*
> *To war and arms I fly.*
>
> *True; a new mistress now I chase,*
> *The first foe in the field;*
> *And with a stronger faith embrace*
> *A sword, a horse, a shield.*
>
> *Yet this inconstancy is such,*
>   *As you too shall adore;*
> *I could not love thee (Dear) so much,*
>   *Lov'd I not honour more."*

He sacrificed his fortune in the king's cause and died in abject poverty. His poems were revived in 1765 in Percy's **Reliques** and have been admired ever since.

In the 17th c its parishioners included Dryden, John Milton, Richard Lovelace and the diarist Evelyn. Samuel Pepys and his eight brothers and sisters were all baptised here. The church was totally destroyed in the Great Fire. The replacement church by Wren took seven years to build between 1671-1678, with the spire, "a madrigal in stone" added in 1703. This, Wren's largest spire, is familiar to most people in England as a Fleet Street pastry cook began the fashion of having a model of it on his wedding cakes, and St Bride's is often referred to as the wedding cake church.

The Society of St Cecilia held its annual music festival here and Dryden composed the ode, **Alexander's Feast** for its members:

> *"Softly sweet, in Lydian measures,*
> *Soon he sooth'd his soul to pleasures.*
> *War, he sung, is toil and trouble;*
> *Honour but an empty bubble.*
> *Never ending, still beginning,*
> *Fighting still, and still destroying,*
> *If the world be worth thy winning,*
> *Think, oh think, it worth enjoying.*
> *Lovely Thais sits beside thee,*
> *Take the good the gods provide thee."*

Samuel Richardson was buried here in 1761 and his crushed coffin and brass memorial plaque were found amongst the bomb debris in 1940. The church was rebuilt to Wren's designs in 1953-57 by Godfrey Allen. A museum was created in the crypt, where one can see parts of the Roman house formerly on this site, and follow the fascinating history of printing and Fleet Street. The museum like most of the rebuilding costs of the church were paid for by national newspapers and the Press Association provides the church's heating from its nearby building. If you go inside you will find most of the pews commemorate dead journalists, and journalists still like to marry here. A recent journalist wedding was that of Colin Wild and Lyn Webster in 1986. **Lyn Webster** is also the author of several novels, including a feminist fantasy based on Alice in Wonderland, **The Illumination of Alice J. Cunningham** (1987) and a study on dreams.

The church is also where the local traffic wardens congregate during their breaks, and they share the church in the daytime with the tramps and the tourists. It will be a pity, now that the newspapers are leaving Fleet Street, if the journalists cease to support St Bride's.

Back into Fleet Street we cross to the other side of the road, where there is the 1931 black glass building of the Daily Express group, the only national newspaper left in Fleet Street. They have sold their building and will be leaving during 1989 to go to their new premises in Blackfriars. The Literary Editor of the Daily Express is Peter Grovenor, while Graham Lord is the Literary Editor of the Sunday Express. London's evening newspaper, The Standard, shares the building, their Literary Editor is John Walsh. At no 135 the Telegraph had its offices until the end of 1987 and their move to their new premises in the Docklands. The Daily Telegraph's Literary Editor has changed recently with Nicholas Shakespeare succeeding David Holloway. Nicholas Shakespeare was formerly the Literary Editor of the short lived London Daily News, Mr Maxwell's newspaper which failed in its circulation battle with the Standard. The Literary Editor of the Sunday Telegraph is Derwent May.

We turn left into **WINE OFFICE COURT**. As you enter there is the Cheshire Cheese pub, rebuilt after the Great Fire in 1667, it has oak beams and the atmosphere of an 18th c London chophouse. It is a delightful pub only spoilt by its fame, as it overflows with people. The pub is a master in self publicity and lists the 15 reigns in which it has flourished while another proclaims proudly its distinguished visitors.

"Here came Johnson's friends, Reynolds, Gibbon, Garrick, Dr Burney, Boswell and others of his circle. In the 19th century came Carlyle, Macaulay, Tennyson, Dickens, Forster, Hood, Thackeray, Cruickshank, Leech and Wilkie Collins. More recently came Mark Twain, Theodore Roosevelt, Conan Doyle, Beerbohm, Chesterton, Dowson, Le Gallienne, Symons, Yeats and a host of others in search of Dr Johnson's The Cheese."

There is no mention of The Cheese in the writings of Dr Johnson or in Boswell's **Life of Johnson**, but as Johnson lived a short distance away in Gough Square he must have set foot in the pub at some time, having, as we know, a predelicition for taverns. The pub has a copy of Dr Johnson's dictionary and the Reynolds' portrait of Johnson hanging up in the bar. Dickens at one period frequented the pub, and mentions Wine Office Court in his historical novel, **A Tale of Two Cities**.

The once famed puddings of the pub made of beef steaks, kidneys, oysters, larks, mushrooms and spices, each weighing over 50lbs, are referred to in Galsworthy's **Forsyte Saga**. The Rhymers Club met at The Cheshire Cheese from 1891. Yeats, Dowson, Le Gallienne, Lionel Johnson, Symons and Davidson would have dinner downstairs before going to rooms upstairs to read their verse.

In 1760-62 **Oliver Goldsmith** had lodgings at no 6 and wrote most of **The Vicar of Wakefield** here. Johnson came to supper with him one evening dressed unusually smartly because he had heard it said, that Goldsmith, who spent more money on clothes than he could afford, had referred to him as an example of slovenly habits and dress.

Wine Office Court leads into **GOUGH SQUARE**, where **Samuel Johnson** rented the house in which his famous dictionary was compiled. He and his wife Hetty moved into no 17 Gough Square in 1746. In the garret, a room running the whole length of the house, he and his six assistants compiled the dictionary from 1747 to 1755. He had entered into an agreement with a consortium of booksellers, headed by the Pall Mall bookseller Dodsley in 1746 to write a dictionary, the first of its kind in England. In

1747 he produced a plan of the work and a dedication to the Earl of Chesterfield in the hope of patronage, which was not forthcoming. Johnson wrote the definition of over 40,000 words, illustrating them with about 114,000 quotations drawn from every field of learning from the time of Sidney onwards. The dictionary was without rival until the Oxford English Dictionary was compiled between 1884 and 1928. Five editions were published in Johnson's lifetime. When it was finished Johnson sent it to one of the booksellers who commissioned it, Andrew Millar, whose shop was in The Strand, and asked the messenger to remark any comment made by Millar:

> "When the messenger who carried the last sheet to Millar returned, Johnson asked him, 'Well, what did he say?' - 'Sir he said, thank God I have done with him.' 'I am glad that he thanks God for anything.'"

Some of the definitions in the dictionary are playfully self mocking, of lexicographers he says, "a writer of dictionaries, a harmless drudge" and, "Grub Street, the name of a street in London, much inhabited by writers of small histories, dictionaries and temporary poems; whence any mean production is called Grub-street." He is rather dismissive of his achievement in the Preface:

> "It is the fate of those who toil at the lower employments of life . . . to be exposed to censure, without hope of praise; to be disgraced by miscarriage, or punished for neglect . . . Among those unhappy mortals is the writer of dictionaries . . . Every other author may aspire to praise, the lexicographer can only hope to escape reproach"

and seemed to see it as inferior to the vocation of a poet:
"But these were the dreams of a poet doomed at last to wake a lexicographer."

Some of his definitions extended past playfulness to clear abuse:

> "Oates. A grain, which in England is generally given to horses, but in Scotland supports the people."

> "Patron. Commonly a wretch who supports with insolence, and is paid with flattery."

Johnson's life was bizarre: his appearance was, his lifestyle and his habits certainly were. He married a widow 20 years older than himself when he was in his early 20s to whom he was devoted. His wife Tetty spent her time mainly in bed drinking gin and taking laudanum while she read trashy popular novels. Her death in 1752 was a grievous blow for Johnson and he mourned her for many years, and never remarried. The house was always full of the destitute people he was fond of supporting, and who his friends referred to as, "Dr Johnson's people". The blind Mrs Williams, with whom Johnson daily took his tea and the impoverished physician Robert Levet, were two amongst many. It was very much a case of the poor helping the poor and in 1858 Johnson only escaped being arrested for debt by sending to Samuel Richardson, the printer and novelist, for help. Richardson's 6 guineas kept Johnson out of prison. It was his poor finances that led to Johnson leaving his house in 1759 for cheaper accommodation in Staple Inn in Holborn. It is this house in Gough Square, alone of all the many houses in which Johnson lived, which has survived. An elegant late 17th century house it is the only original house left in the square. Carlyle visited the house in 1832 and began the fashion of men of letters going in search of Dr Johnson. It was purchased in 1910 by the newspaperman, Cecil Harmsworth, and it was restored to its original condition and opened to the public in 1914. Its management was taken over in 1929 by the Dr Johnson's House Trust. Gradually 18th c artefacts and Johnson memorabilia have been acquired including a First Edition of the Dictionary, many portraits of Johnson and his circle, objects collected by him including a piece of the Great Wall of China, the chair from the Old Cock Tavern in Fleet Street in which he liked to sit, and his silver teaspoons and sugar tongs. It is open Monday to Saturday, from 10.30 to 4.30 or 5. There is an entrance fee. The adjoining house used by the curator is reputed to be the smallest house in the City.

Also in the square are the modern offices and recording studios of LBC, the commercial radio station for London which has several book programmes and is generous in the time it gives to books and authors on its programmes.

Gough Square leads into **JOHNSON'S COURT**,

named after the tailor who used to own it, and not after **Samuel Johnson** who lived here at no 7 from 1765 until 1776. **Johnson** was by now relatively prosperous having been granted a pension of £300 a year in 1762 by the crown. He deliberated on whether it was just for him to change his allegiance from the deposed house of Stuart to that of Hanover, and concluded, "I think that the pleasure of cursing the House of Hanover and drinking King James' health, are amply overbalanced by £300 per year". He lived with his "people" and his black servant, Frank Barber, the life of a great man of letters that Boswell records for posterity. It is Boswell who relates that in 1776:

> *"Having arrived in London late on Friday, the 15th March, I hastened next morning to wait on Dr Johnson at his house; but found he was removed from Johnson's Court, no 7, to Bolt Court, no 8, still keeping to his favourite Fleet-street. My reflection at this time upon the change as marked in my Journal, is as follows: felt a foolish regret that he had left a court which bore his name; but it was not foolish to be effected with some tender regard for a place in which I had seen him a great deal, from whence I had often issued a better and a happier man than when I went in."*

The house is no longer there but there is a plaque marking the site. The magazine John Bull was started here in 1820 and the radical Monthly magazine founded in 1796 had its office here when in 1832, the 20 year old **Charles Dickens** put his first sketch through its letter box one dark night. The first he knew of its acceptance was by seeing it in the magazine, under the altered title **A Dinner At Poplar Walk**. Contributions were unpaid but Dickens later joined the magazine and wrote for it some of the pieces which appear in the first series of **Sketches by Boz**, which were published in book form when Dickens was 24. The magazine's publisher, Chapman and Hall went on to publish some of Dickens' novels. They also offered to publish Thomas Hardy's first novel, **The Poor Man and the Lady**, if Hardy would subsidize the cost of publication. Hardy could not afford the terms and the novel was never published, with Hardy later destroying the manuscript.

Back into Fleet Street, where between the alleyways of Johnson Court and Wine Office Court there is **BOLT**

COURT. **Dr Johnson** lived at no 8 from 1776 until his death in 1784. It was the first of his homes to have a garden and he took a great delight in watering it. The house was as usual crammed with books and "whole nests of people" who depended on his charity for their livelihood. Here he wrote his major literary work, **The Lives of the Poets** (1779-81) the only one of his many books which is read today. Paradoxically Dr Johnson's overwhelming fame is not based on his own work but on the portrait of his gargantuan personality by Boswell. His fame is everywhere while his books are nowhere to be seen. The house was burnt down in 1819.

William Cobbett (1763-1835) occupied no 11 in 1802, where he founded his **Political Register**, a weekly Tory newspaper which became by 1809 thoroughly radical. One of his articles criticising flogging in the army led to his imprisonment for two years, during which time he continued publishing his paper. By 1816 the circulation was 50,000 per week, remarkably high for the time. He published Parliamentary Debates, giving the proceedings in parliament, which was taken over by his printer Luke Hansard. He set off to examine rural conditions in England and the accounts of his travels on horseback between 1822 and 1826 were published in his newspaper, and collected together under the title of **Rural Rides** (1830). His spleen has many targets in the book, including the monstrous swelling of the 'Great Wen' of London. His style was commended by Hazlitt as, "plain, broad, downright English".

Proceeding up Fleet Street we come to **CRANE COURT**. The Royal Society held their meetings here from 1710 to 1780, and Newton attended them regularly. The house was later rented by the Philosophical Society, and **Coleridge** delivered his famous twelve lectures on Shakespeare in the main room, beginning on 18 November 1819. During his lectures he had this to say about reviewers:

> *"Reviewers are usually people who would have been poets, historians, biographers, &c., if they could; they have tried their talents at one or at the other, and have failed; therefore they turn critics."*

The next turning up is **FETTER LANE**. **Tom Paine** (1737-1809) the radical writer lived at no 77. In reply to Burke's **Reflections on the French Revolution** he wrote his far-sighted **The Rights of Man** (1791-2) demolishing Burke's arguments for their "rancour, prejudice and ignorance". It led to Paine fleeing England to escape arrest. At one time **Thomas Hobbes** (1588-1679) lived in the street. He was the author of **The Leviathan** (1651), a philosophical treatise which advocates a sovereign with absolute power, whose task it is to ensure society's well-being, and keep man from doing what is destructive of life. It was replied to in James Harrington's **Oceana** (1656).

Continuing up Fleet Street we come to the church of **St Dunstan in the West**. **John Donne** was the rector from 1624 until his death in 1631, while he was dean of St Paul's Cathedral. The most brilliant of the metaphysical poets Donne is also remembered for his sermons and meditations. It is John Donne who said in his **Meditation XVII:**

> *"No man is an Island, entire of it self; every man is a piece of the Continent, a part of the main; if a clod be washed away by the sea, Europe is the less, as well as if a promontory were, as well as if a manor of thy friends or of thine own were; any man's death diminishes me, because I am involved in Mankind; And therefore never send to know for whom the bell tolls, It tolls for thee."*

The first biography of John Donne was written by his friend and member of the vestry of St Dunstan's, **Izaak Walton** (1593-1683). It is gentle and admiring in tone and appeared in 1640. It is from this book that we learn that the august dean of St Paul's posed for his portrait wearing his funeral shroud:

> *"Several Charcole-fires being first made in his large study, he brought with him into that place his winding-sheet in his hand, and, having put off all his cloaths, had this sheet put on him, and so tyed with knots at his head and feet, and his hands so placed, as dead bodies are usually fitted to be shrouded and put into their coffin, or grave.*
>
> *Upon this Urn he thus stood with his eyes shut, and with so much of the sheet turned aside as might show his lean, pale death-like face, which was purposely turned towards the East,*

from whence he expected the second coming of his and our Saviour Jesus."

It is not possible to see this picture but we can see the famous Nicholas Stone statue modelled on the portrait later on the tour in the ambulatory of St Paul's Cathedral.

Izaak Walton wrote the biographies of other churchmen — **Wotton** (1651), **Hooker** (1665), **Herbert** (1670) and **Sanderson** (1678). He was peculiarly well placed to do so, as he passed most of his time "in the families of the eminent clergymen of England", and married a great-grandneice of Cranmer in 1626, and in 1647 he married Ann Ken, a half-sister of Thomas Ken. They are a major step forwards in this genre and are consciously artistic. Walton is however best known for his book on fishing, **The Compleat Angler**, published in 1653, but expanded and rewritten for the second and definitive edition. It was published by the press in St Dunstan's Churchyard owned by Richard Marriott. This, the bible of fishermen, contains a lot of philosophical musings and some interesting digressions, to render it a book of general interest.

> "Sir Henry Wotton . . . was also a most dear lover, and a frequent practiser of the art of angling; of which he would say, 'it was an employment for his idle time, which was then not idly spent . . . a rest to his mind, a cheerer of his spirits, a diverter of sadness, a calmer of unquiet thoughts, a moderator of passions, a procurer of contentedness; and that it begat habits of peace and patience in those that professed and practised it'."

His aphorism could fill a dictionary of quotations, as he tells us: "I love such mirth as does not make friends ashamed to look upon one another next morning", and, "Good company and good discourses are the very sinews of virtue". "No man is born an artist, so no man is born an angler." Walton excelled in both callings, and earned sufficient from his trade as an ironmonger and a linen draper to retire in comfort to Winchester, where he is buried and commemorated in the Cathedral.

The church narrowly escaped being burnt in the Great Fire, the flames getting within yards of the church. **Samuel Pepys** occasionally worshipped in the church and the entry for August 18 1667 is especially interesting. It is a Sunday:

> "I walked towards Whitehall; but being weary, turned into St. Dunstan's church, where I hear an able sermon of the minister of the place. And stood by a pretty, modest maid, whom I did labour to take by the hand and the body; but she would not, but got further and further from me, and at last I could perceive her to take pins out of her pocket to prick me if I should touch her again; which seeing, I did forbear, and was glad I did espy her design. And then I fell to gaze upon another pretty maid in a pew close to me, and she on me; and I did go about to take her by the hand, which she suffered a little then withdrew. So the sermon ended and the church broke up, and my amours ended also; and so took coach home, and there took up my wife and to Islington with her."

In 1671 a clock was erected, paid for by the parishioners, as a thank-offering for the church having escaped unscathed the Great Fire. It was reputed to be the first London clock to have the minutes marked on the dial and the first with a double face, and was a notable London sight. There are frequent references to it before it was sold to the Marquess of Hertford in the 19th c. The loss of this famous London landmark moved the essayist Charles Lamb to tears. It is mentioned in Oliver Goldsmith's, **The Vicar of Wakefield** and in several works by Dickens including, **Barnaby Rudge** and has a starring role in his Christmas Book, **The Chimes**. It surprisingly appears in Walter Scott's novel, **The Fortunes of Nigel**, which is set in the reign of King James I, a good forty years before the clock existed. A description of the clock's two figures appears in Cowper's **Table Talk** (1782):

> "When Labour and when Dullness, club in hand
> Like the two figures of St Dunstan's stand
> Beating alternately in measured time
> The clock tintinnabulum of rhyme"

In 1830 the church was demolished and John Shaw's new church was built on a site 30 feet smaller to allow for Fleet Street to be widened. The present church is a Gothic revival church. The old clock was bought in 1935 by Lord Rothermere and now protrudes out from St Dunstan's yet again. The interior, though not particularly striking, is well worth a visit to see some of the monuments from the old church, especially the one to a solicitor:

> *"To the Memory of Hobson Judkin Esq..*
> *The Honest Solicitor."*

There is a bust of John Donne on the east side of the porch, and a plaque and memorial window commemorating Izaak Walton.

We leave Fleet Street by turning left up Chancery Lane, hopefully in full agreement with Charles Lamb: "The man must have a rare recipe for melancholy, who can be dull in Fleet Street", even if we cannot go as far in praise of Fleet Street as Samuel Johnson and James Boswell, as they walked in Greenwich Park during a fine July day:

> *"Dr Johnson – Is not this very fine? Boswell – Yes sir, but not equal to Fleet-street. Dr Johnson – You are right sir."*

CHANCERY LANE named after a house in the street which was used from the 14th c by the Keeper of the Rolls of Chancery. It was demolished in 1896 and The Public Records Office is now on this site.

THE PUBLIC RECORDS OFFICE

The wealth of documents about state affairs and legal matters were scattered around some fifty different buildings at the beginning of the 19th c, until an Act of Parliament of 1838 organised their storage centrally and the building of a public records office. This was built in a fortress-like Tudor style, similar to the 19th c additions to the Tower of London, by Pennethorpe in 1851-66, with an extension by John Taylor in 1891-96. The continued accumulation of documents led to the records being divided between Chancery Lane and a new building in Kew opened in 1977 to house records of modern government departments and public offices. After thirty years most government documents are available for public inspection. To use the archives (open Mon-Fri 9.30 - 5, Sat till 1) one needs a Reader's Ticket.

The Record Office Museum (open 1 - 4 Mon to Fri) is very much worth seeing. It contains the two vellum volumes of the **Domesday Book,** the statistical survey of England made for taxation purposes by William the Conqueror over 900 years ago in 1086. Amongst the other interesting exhibits there are in Case U a letter written in c 1220, one of the earliest extant examples of the use of paper in Europe, and the **Abingdon Indulgence** (1476) the oldest document printed in England. Case W has William Shakespeare's signature (1612) and John Bunyan's preaching licence. Case Y contains memorials of Shelley. Case XI Shakespeare's Will. It was transferred from Somerset House in the Strand along with those of Pitt, Burke, Dr Johnson and Newton.

It was at this end of the street (near Fleet Street) that **Jacob Tonson** started his bookshop in 1678. He published here the works of Dryden, Congreve, Vanbrugh, Addison and Steele. Tonson also bought the copyright of Milton's **Paradise Lost** of which he published a fine illustrated edition in 1688. The book was originally published by Samuel Simmons by the sign of the Golden Lion in Aldersgate Street. In the contract signed on 27 April 1667

Milton received £5 on signature, with a further £5 to be forthcoming when the first edition of 1,300 copies was sold out. If there was a second or a third edition Milton would receive a further £5 on each reprinting, but after 3,900 copies were sold there would be no more royalties for the author. **Paradise Lost** brought Milton fame in his own lifetime as a poet, he was, since the 1650s, one of the most famous men in England through his polemical writings and a tourist attraction for visitors to London.

It was Jacob Tonson who founded the Kit-Cat Club, its members being influential Whig patriots who wanted to ensure a Protestant succession after the reign of William III. The name came from Christopher Cat, a pastry cook near Temple Bar, at whose house the club met from 1700 onwards. His mutton-pies were called Kit-cats. Amongst the members according to Alexander Pope, there were Steele, Addison, Congreve, Garth, Vanbrugh and the painter Kneller, who painted portraits of the members which now hang in the National Portrait Gallery. As the dining-room was low the portraits had to be less than half-size, and we still refer to portaits of this size as kit-cats. The club ended in 1720.

Famous people who have lived in Chancery Lane include **Cardinal Wolsey**, whose house was at the top of the lane. He would leave his house at eight o'clock each morning and on his crimson-caparisoned mule he would journey to Westminster, escorted by his entourage of two pillow bearers, two cross bearers and four footmen, and carrying an orange filled with vinegar to ward off the smell of the streets and the crowds. For details of how Wolsey lived we get most of our information from a gentleman in Wolsey's household, **George Cavendish** (1499-1561), who wrote a remarkable biography of his employer, which circulated in manuscript form before being published in 1641. **The Life and Death of Cardinal Wolsey** contrasts the magnificence of the cardinal's life with his subsequent disgrace, showing "the wondrouse mutabilitie of vayn honours . . . And the tykkyll trust to worldly prynces".

Izaak Walton lived in the street in 1627-44 and wrote his **Life of John Donne** here. **William Pickering** (1796-1854), the publisher of the Diamond Classics and the

Aldine Press, famous for its 53 volume edition of the English poets was at no 57 in 1824. He was the first publisher to bind books in cloth.

We turn off from Chancery Lane down **CAREY STREET** opposite the Public Records Office. **Henry Mayhew** (1812-87) was articled here to his father as a solicitor. His time there was "very little to the satisfaction of any of the parties concerned" and he soon gave up law for journalism and drama. He wrote many plays and farces, some of which enjoyed great success. In 1841 he was a co-founder and briefly co-editor of Punch, and wrote many novels and non-fiction works on diverse subjects before turning his attention at the end of the 1840s to philanthropic journalism. His series of 82 articles for the Morning Chronicle were published as **London Labour and the London Poor** (1851). His descriptions of the daily horrors endured by the poor — starvation, disease, and transportation — did much to stir public opinion towards reform. **The Criminal Prisons of London** followed in 1862 and **London Children** in 1874.

We turn right off Carey Street to enter Lincoln's Inn. The premises on either side of Lincoln's Inn Archway are of Wildly & Son, the legal booksellers who have been here since 1830. It is a delightfully old-fashioned shop with a very good second-hand law department in addition to the up to date stuff. It always has a good stock of period prints of the area and caricatures of famous lawyers, and so is worth browsing round for the non-lawyer.

LINCOLN'S INN

The name most likely comes from Henry de Lacy, 3rd Earl of Lincoln, one of Edward I's advisers who owned land nearby, and the Earl's crest — a lion rampant purpure — appears in the arms of the Honourable Society of Lincoln's Inn. The lawyers rented the land from the Bishops of Chichester from the early part of the 15th c for £6 13s 6d per year. The freehold of the property was bought in 1580 for £520. We enter by **NEW SQUARE** built in 1683-93, a very pleasant garden square, the nicest in all the Inns of Court. **Arthur Murphy** (1727-1805) lived at no 1 from 1757 to 1788. Murphy found it difficult to gain admittance into an Inn of Court as he had formerly been an actor at Covent Garden and Drury Lane, and was refused at Grays and Middle Temple before Lincoln took him. He was called to the bar in 1762 and practised as a barrister. He wrote many farces, comedies and tragedies none of which are now performed and he is remembered for his friendship with Dr Johnson. He met Johnson in 1754 and the two men became lifelong friends. It was through Murphy that Johnson met the Thrales. Murphy wrote several biographies including those of Johnson and David Garrick.

Charles Dickens worked here briefly as a solicitor's clerk for Charles Molby when he was 14.

At the end of the square on the right we have the **Old Hall** built in 1489-92. It served as the Court of Chancery from 1733 to 1873, and is the venue for much of the lawsuit of Jarndyce v Jarndyce in Dickens' wonderfully atmospheric and foggy novel, **Bleak House**. "Jarndyce and Jarndyce still drags its dreary length before the Court, perennially hopeless." It is lost in the fog of the English legal system: "At the very heart of the fog sits the Lord High Chancellor in his High Court of Chancery."

Past the Old Hall, with its spendid roof and portraits, where the students of the Inns of Court have some of their lectures, we come to the Chapel.

THE CHAPEL was built in 1619-23, and according to Aubrey, **Ben Jonson**, working as a bricklayer with his

Lincoln's Inn Chapel's Undercroft

The Gateway of Lincoln's Inn

stepfather, helped to build it, with a trowel in one hand and a book always near at hand. The chapel might have been built to the designs of Inigo Jones and it replaced the previous chapel. It is an early example of 17th c Gothic. The foundation stone was laid by **John Donne**, who held the divinity readership of Lincoln's Inn. Donne had entered the Inn from Thavies Inn in May 1592, and it is probably during the period of his law studies that he apparently renounced his Catholic faith. A young man of learning and wit he spoilt his career chances by his secret marriage to Ann More, who was under age, and despite his important friends and patrons he was never able to gain employment at court and was persuaded by King James I to take holy orders which he did in 1615. Cambridge University, much to their annoyance, as they regarded Donne as a careerist without any real vocation, were coerced into giving him a doctorate in divinity. His friends obtained for him several livings inside and outside of London and through the favour of the king's favourite Buckingham, was made dean of St Pauls in 1621. When the chapel was completed Donne preached the consecration sermon on Ascension Day 1623. The chapel's undercroft was the scene of a secret meeting of 80 Members of Parliament in 1659, the first move in the Restoration of the monarchy. The chapel has been much restored and is still in use. Its services are open to the public and each December it has a truly wonderful carol service with the senior judges of the Inn reading the lessons. The antiquarian **Elias Ashmole** married in the chapel in 1668. His collection of curiosities bequeathed to him by Tradescant was presented by him in 1682 to Oxford University, where he had been a student at Brasenose.

We continue round into **OLD SQUARE** where the offices of Kenge and Carboys were situated in Dickens' novel, **Bleak House**, and in **Pickwick Papers** Dickens gave Serjeant Snubbins an address in this square.

Old Square leads up to **Stone Buildings** (1774-80). **William Pitt the Younger** (1759-1806) had chambers here. He was called to the bar in 1780. He entered parliament at 22, became Chancellor of the Exchequer at 23, and Prime Minister at 24. Fox and his friends called Pitt's administration the mince pie government, because Pitt came to power in December and they thought by the time the mince pie season had finished he would be out of office. The mince pie administration lasted almost 20 years.

In Trollope's novel **The Prime Minister** (1876) Mr. Wharton had his chambers here. **Anthony Trollope** combined his career in the Post Office with the writing of novels, and said, "Three hours a day will produce as much as a man ought to write". This he did in the morning before going off to work. His political and clerical novels still appeal although few would claim that Trollope was a great writer.

We turn away from Stone Buildings and go towards the red brick 19th c complex which houses the New Hall, Library and Treasury, and past them to the splendid gardens, unfortunately not open to the public. Pepys liked to stroll here and Steele sings their praises in The Tatler.

To leave retrace your steps to the Chapel and pass through the **Gatehouse** built in 1517-21 by Sir Thomas Lovell, whose coat of arms appear over the door with those of Henry VIII and the Earl of Lincoln. **Sir Thomas More**, a bencher of the Inn, contributed to the building costs. The rooms above were occupied in 1617 by an 18 year old law student, Oliver Cromwell. Cromwell's son Richard was also a student at Lincoln's Inn.

Distinguished members of Lincoln's Inn include **Sir Thomas More** (1478-1535), who entered in 1496, and combined his study of law with literature.

Richard Edwards (1523-66) who became master of the children of the Chapel Royal. He entered in 1547 but did not practise. He wrote several plays, all lost except **Damon and Pithias** (1571), a rhymed play, but is principally remembered for his collection of the works of minor Elizabethan poets, **Paradyse of Dainty Devises**, published posthumously in 1576.

Thomas Lodge (1558-1625), poet, romance writer and adventurer, the son of a Lord Mayor of London, entered in 1578. He is principally remembered for his romance, **Rosalynde** (1590), which was "hatcht in the stormes of the Ocean, and feathered in the surges of many perilous seas". Shakespeare dramatized Lodge's romance in **As You Like It**. A pastoral romance with some beautiful lyrics such as:

> *Love, in my bosom, like a bee,*
> *Doth suck his sweet."*

and the charming description of Rosalynde:

> *Heigh o, would she were mine!*

it is more varied than many Elizabethan romances with a variety of rhetorical speeches and descriptions.

Christopher Brooke, a minor poet shared his chambers with **John Donne** (1572-1631), later chaplain of the Inn and the greatest of our non-dramatic poets.

George Wither (1588-1667), entered in 1606 but soon renounced law for literature. His satire **Abuse stript and whipt** (1613) earned him imprisonment in the Marshalsea in Southwark. His satires led to his imprisonment again in 1621 and 1661, and he was captured and imprisoned during the civil war by the royalists. Today he is remembered for his verse, especially **Fidelia** (1619), a poetical epistle from a faithful nymph to her inconstant lover, which contains the song:

> *"Shall I, wasting in despair,*
> *Die because a woman's fair?*
> *Or make pale my cheeks with care,*
> *'Cause another's rosy are?*
> *Be she fairer than the day,*
> *Or the flow'ry meads in May;*
> *If she think not well of me,*
> *What care I how fair she be?*

The song appeared in Percy's **Reliques** (1765) leading to revival in the appreciation of Wither's poetry, and Charles Lamb in the next century did a lot to make his verse popular again. **Sir John Denham** (1615-69) entered in 1634 and was called to the Bar in 1639. A royalist he fled England in 1648 but returned at the Restoration and was appointed the surveyor-general of works, where his deputy was the young Christopher Wren. He was the author of the tragedy, **The Sophy** (1641), verses, satires and translations, notably of Virgil. His is chiefly known for his topographical peom **Cooper's Hill**, (1642) which contains the well known address to the Thames, "O, could I flow like thee". It began a new genre, of which Pope's, **Windsor Castle** is the best known example. In his poem **Of Prudence** appear the lines:

> *"Youth, what man's age is like to be doth show;*
> *We may our ends by our beginning know."*

Disraeli, later Lord Beaconsfield (1803-81) entered in 1824, and kept nine terms, but removed his name in 1831. He had chambers in Old Buildings.

Charles Reade (1814-84) entered in 1835 and was called in 1842. He became a theatre manager in 1851 and began writing plays. In 1853 he published **Christie Johnstone** the first of his "reforming novels" advocating prison reform, and it was as a reforming novelist that he was best known during his lifetime. Today it is the historical novel, **The Cloister on the Hearth** (1861) set in 15th c Holland, with its catch phrase of, "Courage mon ami, le diable est mort!" which is the most read of his novels. Reade thought his best work was, **Griffith Gaunt** (1866) which is once again coming back into fashion and many modern critics rate it highly. Set in 18th c England it was unusually frank for its time and Reade was prosecuted in a case which Dickens "as a husband and father" refused to help defend him. The critics of his day placed his work even above that of George Eliot, today his historical novels are read and admired without anyone arguing that he is a great novelist.

Sir Henry Newbolt (1862-1938), who was called to the Bar in 1887, practised 12 years before dedicating himself to his writing. He wrote several novels, short stories and nautical histories, but is remembered for his stirring verse, especially **Drake's Drum** (1896):

> *"Take my drum to England, hang et by the shore,*
> *Strike et when your powder's runnin' low;*
> *If the Dons sight Devon, I'll quit the port of Heaven,*
> *An drum them up the Channel as we drummed them long ago."*

And the verses that every schoolboy learns by heart:

> *"There's a breathless hush in the Close to-night –*
> *Ten to make and the match to win –*
> *A bumping pitch and a blinding light,*
> *An hour to play and the last man in.*
> *And it's not for the sake of a ribboned coat,*
>   *Or the selfish hope of a season's fame,*
> *But his Captain's hand on his shoulder smote –*
>   *'Play up! play up! and play the game!'"*

Through the Gothic gateway and up Chancery Lane we turn right into Holborn and walk down until we see a splendid half-timbered building, above a parade of shops, **STAPLE INN**. A hostel for wool-staplers in the 14th c, it became an Inn of Chancery early in the 15th c. The present buildings date from 1586 and have been restored many times. The buildings suffered war damage and were restored in 1950, but the 16th c Hall had to be destroyed. It is now owned by Prudential Assurance Co and occupied by the Institute of Actuaries. If one enters the two small court-yards of the Inn one leaves the hustle and bustle of the town behind and experiences a dignified and almost unbelievable quiet tranquillity, a tranquillity which has been undisturbed for centuries. In Dickens' last and unfinished novel, **Edwin Drood** (1870) we have this description in Chapter 11:

> *"It is one of those nooks, the turning into which out of the clashing street, imparts to the relieved pedestrian the sensation of having put cotton in his ears, and velvet soles on his boots. It is one of those nooks where a few smoky sparrows twitter in smoky trees, as though they called to one another, 'Let us play at country', and where a few feet of garden mould and a few yards of gravel enable them to do that refreshing violence to their tiny understandings."*

And in Dickens' novel, **Bleak House**, poor Mr Snagsby comes to Staple Inn in search of a quiet haven from his problems.

Samuel Johnson had lodgings here in 1759 when his inability to pay the annual rent of £30 led to him leaving his home in Gough Square. The house where he resided was destroyed in the bombings. It was here that he learnt the grievous news of his mother's death, and he wrote **Rasselas, The History of a Prince of Abyssinia**, during the evenings of a week to pay for his mother's funeral and pay her debts. The work's appeal is its wise and humane melancholy. It is didactic and stresses that happiness is unobtainable, despite the efforts of the wealthy, the philosophic and of hermits to find it. It is rarely read today but the discussion of the poet's role by Imlac has become famous and much quoted:

> *"The business of a poet,"* said Imlac, *"is to examine, not the individual, but the species; . . . he does not number the streaks of the tulip, or describe the different shades in the verdure of the forest. He must write as the interpreter of nature, and the legislator of mankind, and considers himself as presiding over the thoughts and manners of future generations; as being superior to time and place."*

It is also in this work that the grieving son and widower put forward one of the best defences for marriage to appear in print:

> *"Marriage has many pains, but celibacy has no pleasure."*

And Johnson talks of, "The endearing elegance of female friendship" and that "Example is always more efficacious than precept". But the overall tenor of the work is best summed up by the lines in Chapter 11:

> *"Human life is everywhere a state in which much is to be endured, and little to be enjoyed."*

When Voltaire's **Candide** appeared that year Johnson remarked on its similarity to **Rasselas**.

Across the road in Holborn stands the large pink-red terracotta Gothic palace of Prudential Assurance. It is one of the last works by one of the greatest of Victorian architects, Alfred Waterhouse, whose Natural History Museum building in Kensington is one of London's prettiest buildings. He died before it could be completed and his son Paul finished it in 1906. It is on the site of another Inn of Chancery, **Furnival's Inn**, which dates back to 1383, and became attached to Lincoln's Inn, who bought the freehold of the Inn in 1547. **Sir Thomas More** was the Reader of the Inn in 1503. When Lincoln's Inn refused to renew the lease the Inn of Chancery was dissolved. A subsequent lessee demolished the Inn and built a new building, but keeping the name of Furnival's Inn. It was acquired in 1888 by Prudential for £150,000, so they could extend their offices over its site.

The young **Charles Dickens** lived here in 1834-7. From being a reporter of parliamentary proceedings Dickens got a job in 1834 on the Morning Chronicle at a salary of 5 guineas a week. His father was again arrested for debt in 1834, and Dickens got him released and moved

The courtyard of Staple Inn

The coade stone figures above the entrance of St Andrew's Holborn

him, his mother and the rest of the family into cheaper lodgings and left home, taking his favourite brother Fred with him into batchelor chambers in Furnival's Inn. It was in this year that he met **Harrison Ainsworth**. Ainsworth was the successful bestselling novelist while the young Dickens was an up and coming journalist, making a name for himself with his **Sketches by Boz**. These sketches were appearing regularly in the newspaper launched in 1835 by the Morning Chronicle, as a daily evening paper. The editor of the Evening Chronicle was an Edinburgh lawyer turned journalist, George Hogarth. Dickens became a friend of the Hogarth family and in April 1836 married Catherine Hogarth at St Luke's Church in Sydney Street, Chelsea. It was necessary for Dickens to obtain a special licence as Catherine was under age. They had a brief honeymoon in a village in Chatham before beginning their married life together in Furnival's Inn. They shared the accommodation with Catherine's younger sister, Mary and Dickens' brother Fred. **Sketches by Boz, Illustrative of Every-Day Life and Every-Day People** were published in volume form in 1836 and 1837 and Dickens received £150 for their copyright; he later bought back the copyright for 11 times that amount. It attracted the attention of a new publisher, Chapman and Hall who approached Dickens with the idea of writing the text for a series of illustrations, which eventually resulted in the comic masterpiece, **Pickwick Papers**. The first instalment of **Pickwick Papers** appeared three days before Dickens' wedding. The series got off to a slow start and only became popular when Dickens introduced Sam Weller as Mr Pickwick's cockney valet. In January 1837 after the birth of their first child Charley the Dickens family, complete with brother and sister-in-law moved to Doughty Street. Charles Dickens was by now famous and not yet 25, the editor of a new magazine, Bentley's Miscellanies, he was writing the last episodes of **Pickwick Papers** and producing for the new magazine the first instalments of **Oliver Twist**.

In **Martin Chuzzlewit** (1843-47) John Westlock had rooms at Furnival's Inn.

Next to the Prudential is **BROOKE STREET**. The site of **Sir Fulke Greville, Lord Brooke's** house. An adviser to Queen Elizabeth I and King James I, he wrote poetry and several tragedies and political treatises. He is best remembered for his **Life of Sir Philip Sidney** which was published posthumously in 1652. James I gave him a peerage in 1621 and granted him Warwick Castle and Knowle Park. In 1628, aged 74, he was murdered by one of his servants in Warwick Castle. The servant then committed suicide. In his **Elegy on the Death of Sir Philip Sidney** Fulke Greville wrote:

> *"Silence augmenteth grief, writing increaseth rage,*
> *Stal'd are my thoughts, which loved and lost, the wonder of our age,*
> *Yet quick'ned now with fire, though dead with frost ere now.*
> *Enraged I write, I know not what: dead, quick, I know not how."*

Lord Brooke's London house disappeared about 1680. On the site of what is now no 39, the boy poet Thomas Chatterton lived briefly, and committed suicide, while still only 17 years of age. **Chatterton** (1752-70) was born in Bristol, his father dying before his birth and he was brought up by his mother, a poor schoolmistress, beneath the shadows of St Mary's Redcliffe. While apprenticed to an attorney the 14 year old Chatterton began publishing pseudo-archaic prose works, which he claimed he had found in a box in St Mary's church. The poems of a 15th c monk followed from the same source. He offered some of the Rowley poems to Dodsley in December 1769, who did not publish them. Many, including Horace Walpole, took the poems to be genuine, but only one of those poems was published in Chatterton's lifetime, **"Elinoure and Juga"**, which appeared in May 1769 in the Town and Country Magazine. In April 1770 he went off to London in 'high spirits' to make his name, and received, so he claimed in his letters to his mother, "great encouragement" from Dodsley and other publishers. In his first two months he earned eleven guineas and sent back a box of presents for his mother and sister. Then with the death of his patron, Lord Mayor Beckford, the 'patriotic' publishers took fright, and the market overstocked with his feverish activity, had no place in the literary 'off season' for any more of his work. So Chatterton soon became penniless and starving but still too proud to accept the meal his landlady offered him, when on August 24 1770 he locked himself in his garret room, tore up his papers and took arsenic. Four months after his arrival in London he was being buried in the pauper's pit of the Shoe Lane Workhouse in Holborn.

The Rowley poems were published in 1777 by Thomas Trywhitt, and immediately controversy arose about whether or not they were forgeries. It was only with the 1871 edition of Chatterton's work by the professor of Anglo-Saxon at Cambridge, Walter Skeat, who convincingly proved they were bogus did the controversy come to an end. Chatterton's life and tragic end excited the interest of the Romantic movement and he became for **Wordsworth**, "the marvellous Boy/The Sleepless Soul that perished in his pride". **Keats** was moved to dedicate his **Endymion** (1818) to Chatterton and his memory, describing the young poet as "the purest writer in the English Language. He has no French idioms or particles, like Chaucer — 'tis genuine English Idiom in English words". The painter Wallis produced his picture of The Death of Chatterton using the poet and novelist, **George Meredith**, as his model. It is not based on any authentic likeness as none survived. The portrait hangs in the Tate Gallery. **Oscar Wilde** concluded his career as a public lecturer with a lecture on Chatterton, ending with a poem to noble Chatterton.

The best novel of 1987 was Peter Ackroyd's **Chatterton** which will prolong interest in the life of the boy-poet well into the next century. In the novel Chatterton's death is not suicide, but a misguided attempt to cure himself of the pox which he inherited from a night of love with his middle-aged landlady, with an over liberal application of arsenic.

We have in the poem **Sentiment** Thomas Chatterton's thoughts about dying:

> "*Since we can die but once what matter it*
> *If Pope or Garter, Poison, Pistol, Sword,*
>   *Slow-wasting Sickness or the sudden burst*
> *Of valve Arterial in the noble Parts*
>   *Curtail the Miserys of human life,*
> *Tho' varied is the Cause the Effect's the same*
> *All to one common Dissolution tends.*"

Passing Staple Inn one sees the huge red and blue late 1950s glass buildings of The Daily Mirror before one comes to the largest parish church in London, **St Andrew's Holborn**. It was not damaged in the Great Fire but was rebuilt by Sir Christopher Wren in 1684-90. The poet **Richard Savage** was christened here in 1696 as Richard Smith, being the illegitimate son of Lady Macclesfield. **Addington** was baptised here in 1757. In 1817 a young jewish boy was baptised here after his father had argued with the rabbi of the Bevis Mark synagogue. The father was **Isaac Disraeli**, his 13 year old son Benjamin, destined to become a bestselling novelist and a Tory Prime Minister. It would have been impossible for Disraeli to have had a political career without being baptised an Anglican, as all but members of the Church of England were excluded from taking up seats in the House of Commons at the time. He became Queen Victoria's favourite Prime Minister. It was Disraeli who said vis-à-vis Victoria, that to get on in life you have to flatter, but to get on with royalty you have to apply the flattery with a bucket and spade.

In 1808 the critic and essayist **Hazlitt** married his first wife Sarah Stoddart, with Mary Lamb as the bridesmaid and Charles Lamb as the best man. Lamb was almost thrown out of the church during the ceremony for his constant laughter.

In the pre-Wren church **Henry Wriothesley**, Earl of Southampton was baptised with Henry VIII as his godfather. Henry Wriothesley later became William Shakespeare's patron and loaned him the money to buy the largest house in Stratford, New Place, where the playwright retired and died in 1616.

The church was badly damaged by bombing in 1941, and was rebuilt in its original form in 1960-1 by the architects Sealey and Paget. The pulpit, font, organ case, chapel altarpiece, communion rails and tomb of Thomas Coram were brought from the Foundling Hospital in Coram Fields, which was demolished in 1926. Particularly charming are the figures of a boy and girl in coade stone at the church's entrance.

We cross over the road and leave Holborn by **Charterhouse Street**, turning left into the private road of **Ely**

Place, one of London's very special and unique streets. It is on the site of the Bishops of Ely's London Palace, built at the end of the 13th c. All the Bishops during the Middle Ages had London palaces, as they had to attend the King's Parliament and fulfil a lot of the functions that diplomats and senior civil servants have today. They were the intellectual elite of the nation. Ely in East Anglia was in the centre of the wool area which provided England's largest export and major source of wealth in the medieval period, so the Bishops could afford to build a truly magnificent palace in London and one of the finest churches in the world, in East Anglia, with its unparallelled octagonal tower, which gets so few tourists today that it became the first church to charge an entrance fee. (£1.60 in 1987). The palace was used by John of Gaunt from 1381 until his death in 1399, after his Savoy Palace had been wrecked in the Peasants' Revolt. It is here that "Old John of Gaunt, time-honour'd Lancaster" makes his famous speech in William Shakespeare's **Richard II.**

> "This royal throne of kings, this scepter'd isle,
> This earth of majesty, this seat of Mars,
> This other Eden, demi-paradise,
> This fortress built by Nature for herself
> Against infection and the hand of war,
> This happy breed of men, this little world,
> This precious stone set in the silver sea,
> Which serves it in the office of a wall,
> Or as a moat defensive to a house,
> Against the envy of less happier lands,
> This blessed plot, this earth, this realm, this England,
> This nurse, this teeming womb of royal kings,
> Fear'd by their breed and famous by their birth,
> Renowned for their deeds as far from home, –
> For Christian service and true chivalry, –
> As is the sepulchre in stubborn Jewry
> Of the world's ransom, blessed Mary's Son:
> This land of such dear souls, this dear, dear land,
> Dear for her reputation through the world,
> Is now leas'd out, – I die pronouncing it –
> Like to a tenement or pelting farm:
> England, bound in with the triumphant sea,
> Whose rocky shore beats back the envious siege
> Of watery Neptune, is now bound in with shame,

*With inky blots, and rotten parchment bonds:
That England, that was wont to conquer others,
Hath made a shameful conquest of itself.''*

There is another reference to Ely Palace in Shakespeare's **Richard III**. Richard, then Duke of Gloucester, says in Act II:

*"My Lord of Ely, when I was last in Holborn,
I saw good strawberries in your garden there;
I do beseech you send for some of them.*

*Bishop of Ely.   Marry, and will, my lord,
with all my heart.'' (Exit)*

The garden of the Bishops of Ely was reputed to be the most glorious in London, of which nothing remains but a place name, Hatton Garden. It was Elizabeth I who in 1576 obliged the Bishop to lease part of the property to her dancing partner and Lord Chancellor, Sir Christopher Hatton, in return for £10 a year, ten loads of hay and a rose picked at midsummer. While the see was vacant in the 1580s Hatton built himself a house in the garden, hence the street name Hatton Garden.

When the last Lord Hatton died in 1772 the property reverted to the Crown. The Bishops palace had become so delapidated that the Bishops moved to Ely House at no 37 Dover Street. Then the palace was demolished, all that is, except for the adjoining chapel, dedicated to St Etheldreda, and terrace houses were built on the site. Today it is an almost intact 18th c close of great charm. It retains its delightful miniature lodge, centrally positioned, with wrought iron gates to either side. In Dickens' **David Copperfield**, Agnes Wickfield stayed here and was visited by David Copperfield.

If you walk down to the end of Ely Place there is the chapel of **St Etheldreda**. St Etheldreda's was built in 1293 as a private chapel for the Bishop of Ely and is named after a 7th century Abbess of Ely. The crypt dates from even earlier, probably from about 1251, with part of the walls believed to be the remains of a Roman basilica. It is dimly lit through fine stained-glass of the east and west windows, and the church has a mystical and medieval feel, enhanced by being run by an order of monks. After various uses it was bought by the Catholic church in 1874, and is the oldest catholic church in England. It is, despite its smallness, one of London's most impressive churches, and should be visited. Its main event is on February 3rd each year, the Blessing of the Throat, commemorating St Blaise, who saved a boy from choking to death on a fishbone. During the ceremony lighted candles are held near those suffering from throat diseases. The street's big event is the Strawberry Fair each summer commemorating those famous strawberries in the Bishop's garden. There is a jazz band, men on stilts, clowns, lots of stalls, refreshments and a lighthearted swinging afternoon in keeping with the reserved character of the street. As it is always held on a Saturday afternoon Holborn is a quiet backwater enlivened by the fair.

At the end of Ely Place is **BLEEDING HEART YARD**. R.H. Barham's collection, **The Ingoldsby Legend** (1840) tells of Lady Elizabeth Hatton being killed by one of her many beaux in 1648. She was found the next morning dead, but with her heart still pumping blood. The place where her house stood in the Gardens of Ely Palace is now the yard named after her bleeding heart. In Dickens' **Little Dorrit** the Yard is the home of the Plornishes, the site of Doyce and Clennam's factory, and the property of the seemingly philanthropic Mr Caseby, a place that we are told in Chapter 12:

> *"with some relish of ancient greatness about it. Two or three mighty stacks of chimneys, and a few large dark rooms which had escaped being walled and subdivided out of recognition of their old proportions, gave the Yard a character. It was inhabited by poor people, who set up their rest among its faded glories, as Arabs of the desert pitch their tents among the fallen stones of the Pyramids; but there was a family sentimental feeling prevailing in the yard, that it had a character."*

If we walk back down Ely Place on the same side as St Etheldreda, there is a narrow opening which leads into a small courtyard and to the pub, Ye Old Mitre, built in 1546. The pub which is tiny, but very picturesque, contains a cherry tree inside, making it unique amongst London's pubs. The courtyard comes out into **HATTON GARDEN**, which Evelyn tells us, in his **Diary** in 1659, "To Lond... to see the foundations now laying for a longe streete, and buildings in Hatton Garden, designed for a little Towne; lately an ample Garden". The restoration dramatist **William Wycherley** had a house here in the 1670s. The founder of the foundlings hospital **Captain Coram** was living in the street in the 1740s, while **Guiseppe Mazzini**, Italian patriot, politician and author of **Il dovere dell'uomo** (The Duties of Man) was living here in exile in 1841-2 at no 5. It was Mazzini's Young Italy Movement that led to Italy's ultimate unification as one state in 1861-70. Turning left we return to Charterhouse Street and descend until we see **SAFFRON HILL** on the left, the site of Fagin's Den in Dickens' **Oliver Twist**. John Dawkins (the Artful Dodger) brings Oliver through London at dead of night to this haven:

> "As John Dawkins objected to their entering London before nightfall, it was nearly eleven o'clock when they reached the turnpike at Islington. They crossed from the Angel into St John's Road; struck down the small street which terminates at Sadler's Well Theatre; through Exmouth Street and Coppice Row; down the little court by the side of the workhouse, across the classic ground which once bore the name of Hockley-in-the-Hole then into Little Saffron Hill; and so into Saffron Hill the Great, along which the Dodger scudded at a rapid pace, directing Oliver to follow close at his heels."

Dickens knew this notorious rookery, a slum district inhabited by thieves and poor immigrants, first from Ireland, and later from Italy. A school for the poor, was started in Little Saffron Hill, and Dickens visited and took a great interest in the Ragged School, and described the area in **Oliver Twist** as, "A dirtier and more wretched place he had never seen".

The Victorian Improvement Schemes of the middle of the 19th c which created Holborn Circus, Holborn Viaduct and Farringdon Road swept away the slums, replacing them with warehouses, and the district developed into a commercial one. The slum dwellers, dispossessed without any compensation headed east to swell the burgeoning slums of the East End.

The name Saffron Hill goes back to the days when the street was still part of the Bishop of Ely's land. The Bishop's famous garden renowned for its fruit, and for saffron, which was first introduced into England in Cambridgeshire during the 14th c, and cultivated soon after in the Bishop's London garden. Saffron and spices in general were in great demand as a flavouring which could conceal the taste of the rancid meat which was the staple diet of the Londoners. The reason why life expectancy was so low was because of the unhealthy diet, the almost total lack of fresh vegetables, salad and fruit. By the beginning of the 18th c the hilly road, like the rest of the Bishop's former estate, had become a ramshackle slum area with only St Etheldreda's and the Mitre Tavern surviving unscathed.

At the end of Charterhouse Street we turn left into **Farringdon Road**, built in 1845-6. Parallel to it, London's first underground railway line, the Metropolitan Railway was opened in 1863, with a station on the road, Farringdon Street. It was built on the cut and cover technique, and is not a deep 'tube' line and often the train comes out into the daylight. The tube system, which is a lot deeper underground began in 1890, connecting Stockwell with the City. One can reflect that as the last public execution in London was at Newgate prison (the site of the Old Bailey) in 1868, and the underground railway had begun in 1863, one could have taken an underground train to view it. A rather stunning example of the progress and the backwardness of Victorian society. The best time to visit Farringdon Road is Saturday morning, for there is a really good second-hand and rare books market in the street. In Mayhew's **London Labour and the London Poor** (1851) he tells of the **Farringdon Market**, a 19th c fruit and vegetable market when 7 year old waifs would come and haggle at dawn with the stallholders to buy water cress, which they would hawk round the streets, crying, "Water-creases, four bunches a penny, water-creases!". A day's earnings would be no more than 3d or 4d.

We leave Farringdon Road where it meets Clerkenwell, turning right to enter the district often described as unknown London or London's forgotten village, but for the energetic they can continue further up the street to no 119, and The Guardian newspaper. Founded in 1821 as the Manchester Guardian it was a weekly newspaper which became a daily in 1855. It was the principal Liberal paper of the 19/20th centuries outside of London. Since 1961 it has been published in London. Its Literary Editor of 28 years standing, Bill Webb, has given prominence to social issues, radical and political works, and generous coverage to translations and books published by the smaller presses, clearly distinguishing his book pages from the rest of the national press. However The Guardian has been caught up in the Fleet Street obsession for change and is revamping itself with Bill Webb becoming the assistant editor of the new 'Personal Page', and his place as Literary Editor will be taken by Waldemar Januszczak, the paper's art critic. He is 33 and is well known for his incisive and outspoken views.

One retraces one's steps and takes the path for Clerkenwell.

CLERKENWELL

Orginally the site of a medieval monastery with a surrounding hamlet. There was a good water supply, the Fons Clericorum or Clerk's Well, which gave its name to the district. At the Dissolution of the Monasteries in 1535-40, the monastic land was given to the new Tudor nobility, and Clerkenwell became an aristocratic suburb near, but outside the City, and in close proximity to Westminster and the Court. The New River project in 1613 gave the City its first piped domestic water supply, which ran through Clerkenwell, and began the process in which the village became a City overspill area. During the reign of Charles II, with the Great Plague (1665) and the Great Fire (1666) and the westwards movement of the Court, the great houses of the nobility were abandoned to the merchants and the tradesmen. It was especially popular with foreign craftsmen, who were prevented by the City Guilds from competing in London, and French Huguenot refugees, amongst others, settled here as Clerkenwell rapidly became an urban conglomeration, a centre for watch and clock-makers, jewellers, printers and allied trades. Brewers of beer and gin settled here because of the good water supply. Fine houses were built, especially around St John's Square, and several spas were opened as gardens of popular entertainment with music and refreshment, including Sadler's Wells and the Islington Spa. Clerkenwell's period of middle class prosperity came to a rapid end in the 19th c where uncontrolled expansion after the Napoleonic Wars led to a rapid increase in population and the once fine streets becoming slums, and the large houses being subdivided into tenements for the poor.

The Victorian wide boulevards were always directed through the slum districts and the new roads and the railways created many homeless in Clerkenwell who migrated to the slums further to the east. With its rampant social problems Clerkenwell became a centre of radicalism and political protest, some of which ended in riots. As the 19th c progressed into the 20th c Clerkenwell declined as an urban and commercial area. There is little commerce, few houses and large prison-like barracks have been erected as council housing estates. Today the growing success in highlighting the richness of the area's history and the growth of the tourist industry, combined with the gentrification of nearby Islington has brought a reversal in the area's decline.

As we proceed up Clerkenwell Road on the left at no 14-16 Farringdon Lane, was the redbrick building of the New Statesman, the weekly magazine founded in 1913 as an organ of the Fabian Society, Socialist in standing but independent in party. Its first editor was **Clifford Sharp,** with **J.C. Squire** (1884-1958), poet, essayist and parodist, the Literary Editor. He and his circle became the literary establishment of the 1920s and 30s, and were detested by the more radical Bloomsbury group and the Sitwells. He and his friends were derogatorily called the Squirearchy. Amongst its regular contributors were the Webbs and G.B. Shaw. In more recent times the editors have included Paul Johnson, Richard Crossman and Anthony Howard, and with a distinguished list of contributors. Its editorial policy of "dissent, of scepticism, of inquiry, of non-conformity" continues. The present Literary Editor is Harriet Gilbert. The magazine has recently moved to no 38 Kingsland Road, London E2.

In the basement of this building there still is the Clerk's Well and a few kind words usually gets you inside to view it. There are records of miracle plays being performed in its vicinity from the 12th c onwards, by the clerks of the local parishes.

We see on the left an opening which will take us into **Clerkenwell Green** which alas is green no longer. In Dickens' **Oliver Twist** Mr Brownlow is robbed here and Oliver discovers the purpose of Fagin's training. In another Dickens novel, **Barnaby Rudge**, the upright locksmith Gabriel Varden and his family live in the vicinity, and a lot of the novel's action takes place in Clerkenwell. The locksmith's apprentice, the vainglorious, pint-sized and anarchic, Simon Tappertit takes an active part in the Gordon Riots. The family servant Miggs is a wonderful Dickens grotesque and as is usual in Dickens reaps what she has sown.

The Green contains one very attractive building, the 18th c Middlesex Sessions House, a late Palladian courthouse. This Georgian building is no longer in use as a court and is now an office. Walking past it one comes to the **Marx Memorial Library**, where the Russian revolutionary leader **Lenin** (1870-1924) wrote his pamphlets on wafer thin paper to be smuggled back into his homeland and provide the spark for the Revolution. It was at a meeting in the library on November 13 1887 held by the London Patriotic Club, addressed by the socialist designer, publisher, and writer **William Morris** that the protest march to Trafalgar Square began which culminated in the scenes of Bloody Sunday. The police with the help of the troops violently dispersed the demonstrators with many people being injured and two killed. One of the capital's newest literary magazines, The Fiction Magazine, has its offices across the green from the library. It has survived and established itself in the hazardous waters of literary periodicals under the editorship of Judy Cooke.

Leaving the Green we proceed up Clerkenwell until we come to St John's Square on our right and St John's Gate on our left, and to the heart of all that is interesting in the area.

ST JOHN'S SQUARE is the site of the priory church of the Knights Hospitallers, the Crusading Order which was dissolved at the Reformation by Henry VIII in 1540. The first priory church was built in about 1100 but it was destroyed during the Peasants Revolt of 1381, and Watt Tyler and his rebels had the prior beheaded on Tower Hill. The priory was rebuilt soon afterwards. It is said when the prior, Sir William Weston, heard of the King's order of dissolution he had a heart attack and died. Many of the Knights of the Order fled abroad, some of them who remained behind were executed. St John's Church was kept by Henry VIII to store his hunting tents, while the rest of the priory buildings were given to the Duke of Northumberland. In Edward VI's reign, his Lord Protector, Somerset blew up most of the priory to use the stone to build his house in the Strand, the present site of the Inland Revenue Offices, still called Somerset House. It later became a private chapel, then a presbyterian church, before a parish church in 1723. Almost parishionerless in 1931 it reverted to the Order of St John, which had been revived in 1831 as a Protestant Order, and best known as St John's Ambulance Brigade. The church, restored after the bombings of World War II, has a fine altarpiece from a 15 c Flemish triptych (the two wings) and an interesting and very well preserved crypt which is really worth visiting. The crypt is 12th century and amongst its monuments there are a memento mori from the tomb of the last prior of the order, Sir William Weston (d 1540) and a fine 16th c alabaster effigy of a Knight of the Order brought from Spain.

Across the road **ST JOHN'S GATE** is a survivor with the crypt and the chapel of St John's Church from the priory buildings. Built in 1504 it is now the Clerkenwell Museum. During the reign of Elizabeth I it served as offices for the Master of the Revels, Sir Edmund Tilney who licensed 30 of Shakespeare's plays. Between 1731-81 it housed the printing works of David Cave's Gentleman's Magazine. It was the first periodical to call itself a magazine, and intended to be a monthly journal of interesting news, essays and anecdotes filched from the innumberable daily and weekly newspapers and journals. By about 1739 it was full of original contributions and no longer functioned as a news digest. It became more serious in tone with essays, reviews, list of books being published and parliamentary reports. It was **Samuel Johnson** who helped to devise a means of evading the official ban on parliamentary reporting by claiming that the reports were from Lilliput. Johnson's accounts of debates in parliament for the magazine, between 1740 and 1743, were largely concocted by himself and always had the 'Whig dogs' getting the worst of it. His impressive parliamentary accounts were rarely questioned and believed to be authentic. When Samuel Johnson first set his eyes on St John's Gate he beheld it with great reverence as Boswell tells us in his **Life of Johnson:**

> *"The Gentleman's Magazine, begun and carried on by Mr Edward Cave, had attracted the notice and esteem of Johnson, in an eminent degree, before he came to London as an adventurer in literature. He told me, that when he first saw St John's Gate, the place where that deservedly popular miscel-*

lany was originally printed, he 'beheld it with reverence'.

It appears that he was now enlisted by Mr Cave as a regular coadjutor in his magazine, by which he probably obtained a tolerable livelihood. At what time, or by what means, he had acquired a competent knowledge both of French and Italian, I do not know; but he was so well skilled in them, as to be sufficiently qualified for a translator. That part of his labour which consisted in emendation and improvement of the production of other contributors, like that employed in levelling ground, can be perceived only by those who had the opportunity of comparing the original with the altered copy. What we certainly know to have been done by him in this way was the Debates in both Houses of Parliament, under the name of, 'The Senate of Lilliput', sometimes with feigned denominations of the several speakers, sometimes with denominations formed of the letters of their real names, in the manner of what is called anagram, so that they might easily be decyphered.

Thus was Johnson employed, during some of the best years of his life, as a mere literary labourer 'for gain not glory', solely to obtain an honest support. He however indulged himself in occasional little sallies, which the French so happily expressed by the term of jeux d'esprit, and which will be noticed in their order, in the progress of this work.

But what first displayed his transcendent powers and 'gave the world assurance of the MAN' was his London, a Poem, in Imitation of the Third Satire of Juvenal: which will for ever encircle his name."

Dr Johnson's name is no longer encircled by his poem, which like most of his work is unread, but by the praise of his biographer, who one might almost say created the MAN. At the time of its publication in 1738 the anonymous poem enjoyed great success, part of it political for its attack on Walpole's administration and the oppression of the poor, "All crimes are safe, but hated poverty":

"Here falling houses thunder on your head,
And here a female atheist talks you dead.
(1.17)

Of all the griefs that harass, the distress'd,
Sure the most bitter is a scornful jest;
Fate never wounds more deep the gen'rous heart,
Than when a blockhead's insult points the dart.
(1.176)

> *This mournful truth is ev'rywhere confess'd*
> *Slow rises worth by poverty depress'd"*
>   *(1.176)*

In his early days in London Dr Johnson found it hard to resist the attractions of the taverns, and a room was furnished for him in St John's Gate so that he could write undistracted and finish his contributions in time. To be doubly sure he would not yield to temptation and repair to the nearby coaching inns of St John Street the precaution was taken of locking him inside the room until he had finished.

It was at St John's Gate that Johnson met another of the magazines contributors, **Richard Savage** (1697-1743), who was to be the subject of his first biography in 1744 which is reprinted in Johnson's last work, **The Lives of the English Poets**. It is a truly remarkable life, at least as recounted by Johnson, with Savage the illegitimate son of Lady Macclesfield struggling to exist as a writer in London. Convicted and pardoned on a murder charge in 1727, he died imprisoned in a Bristol goal. He is the author of 2 plays, **Love in a Veil** (1719), and **The Tragedy of Sir Thomas Overbury** (1724), various odes and satires. His best work comes in the poem **The Wanderer** (1729) described by Johnson as "a heap of shining material thrown together by accident, which strikes with the solemn magnificence of the stupendous ruin". His most quoted lines appear in the poem, **The Bastard** (1728), where he attacks his 'Mother, yet no Mother' and has the line "No tenth transmitter of a foolish face", and the well known:

> *"Perhaps been poorly rich, and meanly great,*
> *The slave of pomp, a cipher in the state."*

Johnson shared Savage's life of the poor poet and they would often wander round the streets of London at night to save the cost of a night's lodging, and when they were in funds they would frequent the taverns and more likely than not the City's low life. Johnson, a very devout man, worried greatly in his last years whether the early years in London, spent in dissipation with Savage, would lead to his eternal damnation, and was very circumspect about what had actually taken place.

The Gentleman's Magazine lost its popularity in the 19th c as a literary magazine, even though it published the work of young writers like Charles Lamb, it seemed antiquated. The magazine however continued as a periodical of general interest until 1914.

Also in St John's Gate, the painter William Hogarth's father had a coffee house. Today it combines the function of a tourist office for the district and a museum of local history and should be visited.

In the nearby Priory House the supplements of The Times have their offices, including The Times Literary Supplement. This began in 1902 as part of The Times before becoming a separate publication in 1910. Its first editor, **Bruce Richmond** (1871-1964) was an invaluable fosterer of new talent, commissioning articles and publicizing the work of Virginia Woolf, T.S. Eliot, J.M. Murry, E. Blunden amongst many others. In his 35 years as editor he established a world-wide reputation for the TLS. Under the editorship of John Gross reviews ceased to be anonymous and now always appear with the name of the reviewer. It is still the no 1 literary publication in Great Britain, if not the world, and covers most of the important works of literature and scholarship, often reviewing foreign works before they are translated, a practice more literary magazines should follow.

Continuing up Clerkenwell Road we reach the junction with Goswell Road, passing on the way St John Street, once famous for its taverns. **ST JOHN STREET** was full of coaching taverns and was the starting point for journeys North to Barnet and the villages beyond. The Three Cups Tavern is mentioned in Daniel Defoe's **Moll Flanders** (1722), while Samuel Pepys supped at the Bottle of Hay. Richard Savage's favourite tavern, the Cross Keys was at no 16. It was here that the 9 year old **Thomas Hardy** stayed with his mother on their way back to Dorset from a visit to his mother's sister in Hatfield. Hardy remembered his mother searching the huge old closets in the room in case any man should be hiding there, before she put out the light in their attic room. His other abiding memory of this first trip to the big city was the cruelty of the men to the beasts in Smithfield Market.

One of Dr Johnson's haunts has survived, the Old Red

Lion at no 418, where he was a frequent customer in his early days in London. Oliver Goldsmith and Tom Paine also frequented this tavern. The street today is a mixture of commerce, little shops and small businesses with no particular character. It leads to the City University.

We enter **GOSWELL ROAD** having turned right. This part of the street, before Aldersgate Street, was once called Goswell Street, and at the beginning of **Pickwick Papers** Mr Pickwick had his lodgings here with Mrs Bardell. When he opened his window, "Goswell Street was at his feet; Goswell Street was on his right hand — as far as the eye could reach; Goswell Street extended on his left: and the opposite side of Goswell Street was over the way". Mrs. Bardell misconstrues the innocent Mr Pickwick's words, seeing an offer of matrimony which, when it did not materialize, leads to the breach of promise case of Bardell v Pickwick. Damages are awarded against the noble Pickwick who goes to prison rather than pay, that is until Mrs Bardell becomes an inmate of the very same prison, as a debtor to her lawyer, bringing a change of heart in the chivalrous Pickwick who buys them both out of prison.

ALDERSGATE STREET was named after one of London's six original gates in the walls of the City. During the Middle Ages the church of St Botolph Aldersgate was built nearby, honouring the then patron saint of travellers, whose intercession was required to guard you from the multiple perils of travelling outside the City walls. The church was the first recorded building in the street, mentioned in 1135. The Gate stood where no 62 is today. There was a workshop above used by the printer **John Day** (1522-84). He produced **The Folio Bible** (1549), the first church service book with musical notation (1560), **Parker's English version of the Psalms, with music by Tallis and others** (1560), Roger Ascham's **Scholemaster** (1570), and the **Works of Tyndale** in 1572. But by far the most famous book that he produced was Foxe's **Book of Martyrs** (1563). In 1660 Samuel Pepys saw the limbs of traitors on the Gate. It was demolished in 1761.

John Milton lived in the street, at Maidenhead Court in 1639, where he educated his nephews and other children in a kind of elite private boarding school, his little academy. It was "a spacious house," he tells us, "for myself and my books where I again with rapture renewed my literary pursuits". It is in this period he wrote his 5 anti-episcopal pamphlets in a vigorous, colourful Ciceronian prose which at times rises to visions of apocalyptic grandeur. They were published in 1641 refuting the writings of Bishops Hall and Ussher. In the Summer of 1642 Milton returned from a short trip to Oxford with a 17 year old bride, Mary Powell, he was almost 34. Their married life began badly and he allowed her, after just six weeks of married life, to go on a visit to her parents on the condition she would return in time for Michaelmas. Mary failed to return, the outbreak of the Civil War and her mother's hostility towards Milton combined to keep her at Oxford. Newly married but estranged from his wife Milton wrote his controversial pamphlet advocating divorce, **The Doctrine and Discipline of Divorce** which was published in 1643 and made him notorious. He argued that people should not find themselves, "chained unnaturally together" and urged in true little Englander fashion, "Let not England forget her precedence of teaching nations how to live". Other pamphlets on divorce followed from Milton's pen as Mary Milton (née Powell) steadfastly refused his entreaties to return. Milton turned his attention towards a certain Miss Davis with whom he fell in love as the Civil War was decided in favour of parliament. One day during the Summer of 1645 Milton was visiting relatives, the Blackboroughs, at their house in the lane of St Martin Le Grand and was told on entering the parlour that there was someone waiting in the next room to see him. The visiting person was his wife Mary, who Milton forgave, no doubt influenced by the beautiful young woman his 21 year old wife had become. He moved into a house in the nearby Barbican, and when he had settled in allowed Mary to rejoin him.

It was during the summer of 1642 when a royalist attack on London seemed imminent and houses began to be barricaded for their protection that Milton wrote a sonnet addressed to a Cavalier marauder. It reminded him how in the days of Alexander the Great invading armies spared the houses of poets, promising him in return for his forebearance immortality by being the subject of his poem. It is said that he pinned it to the door of his house in Aldersgate Street as its sole protector:

> "Captain or colonel, or knight in arms,
> Whose chance on these defenceless doors may seize,
> If deed of honour did thee ever please,
> Guard them, and with him within protect from harm,
> He can requite thee, for he knows the charms
> That call fame on such gentle acts as these,
> And he can spread thy name o'er lands and seas,
> Whatever clime the sun's bright circle warms.
> Lift not thy spear against the muses' bower,
> The great Emathian conqueror bid spare
> The house of Pindarus, when temple and tower
> Went to the ground: and the repeated air
> Of sad Electra's poet had the power
> To save the Athenian walls from ruin bare."

In was in Aldersgate Street, next door to the Golden Lion that Samuel Simmons published **Paradise Lost** in 1667, establishing Milton's fame as a poet in England. Paradoxically from his youth Milton's Latin and Italian verses had established his reputation in Europe, especially in Italy. In England it was only his late epic poems that proved his genius as a poet, something Milton had always taken for granted.

In 1648, the Cavalier poet **Richard Lovelace** was kept in prison in Petre House, which after the Great Fire became the home of the Bishop of London. The house was burnt down in 1768. It was at a Moravian meeting house here in 1728 that **John Wesley** (1703-91) experienced a revelation:

> "Went very unwillingly to a society in Aldersgate Street where one was reading Luther's Preface to the Epistle to the Romans. About a quarter before nine while he was describing the changes which God makes in the heart through faith in Christ, I felt my heart strangely warmed."

What was once a very fine street in the 17th and 18th c is a rather dreary characterless road, with the east side of the street now part of the Barbican development. We turn into the modern complex of apartments, theatres, concert halls and exhibition halls which is the Barbican today.

THE BARBICAN

Named after part of the City of London's ancient fortifications, probably a watch tower, which was pulled down, according to John Stow, in 1267 by Henry III after the war with the barons.

John Milton lived here between 1645-49. His collected poems were published in 1645 at the sign of the Prince's Arms in St Paul's Churchyard. It took 15 years for the first edition to sell out. Milton's house was crowded, his father lived here with Milton, his wife and his pupils when in June 1646 his father and mother-in-law and their 5 children arrived on his doorstep. After the vicissitudes which they had caused in his marriage Milton would have been well within his right to show them the door, but being dispossessed by the Civil War Milton took them in. At the end of the month Milton's first child Anne was born. It was discovered later that she was lame and what we would describe today as mentally retarded. On January 1st 1647 Milton's father-in-law died aged 50 and was buried at the parish church, St Giles Cripplegate. On March 15th Milton's father died aged 83 and was buried at St Giles. Later that year his mother-in-law and her 5 children moved out, leaving her son-in-law's young family with a little space and much needed tranquillity. His pamphlet **The Tenure of Kings and Magistrates** was published on the 13th of February 1649. It contains many memorable lines:

> *"None can love freedom heartily, but good men; the rest love not freedom but licence.*
>
> *No man who knows aught, can be so stupid to deny that all men naturally were born free."*

It defended the execution of the King, Charles I, as just and supported the King's executioners. It resulted in him being given the position of Secretary of Foreign Tongues. A house went with the position and he and his family moved to Petty France, a house with a pretty garden near the parliament in Westminster.

The street and the surrounding area of the Barbican were bombed in World War I and devastated in World War II. It was hoped to create a 'genuine residential neighbourhood, incorporating schools, shops, open spaces and amenities' on this 35 acre site, even if it meant, 'foregoing a more remunerative return on the land'. The land was compulsorily purchased in 1958 and flats, some in tower blocks over 400 ft high were built to accommodate 6,500 people. This middle class enclave in the heart of the City has not quite worked out as intended, and the Barbican operates as a kind of pied-à-terre for businessmen in the week, and on the weekend it is like the rest of the City, deserted. Some of the flats have also become offices. In the midst of this complex a vast cultural centre was built, a kind of London equivalent to the Lincoln Center in New York, or the Pompidou Centre in Paris. It contains an art gallery, a concert hall for the London Symphony Orchestra, and a theatre for The Royal Shakespeare Company who left the Aldwych in 1982 for their new home. The largeness of the scale makes the Barbican quite a forbidding place and is disconcertingly easy to get lost and wander in endless circles in its midst. Despite that the Londoners are slowly warming to its attractions. It contains the superb Museum of London (closed on Monday) which is the best laid out and presented museum in London and the most interesting museum for anyone with a fascination for London and its history. From prehistoric to modern, every period of London life is richly presented and documented. The exhibits include part of London's Roman Wall and the Lord Mayor's coach which disappears when the Lord Mayor is in need of it for an official function. There is a wonderful parade of Victorian shops, and a sound and light performance of the Great Fire. It is the most visual and thematic of our museums and by far the best museum to visit with young children. Almost lost in the Barbican maze is the church of St Giles Cripplegate.

ST GILES WITHOUT CRIPPLEGATE

An 11th c church dedicated to the patron saint of cripples, St. Giles. It was rebuilt twice during the 16th c, and survived unscathed the Great Fire only to be destroyed by the bombings of World War II. It was rebuilt as the parish church of the Barbican Development. The interior is somewhat disappointing. Outside in what was the churchyard there is a bastion of the old City wall. In and around the Barbican there are large sections remaining of the old wall which are well signposted and one can pass an enjoyable afternoon following the line of the wall, with the help of The London Wall Walk booklet produced by the London Museum.

Oliver Cromwell married Elizabeth Bourchier at St Giles in 1620. **John Foxe** (1516-87) was buried here, he was the author of **Actes and Monuments of these latter perillous dayes, touching matters of the Church**, popularly known as the Book of Martyrs. It was first published in Latin at Strasbourg in 1559, an English version appearing in 1563. The book deals with the history of the Christian church from the earliest times, giving special attention to the suffering of Christian martyrs of all ages, especially those of Queen Mary I's reign, who were Protestants. A former Oxford don he left England during the reign of Queen Mary and on his return after her death he became a priest. He wrote a verse drama, **Christus Triumphans** (1556) and several other Latin works of little interest today. His **Book of Martyrs** is still in print in a greatly abbreviated form. Also buried here were:

Martin Frobisher (1435-94) the Elizabethan explorer and sailor whose accounts of his adventures appeared under the title **The Three Voyages** and was edited by Stefansson.

John Speed (1552-1629) historian and cartographer. He published a **Historie of Great Britain** (1611) and an atlas of his maps in 1611, under the title of **The Theatre of the Empire of Great Britain**, which has been of great importance and is still in demand.

John Milton was buried here in 1674 next to his father.

His funeral on the Sunday of the 12th November was a big affair, with Andrew Marvell and John Dryden amongst the mourners. A small square stone in the church marks the site of his grave. His grave was opened and desecrated in 1793, accounts vary of the exact circumstances:

"A journeyman named Holmes procured a mallet and chisel, and forcing open the coffin so that the corpse (which was clothed in a shroud, and looked as if it had only just been buried) might be seen. Mr Fountain, one of the overseers, then endeavoured to pull out the teeth but, being unsuccessful, a bystander took up a stone and loosened them with a blow. There were only five in the upper jaw, but they were quite white and good. They, together with some of the lower ones Mr Fountain, (and two other men) divided between them. A rib bone was also taken and the hair from the head which was long and smooth was torn out by the handful. After this the caretaker Elizabeth Grant took the coffin under her care charging sixpence to anyone who wished to view it. Later she reduced her fee to threepence and finally to twopence."

Holman Hunt (1827-1910), the pre-Raphaelite painter was christened here in 1827. Famous for his picture, The Light of the World, of which there are three versions, he also painted many pictures with literary subjects drawn from the works of Shakespeare, Tennyson, Keats and Bulwer-Lytton. His autobiographical **Pre-Raphaelitism and the Pre-Raphaelite Brotherhood** (1905) is a full but personal history of the movement. We make our way back into Aldersgate Street where we turn right down Carthusian Street to Charterhouse Square.

CHARTERHOUSE SQUARE

The square was once 13 acres of land adjoining Pardon Churchyard which Sir Walter de Manny gave to the City of London in 1350-1 as a burial ground for victims of the Black Death. In 1370 a Carthusian monastery was founded on the site as the House of the Salutation of the Mother of God, otherwise known as the Charterhouse. Henry Yevele, one of the architects of Westminster Abbey, took charge of the building operations. Most of the two storey houses, 'cells' were finished by 1398. Sir Walter de Manny was buried in the chapel in 1372, and John of Gaunt endowed 500 masses to be said for his soul. Between 1499 and 1503 **Sir Thomas More** used to pray at the monastery and wore a hairshirt as an act of penance. At the Reformation the prior and several other monks from the Charterhouse were hung at Tyburn, and while still alive, cut down and quartered. The monastery was surrendered to the King and used for storing his hunting accoutrements. After a succession of aristocratic owners it was bought by Thomas Sutton in 1611, who was esteemed the richest commoner in England, for £13,000. Sutton endowed it as a school for 44 poor boys and a hospital for 80 poor gentlemen. The school moved to Godalming in 1872. The old buildings were bombed in 1941 and restored after the war, with St Bartholomew's Medical School built over the site of the old cloister. The charterhouse pensioners still live in the surviving old buildings, their number is now limited to 40. To qualify they must be bachelors or widowers, members of the Church of England, and over 60 years old; and they must have been officers in the Army or Navy, clergymen, doctors, lawyers, artists or professional men. They occupy chambers in Master's Court and Wash-House Court. On Wednesday afternoon it is possible to visit the Charterhouse during the summer months, though most passers-by find it hard to resist a stroll in the cloistered calm of the alms houses. Charterhouse Square with its Charterhouse is one of London's most pleasant squares, rarely crowded it is deserted on the weekends and evenings and allows the visitor perfect calm and tranquillity, and an opportunity to enjoy one of London's forgotten corners.

Richard Crashaw (1612-49) was a pupil at Charterhouse. He was a fellow at Peterhouse Cambridge but fled England when he was converted to catholicism and lived first in Paris and then in Rome, as an attendant on Cardinal Palotte. A mainly religious poet he published a volume of Latin poems, **Epigrammatum Sacrorum Liber**, which has the famous line on the Miracle at Cana, "The modest water saw its God and blushed (Nympha pudica Deum vidit et erbuit)". His main work **Steps to the Temple** appeared in 1646, and was revised and extended and appeared posthumously as **Carmen Deo Nostro** at Paris in 1652. His poems range from the metaphysical dramatic intense style of John Donne to what some have called the ultimate English baroque. He is one of the most melodious poets of his day. His most anthologised poems are **The Weeper: a poem on Mary Magdalen:**

> "*Two walking Baths, two weeping motions;*
> *Portable and compendious oceans.*"

Wishes To his (supposed) Mistresse:

> "Who ere shee bee,
> That not impossible shee
> That shall command my heart and mee.
> Where ere shee lye,
> Lock't up from mortal Eye,
> In shady leaves of Destiny:"

and **His Hymn to St Theresa:**

> "*Love thou art absolute sole Lord*
> *Of Life and death.*"

Other famous pupils included **Richard Lovelace** (1618)-57) the cavalier poet, **Richard Steele** (1672-1729) and his friend **Joseph Addison** (1672-1719).

Addison distinguished himself as a classical scholar with his Latin poems praised by Dryden. He had a political career and was a Member of Parliament from 1708 until his death, and was a close friend of Jonathan Swift and a prominent member of the Whig Kit-Cat Club. His neo-

The Charterhouse

A courtyard in the Charterhouse

classical tragedy **Cato** (1713) was successful, partly for political reasons, unlike his comedy **The Drummer** (1715) which failed badly. In the last year of his life he fell out with his life-long friend Steele, with whom he collaborated to produce The Tatler, The Spectator and The Guardian. He was buried in Westminster Abbey. He is remembered today for his contributions to The Tatler and The Spectator, and his creation of Sir Roger de Coverley:

> *"As Sir Roger is landlord to the whole congregation, he keeps them in very good order, and will suffer nobody to sleep in it (the church) besides himself; for if by chance he has been surprised into a short nap at sermon, upon recovering out of it, he stands up, and looks about him; and if he sees anybody else nodding, either wakes them himself, or sends his servant to them."*

But for most students of English Literature Joseph Addison is Pope's much satirised Atticus, in his **Epistle to Dr Arbuthnot** (1735):

> *"Were there one whose fires*
> *True genius kindles, and fair fame inspires;*
> *Blest with each talent, and each art to please,*
> *And born to write, converse, and live with ease:*
> *Should such a man, too fond to rule alone,*
> *Bear, like the Turk, no brother near the throne,*
> *View him with scornful, yet with jealous eyes,*
> *And hate for arts that caus'd himself to rise;*
> *Damn with faint praise, assent with civil leer,*
> *And, without sneering, teach the rest to sneer;*
> *Willing to wound, and yet afraid to strike,*
> *Just hint a fault, and hesitate dislike.   (I.193)*
>
> *Alike reserv'd to blame, or to commend,*
> *A tim'rous foe, and a suspicious friend;*
> *Dreading ev'n fools, by flatterers besieged,*
> *And so obliging, that he ne'er oblig'd;*
> *Like Cato, give his little senate laws,*
> *And sit attentive to his own applause.   (I.207)*
>
> *Who but must laugh, if such a man there be?*
> *Who would not weep, if Atticus were he!"*
> *(I.215)*

John Wesley (1703-91) and **Sir William Blackstone** (1723-80) were both former pupils.

William Makepeace Thackeray (1811-63) does not seem to have enjoyed his time at Charterhouse. He talked of the brutality of public school life, calling his masters Birch and Swishtail and the school Slaughterhouse. It is Thackeray who puts the school and its alms houses into literature in his novel **The Newcomes** (1853-5), the school is called Grey Friars. The hero of the novel Colonel Newcome as a boy was a pupil at the school and as an old man finishes as a Poor Brother in an alms house where he dies:

> *"At the usual evening hour the chapel bell began to toll, and Thomas Newcome's hands outside the bed feebly beat time. And just as the last bell struck, a peculiar sweet smile shone over his face, and he lifted up his head a little, and quickly said 'Adsum' and fell back. It was the word we used at school, when names were called; and lo, he whose heart was as that of a little child, had answered to his name, and stood in the presence of his Master."*

The manuscript of **The Newcomes** is in the library of the school's new building at Godalming. The writer and caricaturist **Sir Max Beerbohm** (1872-1956) was a pupil at the new location. He said of his schooldays: "My delight in having been at Charterhouse was far greater than my delight in being there." He is best remembered as one of Oscar Wilde's circle and for his novel of life in Oxford, **Zuleika Dobson** (1911) and his essay on **Swinburne**.

The playwright **Elkanah Settle** (1648-1724) spent the last six years of his life as a Charterhouse pensioner. His bombastic oriental melodramas were so successful they rivalled those of Dryden in the public esteem, and the two playwrights put a lot of effort into satirizing and belittling each other's work. Settle is Doeg in the second part of Dryden's **Absalom and Achitophel:**

> *"Doeg, though without knowing how or why,*
> *Made still a blund'ring kind of melody;*
> *Spurr'd boldly on, and dash'd through thick and thin,*
> *Through sense and nonsense, never out nor in;*
> *Free from all meaning, whether good or bad,*
> *And in one word, heroically mad."*

Settle became City poet and wrote short farces for performance at St Bartholomew's Fair in Smithfield.

We leave Charterhouse Square and enter into Smithfield.

SMITHFIELD

This was a large open space just outside the City Walls used for tournaments and major public events. In the first history, or account of London we have, **William Fitzstephen**, a clerk for St Thomas Becket, describes the area in 1173 as, "a smooth field where every Friday there is a celebrated rendez-vous of fine horses to be sold". It was to this horse market that Sir John Falstaff sent his servant Bartolph to buy his horses in Shakespeare's **Henry IV, Pt 2**. Other animals were traded at the market and by 1400 the City was granted the tolls of the market by charter. Great tournaments took place in the smooth fields, including one for 7 days in 1384 in honour of Alice Perrers, Edward III's mistress. Bartholomew's Fair was held here from 1123 until 1855. It was founded by Rahere, court jester to Henry I and became the greatest cloth fair in the country, and was held annually for three days on the eve of St Bartholomew's Day. By the 17th c the fair had become more important as a centre of general entertainment than as a cloth fair. It was a cross between today's circus and fun fair. We have an account of the fair in Ben Jonson's play, **Bartholomew Fair**.

First performed by the Lady Elizabeth Men in 1614 the comedy follows the fortunes of various visitors to the fair, including Littlewit, his wife Win-the-fight, his mother-in-law Dame Purecraft and the Puritan Zeal-o-the-land Busby. It gives a vivid account of the Fair's entertainments, with the attendant bawds, cutpurses and tricksters who pray upon the stallholders and their customers.

Elkanah Settle wrote farces for the fair, called drolls: scenes from plays expanded into mini-plays. Later that century both **Pepys** and **Evelyn** give descriptions of the Fair in their **Diaries**, with Pepys commenting on the re-introduction of the old sport of wrestling. It appealed to both rich and poor alike with the Prince of Wales visiting the fair with great pomp in 1740. In George Stevens' **Songs** (1772) he tells us: "While gentle folk strut in their silver and satins we poor folk are tramping in straw hat and pattens." The essayist **Charles Lamb** took his friends **William** and **Dorothy Wordsworth** to the Fair in 1802, and half a life-time later William Wordsworth can still remember the "chattering monkeys, the hurdy-gurdy and children whirling in their roundabouts at The Fair" (**The Prelude 1850**). The fair was suppressed in 1855 by the City authorities because of its rowdiness. It is interesting to reflect that the Puritans allowed the fair to continue while the Victorians felt the need to suppress it.

It was at Smithfield that Watt Tyler and his peasant rebels met the boy king, Richard II and his entourage to make their grievances known, especially against the much hated Poll Tax. Tyler increased his demands and the Lord Mayor of London William Walworth fearing for the life of the King, pulled Tyler from his horse and stabbed him, aided by another of the King's party, Standish. The 14 year old Richard, displaying admirable courage and leadership, offered himself to the rebels as their captain, and in their confusion succeeded in leading them north to the fields at Clerkenwell, where they were persuaded to disperse without bloodshed. The anarchy of the peasants' revolt and their execution of government officials, including the Archbishop of Canterbury and many lawyers, and the pillaging and destruction caused in London were sufficient for the Poll Tax to be withdrawn and to have a salutary effect on the minds of England's rulers for many generations to come. It was undoubtedly the worst and most bloody event of popular violence that London has ever seen. The dagger of the Lord Mayor which killed Watt Tyler can be seen in the Fishmonger's Hall in Thames Street; William Walworth was a distinguished member of the Company of Fishmongers.

The large expanse of Smithfield made it suitable as a place of public execution, and for over 400 years the gallows stood here until the beginning of the 15th c when they were moved to Tyburn (where Marble Arch is today.) It has always been a very good place for burning people, especially witches and heretics. While they were being roasted or boiled alive a priest would be near at hand trying to get the victim to recant. There are firsthand accounts of Henry V, when Prince of Wales, trying to get John Bailey to recant during his execution. The Greenwich priest John

Forest was put in a cage and roasted alive for refusing to accept Henry VIII as the head of the Church of England in 1538. In the reign of Mary I, Henry VIII's catholic daughter, 200 protestant martyrs were burnt in 1554-8. Not all the burnings were for religious reasons, **Evelyn** tells of seeing a woman burned at Smithfield for poisoning her husband.

The area also lent itself to fighting and duelling which became such a problem that it was urbanised in 1615, with paving stones, railings and sewers being provided. In 1638 the cattle market was officially established by Royal Charter. The stampeding cattle driven by drunken herdsmen became a frequent complaint in the streets which grew up around the market as London spread out in the 17th c. The panic-stricken animals would often take refuge in shops and houses, giving rise to the expression a bull in a china shop. The problem was greatly discussed and proclamations issued but it was only in 1855, that the sale of live cattle and horses was finally ended. The cattle used to be slaughtered in the market with the bloody debris blocking the drainage channels. What it must have been like we can gauge from Charles Dickens' account in **Oliver Twist:**

> "The ground was covered, nearly ankle-deep, with filth and mire; a thick steam perpetually rising from the reeking bodies of the cattle . . . the unwashed, unshaven and dirty figures constantly running to and fro, and bursting in and out of the throng, rendered it a stunning and bewildering scene, which confounded the senses."

Thomas Hardy remembered for the rest of his life the brutality of the men at the market to the beasts which he had seen on his first visit to London as a 9 year old boy.

A dead meat market was created in a new building by Horace Jones, built on the model of Paxton's Crystal Palace. It was opened in 1866 as the London Central Meat Market, with underground links to the main railway stations. The entire poultry section was burnt down in 1958 and a replacement market hall was completed in 1963. Smithfield is the only major market still in London and employs over 3,000 people and sells over 350,000 tons of meat every year, making it the largest meat market in

Entrance to St Bartholomew's Smithfield

Period houses in Cloth Fair Smithfield

Europe. The market is open through the night until about midday, by 5 a.m. the market is in full swing. The cafes and pubs in the vicinity provide wonderfully large breakfasts and in the early hours of the morning the area is alive with activity. The pubs are licensed from 6.30 a.m., and many of the porters can enjoy a drink with their breakfast. For the casual visitor it is often a shock to find when they want a drink the pubs have closed for the day. It will be a sad day for London when its last great market is shifted out to some faceless new home. Later on the tour we will see Horace Jones' other market buildings, the splendid Leadenhall Market.

Adjacent to the market is the church of **St Bartholomew the Great** the oldest working church in London, the only surviving part of the Augustinian prior, founded by Henry I's jester, Rahere in 1123. We enter the church by the beautiful half timbered gateway and enjoy the idyllic calm of this ecclesiastical backwater, which gets surprisingly few visitors. The tomb of Rahere the jester is here, and a very attractive 15th c font, but the church's most interesting feature is the Norman 12th c choir. The painter **William Hogarth** (1697-1764) was baptised in the church in 1697, and more recently the poet **Vernon Watkins** was married here during World War II. The best man was **Dylan Thomas** (1914-53) that is he would have been if he had not failed to turn up at his best friend's wedding. It took Thomas two weeks to send his apologies in a letter he crumpled up to make it look as if he had been carrying it around since the wedding and finally got round to posting. Surprisingly Watkins forgave Thomas and their friendship continued, and it was Vernon Watkins who edited Dylan Thomas' **Complete Works** after his death, and wrote at very short notice Thomas' obituary in The Times. Dylan Thomas' many letters to Vernon Watkins are in the British Museum and is the most important collection of the poet's letters in the UK, most of his letters, manuscripts and worksheets are held in American Universities, with Texas having the largest collection.

As a poet **Vernon Watkins** (1906-67) had a strong lyrical gift, with many of his poems rooted in Welsh folklore and mythology as in his first collection, **The Ballad of Mari Lwyd** (1941). An edition of **Selected Poems**

(1967) gives a varied selection of the poems he wrote between 1933 and 1960. He was one of T.S. Eliot's discoveries as Poetry Director of Faber and Faber.

The Lady's Chapel of the priory church was used as a printer's office in the 18th c and **Benjamin Franklin** worked here for a time when he came to England in 1757. Franklin set up his own press in America. The chapel is once again part of the church. The nearby Butcher's Company holds its annual service in the church.

Near to the church there is a monument commemorating the execution of the Scottish patriot Sir William Wallace in 1305. After his trial in Westminster Hall he was hanged, drawn, beheaded and quartered in public at Smithfield. His quarters were sent to Newcastle, Berwick, Stirling and Perth. Past this monument we arrive at **St Bartholomew's Hospital**, the large teaching hospital which has the distinction of being the capital's oldest hospital, founded by Rahere in 1123. The jester had an attack of malaria during a pilgrimage to Rome and made an oath that if he survived his illness he would build a hospital in London on his return. Watt Tyler was brought here after being stabbed by the Lord Mayor during the Peasant's Revolt, but before he could be treated the King's men dragged him outside the hospital and beheaded him. The priory attached to the hospital was dissolved by Henry VIII, who petitioned by Sir Richard Gresham, consented to the hospital's continuation and it was refounded in 1544 as a non religious body. It is for this reason that the statue of Henry VIII appears over the hospital, the only statue of Henry VIII in London. Dr Roderigo Lopez was appointed the hospital's physician in 1568, his career as London's leading doctor came to an end when he was accused of trying to poison Queen Elizabeth I, and was hung at Tyburn in 1594. He was one of the inspirations for Marlowe's play, **The Jew of Malta**.

The hospital was rebuilt in four blocks round a courtyard by James Gibbs in 1730-59, and one of its governors **William Hogarth** presented his large paintings The Good Samaritan and the Pool of Bethesda to the hospital in the hope of attracting commissions for his work. If one asks one can go in and see Hogarth's paintings which now decorate the main staircase.

Bust of Charles Lamb at Holy Sepulchre's Newgate

Statue of gluttony at Cock Lane

Inside the hospital entrance is the church of **St Bartholomew the Less**, the chapel of the hospital. The church was rebuilt several times, with George Dance creating an octagon in wood within a square for the interior in 1789. The church was bombed in the war and was restored in 1956.

John Shirley (1366-1456) and his wife are buried in the church. They are depicted in a brass in the habit of pilgrims. He was the scribe for many works of Chaucer and Lydgate, a great traveller and translator of a number of works from Latin and French into English.

Thomas Watson (1557-92), one of the first English poets to use the sonnet form was buried in the church. He made Latin versions of Greek and Italian works, including Tasso's **Aminta** (1585) and Sophocles' **Antigone** (1581). He also published **The First Sett of Italian Madrigals Englished** in 1590 which Byrd set to music. He was a close friend of **Christopher Marlowe**, and coming to Marlowe's assistance in a street fight killed a man. He appears in Spenser's **Colin Clouts come home againe**, as Amyntas. Although his **Tears of Fancie** (1593) and **Hecatomphia** (1552) collections of sonnets are no longer read today they were an important influence on **Shakespeare** and the other major poets of his day.

John Lyly (1554-1606) was also buried here.

Smithfield turns into **Giltspur Street** which was the main route from the City to the smooth fields and the jousting tournaments. The street was named, according to the historian John Stow, after the passing knights as Knightrider Street. The change to Giltspur probably reflects that the makers of spurs resided in the street advertising their wares with the sign of a gilt spur.

Off on the right is **Cock Lane** where about ten feet up on the corner is the gilt statue of a little boy marking Pie Corner where the Great Fire stopped in 1666. The street became famous when an 11 year old girl claimed to have heard a ghost at their house in the lane in 1762. This aroused great interest and **Dr Johnson** was one of the important personages invited to investigate the phenomenon, which proved to be the child's hoax. Dr Johnson gives **An account of the Detection of the Imposture in Cock Lane** which was published in The Gentleman's

Magazine. **Charles Churchill** (1732-64) the satirical poet and friend of Wilkes, used the incident in **The Ghost**, where Johnson is portrayed as Pomposo, a credulous visitor:

> *"He for subscribers baits his hook,*
> *And takes your cash; but where's the book?*
> *No matter where; wise fear, you know,*
> *Forbids the robbing of a foe;*
> *But what, to serve our private ends,*
> *Forbids the cheating of our friends."*

Giltspur Street meets Newgate Street and on the right there is the church of **St Sepulchre**. On the corner of Newgate Street and Giltspur Street the rebuilt Watch House of the church has the bust of **Charles Lamb** which was moved from Christ Church (destroyed in the war) and erected in its present position in 1962. Lamb went to the school of Christ Church, the famous Bluecoat School. The inscription reads, 'Perhaps the most loved name in English Literature, who was a Bluecoat boy here for 7 years'. The church originally built in the 12th c, was rebuilt in the 15th c and has been restored several times, including a restoration by Wren in 1670-77. The bells of the church were tolled on the occasion of an execution at Newgate, and before 1774 criminals on their way to Tyburn to be hung were presented with a nosegay at St Sepulchre on the outset of their final journey.

Across the road are the Central Criminal Courts, better known as **The Old Bailey**. This was the site of **Newgate Prison**, and there was a prison on this site from the 12th c until 1902. For most of these years it served as London's main prison. **Sir Thomas Malory** (d 1471) was in prison here for murder, theft and rape and wrote **La Morte D'Arthur** to help pass his many years of imprisonment. His cycle of Arthurian legends were finished in 1470 and printed by Caxton in 1485, divided into 21 books. He was buried in the nearby monastery of Grey Friars where he was permitted to use the library.

George Wither (1588-1667) poet and pamphleteer, had several spells in prison for his satires including 3 years in Newgate 1660-63 when his **Vox Vulgi** was considered seditious.

Titus Oates (1649-1705) the fabricator of the Popish Plot in 1678, was imprisoned in Newgate. The existence of the plot was widely believed at the time and many people were falsely accused and imprisoned, including Samuel Pepys. Thirty-five people were tried and executed for their complicity in the non-existent plot and Oates was a national hero. After two years the hysteria subsided and a reaction set in, and in May 1683 Titus Oates was fined £100,000 for calling the Duke of York (later James II) a traitor, and being unable to pay was imprisoned. In May 1685 he was found guilty of perjury and was pilloried, flogged and imprisoned for life. He was released from Newgate Prison when James II was deposed by the Glorious Revolution, and was even awarded a pension. He appears in Dryden's **Absalom and Achitophel** as Corah.

William Penn (1644-1718), the son of an admiral, was a devout Quaker and the founder of Pennsylvania. His writings include **The Sandy Foundation** (1668) an attack on the orthodox doctrines of the Trinity and Atonement, and on the Calvinist theory of justification. This work led to his imprisonment in the Tower where he wrote his Quaker classic, **No Cross, No Crown** (1669) an eloquent and learned dissertation on Christian Duty. In 1671 he was imprisoned in Newgate for six months for his illegal preaching. In 1682 he went to the New World and founded and governed his colony from the city of Philadelphia for two years with great enlightenment before returning to England to exert himself for his persecuted brethren. In 1686 he managed to have freed all persons imprisoned for their religious beliefs including 1200 Quakers. His last years under William III were full of problems, accusations of treason, and he was imprisoned for nine months in the Fleet Prison. He wrote more than 40 books and pamphlets on religious subjects.

Daniel Defoe (1660-1731) was educated at the dissenting academy in Stoke Newington and his satire **The Shortest Way with Dissenters** (1702), was so misunderstood that the High Church party in power at the beginning of Queen Anne's reign fined, pilloried and imprisoned him from May to November 1703. The irony of a Dissenter demanding the total and savage suppression of dissent was lost on his accusers. While in Newgate

Prison he wrote his **Hymn to the Pillory**, a mock-Pindaric ode which was sold in the streets to sympathetic crowds. Often seen as the first ever journalist he began his **Review** in prison, a thrice weekly newspaper about foreign and commercial affairs which lasted until 1713.

Richard Savage (1697-1743) had one of his many spells of imprisonment in Newgate in 1727, not for debt but for killing a man in a brawl. He was later pardoned.

Jonathan Wild (1682-1725), the Thief-Taker General was imprisoned here before being hanged at Tyburn for his crimes. He is the hero of Fielding's satire, **Jonathan Wild.**

Jack Sheppard (1702-24) the audacious cockney highwayman who was caught five times and managed to escape four times, before being hung at Tyburn in front of 200,000 spectators, as a kind of folk hero. His last escape from Newgate was from the cell on the third floor tower above the gate on Newgate Street. He had been handcuffed, manacled and chained to the floor but still managed to get out of Newgate Prison. While waiting for his execution he was painted by Sir James Thornhill, and many ballads, plays and tracts, including one by **Daniel Defoe** were written about him. In the 19th c **Harrison Ainsworth** wrote a bestselling novel based on his life.

In 1774 **The Newgate Calendar** was published giving an account of the inmates' crimes from 1700, concentrating on the most notorious. Similar collections appeared during the next 50 years, and they provided the source for the Newgate novels of **Ainsworth, Bulwer-Lytton, Fielding** and **Godwin. Thackeray** countered the genre in his novel **Catherine** (1839-40) taking a story from the Newgate Calendar about the murderess Catherine Hayes, he made it as grim and sordid as possible. Dickens' **Oliver Twist** is an example of the Newgate genre, although later Dickens tried to distance himself from any implication that he made crime glamorous and was the author of a Newgate novel.

A new prison was built by George Dance which was burnt down in the Gordon Riots which are brilliantly dramatized in Dickens' novel, **Barnaby Rudge**. The poet **George Crabbe** an eyewitness "never saw anything so dreadful. You have no conception of the phrensy of the multitude". The prison was rebuilt in 1780-3 and the instigator, however innocently, of the anti-Catholic riots, George Gordon, was arrested and tried by his peers at the House of Lords and acquitted on the crime of High Treason. He changed his faith to that of Abraham and called himself Israel Abraham George Gordon. The jewish lord was convicted in 1787 for libelling Marie Antoinette and escaped to Holland from where he was extradited and taken to Newgate prison where he died of goal fever in 1793. Dickens' portrait of him in his novel is sympathetic. The new prison had a large open area in front of it and on the recommendation of the Sheriffs the place of execution was transferred here from Tyburn (Marble Arch), and public executions were conducted in the side street called Old Bailey from 1783 until 1868. They were an immensely popular spectacle. From 1868 executions took place inside the prison.

Charles Dickens had a 'horrible fascination' for Newgate and visited the prison several times, and made use of it in his novels. We see Fagin in **Oliver Twist** waiting for his end in the condemned cell, and Pip in **Great Expectations** is shown inside 'the grim stone building' to view the yard where the gallows are kept and 'the Debtors Door', out of which culprits come to be hanged. And of course it figures prominently in **Barnaby Rudge**.

Thackeray's novel **Henry Esmond** makes use of Newgate Prison also.

The prison was demolished in 1902 to make way for the Central Criminal Courts, known colloquially as the **Old Bailey**. From 1539 there stood an Old Bailey Sessions House next to the prison exercising criminal jurisdiction over London. The odours from the nearby prison were so great that the judges used to carry posies of sweet smelling flowers to combat the stench. The hanging judge, later James II's Lord Chancellor, **Judge Jeffreys** (1648-89) was a resident judge here in 1671, and Recorder in 1678. The most famous fictional trial here was of the dashing and highly principled Charles Darnay in Dickens' **A Tale of Two Cities**. The public, as they are today, were allowed to watch the trials but with a difference:

"For people then paid to see the play at the Old Bailey, just as they paid to see the play in Bedlam – only the former entertainment was much the dearer."

The most sensational and infamous of the Old Bailey trials were those of **Oscar Wilde** (1854-1900), in 1895. Wilde's headstrong friend Bosie goaded Wilde into suing his father for criminal libel after he left a card for Wilde at the Albermarle Club which said "To Oscar Wilde posing as a Sodomite". The trial began at the Old Bailey on the 3rd April 1895, before Mr J. Henn Collins. The defence counsel Carson was once Wilde's friend and fellow student at Trinity College Dublin, and won the argument even if Wilde triumphed in the literary discussion.

Carson read a passage from **Dorian Gray** and demanded: "Did you write that?" Wilde replied that he had the honour to be its author. Carson put the book down with a sneer and turned over some papers. Wilde seemed lost in thought. Presently Carson read aloud a piece of verse from one of Wilde's articles: "And I suppose you wrote that also, Mr Wilde?" Wilde waited until you could hear a pin drop and then said, very quietly: "Ah no Mr Carson, Shakespeare wrote that". Carson blushed scarlet. He turned the pages again and read another piece of verse and said: "And I suppose Shakespeare wrote that also, Mr Wilde?"

"Not as you read it, Mr Carson", replied Oscar Wilde.

Unfortunately for Wilde, Queensberry's detective had been thorough and Wilde's predilection for entertaining common boys in expensive hotels made an only too vivid contrast with his elitist view of art. Wilde withdrew from the case but the judge still made a ruling, stating that Queensberry was justified in calling Wilde a sodomite in the public interest.

After the trial Wilde went to the Cadogan Hotel in Sloane Street where Lord Alfred Douglas, 'Bosie' had been staying for 5 weeks. A sympathetic reporter from the Star arrived and told Ross that a warrant for Wilde's arrest had been issued. Urged on all sides to flee England on the boat train to France, Wilde prevaricated initially before settling in his armchair and declaring, "'I shall stay and do my sentence whatever it is". He was arrested at 10 past 6 by two detectives on a charge of committing indecent acts and taken to Bow Street police station. Preliminary hearings took place in April with Wilde being transferred to Holloway Prison. He was sent for trial on the 26th April 1895. Two days before the trial there was a bankruptcy sale of Wilde's possessions at his Tite Street home, forced by Lord Queensberry, who wanted his £600 legal costs from Wilde.

At his trial Wilde was asked by the prosecuting counsel Gill, during cross-examination, what was the love that dare not speak its name, a line from a poem by Bosie. Wilde rose to the occasion, brushing aside the lies, prevarications and denials, he replied:

> "The 'Love that dare not speak its name' in this century is such a great affection of an elder for a younger man as there was between David and Jonathan, such as Plato made the very basis of his philosophy, and such as you find in the sonnets of Michelangelo and Shakespeare. It is that deep, spiritual affection that is as pure as it is perfect. It dictates and pervades great works of art like those of Shakespeare and Michangelo, and those two letters of mine, such as they are. It is in this century misunderstood, so much misunderstood that it may be described as the 'Love that dare not speak its name,' and on account of it I am placed where I am now. It is beautiful, it is fine, it is the noblest form of affection. There is nothing unnatural about it. It is intellectual, and it repeatedly exists between an elder and a younger man, when the elder man has intellect, and the younger man has all the joy, hope and glamour of life before him. That it should be so the world does not understand. The world mocks at it and sometimes puts one in the pillory for it."

A truly magnificent speech which a clever writer could concoct at his desk but few could produce while under pressure, especially in a court of law facing a hostile counsel and imminent imprisonment.

It is interesting to quote the reaction of Max Beerbohm, one of Wilde's circle who was in court. He wrote to Reggie Turner:

> "Oscar has been quite superb. His speech about the Love that dare not tell his name was simply wonderful and carried the whole court right away, quite a tremendous burst of applause. Here was this man, who had been buffeted, perfectly self-possessed, dominating the Old Bailey with his fine presence and

musical voice. He has never had so great a triumph, I am sure, as when the gallery burst into applause – I am sure it affected the jury."

Wilde's activities with young boys in the Savoy and elsewhere were harder to shrug off, although he occasionally won the round he lost the bout on whether his denials should be believed:

"Why did you take up with these youths?
Wilde: I am a lover of youth (laughter)

You exalt youth as a sort of God?
Wilde: I like to study the young in everything. There is something fascinating in youthfulness.

So you would prefer puppies to dogs and kittens to cats?
Wilde: I think so. I should enjoy, for instance, the society of a beardless, briefless barrister quite as much as that of the most accomplished Q.C. (laughter)"

At the end of the case the judge put four questions to the jury:

i) Do you think that Wilde committed indecent acts with Edward Shelley and Alfred Wood and with a person or persons unknown at the Savoy Hotel or with Charles Parker?

ii) Did Taylor procure or attempt to procure the commission of these acts or any of them?

iii) Did Wilde or Taylor or either of them attempt to get Atkins to commit indecencies?

iv) Did Taylor commit indecent acts with Charles Parker or with William Parker?

The jury after four hours of deliberation could not make up its mind, and according to a juror talking at his club, the Pall Mall, it was 10 to 2 in favour of convicting Wilde. Max Beerbohm and Bosie said they heard only one juror had voted to acquit Wilde. A new trial was ordered and bail was refused. It was argued that it would be in the public interest (to protect their morals) not to have a retrial, but because of the rumours about Lord Rosebery (the Prime Minister) being implicated homosexually with Bosie's older brother, who had committed suicide, it was decided to go ahead.

Baron Pollock at a hearing in chambers granted bail on sureties of £5,000. Rooms were hired for Wilde at the Midland Hotel, St Pancras, but he was asked to leave the hotel when a gang of the Marquis of Queensberry's hooligans threatened the manager of the hotel. The same events were repeated at the next hotel they tried, so at midnight Wilde went to no 146 Oakley Street, Chelsea where his mother and brother Willie and his wife lived, and was taken in. After ten days he left to stay with the Leversons, finding his brother's moralizings hard to support. Mrs Leverson informed the servants who their guest was, giving them the chance to resign, which none took. Many urged Wilde to flee including his wife Constance, but Wilde was determined to see it through, even though everyone forecast disaster for him.

On May 25th Oscar Wilde, at the retrial, was sentenced to two years imprisonment under the 1885 Criminal Law Amendment Act, which for the first time made it an offence for consenting adult males to indulge in indecent relations. From Holloway he was taken to Pentonville Prison, then to Wandsworth and finally to Reading. One of the worst moments of his imprisonment Wilde tells us in **De Profundis** was his time spent on Clapham Railway Station, handcuffed and in prison clothing while he waited for the Reading train in the rain. A man recognised Wilde and spat at him. "For a year after that was done to me I wept every day at the same hour and for the same space of time."

His imprisonment ruined Wilde's health and his creative talents, and he spent the last three years of his life on the continent, always short of money, snubbed and avoided by his friends, a victim of his own brilliance and of the society he had once so wonderfully entertained.

There was no great work to come out of his prison years, parts of **De Profundis**, his letter written in the last months of his imprisonment and his **Ballad of Reading Goal** are truly moving, but little to show for so much suffering.

The Ballad of Reading Goal was published in February 1898 by Smithers, with the author given as **C.3.3.** The book sales were amazingly high for a poem, and it was favourably reviewed in the press. On the 7th edition in 1899 Wilde's name was added as the author, in brackets, beside the prison number C.3.3.

And as one stands outside the Old Bailey Wilde's words ring out in one's ears:

> *"I never saw a man who looked*
> *With such a wistful eye*
> *Upon that little tent of blue*
> *Which prisoners call the sky."*

In 1960 the Old Bailey was the venue for another celebrated literary trial, this time of a book, and not an author, when **Penguin Books** were prosecuted under the Obscene Publications Act 1959 for having published the full text of D.H. Lawrence's **Lady Chatterley's Lover**. The witnesses for the defence included E.M. Forster, R. Hoggart and H. Gardner with others like T.S. Eliot prowling the corridors of the Old Bailey waiting to be called. The acquittal of Penguin Books had a profoundly liberating effect on both writing and publishing in this country. The case produced the celebrated quote from the prosecuting counsel when he asked the jury whether **Lady Chatterley's Lover** was a book they would wish their wives and servants to read. The defence of literary merit overcame the hostility of the judge and the judge's wife to this very minor work of D.H. Lawrence. It was also pleaded successfully in **Last Exit to Brooklyn** in 1968, and on appeal the publisher John Calder was found not guilty under the same act.

Proceeding down Newgate Street the next turning leads to **Little Britain**. The street was named after the town house of the Dukes of Brittany erected at the end of the 13th c. (The street was formerly called Brettonestrete.) It was a street of booksellers from 1575 to 1725, and one of the booksellers in the 17th c was an especially close friend of **John Milton**. Millington the bookseller of Little Britain would come each day to take the blind ageing poet out on his walk, and leaving Milton's house on Artillery Row (now Bunhill Row) they would stroll arm in arm on the vast nearby common of Bunhill Fields. This was the period of the 1660s when **Paradise Lost** was published. The book was praised in the House of Commons by **Sir John**

Oscar Wilde (1854-1900)

Samuel Taylor Coleridge (1772-1834)

Denham and when the Earl of Dorset "was in Little Britain, beating about for books to his taste" he came upon it. "He was surprised with some passages he struck upon by dipping here and there and bought it." Not an immediate commercial success the sales of **Paradise Lost** were such that every educated man in England must have possessed a copy by the end of the decade. Milton briefly had lodgings in Little Britain in 1662.

The Spectator, the periodical founded by Steele and Addison, was first printed in this street by Samuel Buckley in 1711. It lasted from March of that year to December of the following year. A further 80 issues were printed by Addison in 1714, but the first period is generally agreed to have been superior.

In 1712 **Samuel Johnson**, aged three, had lodgings in this street with his mother, when he was brought down to London to be cured of the Queen's Evil, by being touched by Queen Anne at the Banqueting Hall in Whitehall. For centuries there had been the unfounded belief that the monarch's touch had the power to free a sufferer from scrofula. After Queen Anne this practice went out of fashion.

Little Britain is where Jagger, the lawyer in Dickens' **Great Expectations** had his offices.

As Newgate Street loops round we see the ruins of the Wren church **Christ Church, Greyfriars**, where the steeple tower and vestry have been restored after the bombings of World War II. Prior to the Wren church of 1684-1704 there stood here a 14th c Gothic church which was the largest church in London after the nearby cathedral of St Pauls and was attached to the monastery of Greyfriars. At the dissolution of the monasteries the church was used as a store house for plundered French wine, and the King's Printer set up his presses in the nave. The church was made into a parish church and was destroyed by the Great Fire in 1666. The large monastery on this site was founded by the first Franciscan monks to come to England in 1224. From the begining the simplicity and piety of the life at the monastery attracted the admiration of the royal family and other rich benefactors. **Richard Whittington**, four times Lord Mayor of London, provided the money to build a library in 1421-5, and presented it with £400 worth of books. It is believed that **Thomas Malory**, a prisoner in the nearby prison had access to the library to write his Arthurian cycle, **Le Morte D'Arthur**. After the dissolution of the monastery a school for 'poor fatherless children' was founded in the monastery buildings in 1553, and called **Christ's Hospital**. Its founder, Edward VI died 10 days after the school was founded. 380 children were collected together and cared for. Initially it was more of a children's home than a school, but a grammar school was later founded and called the **Bluecoat School** because of the children's uniforms of long blue coats and yellow stockings. In the 17th c pupils from the school were hired out as mutes for funerals. The school was almost totally destroyed in the Great Fire and rebuilt under the supervision of Sir Christopher Wren. A new building for girls was constructed in the countryside at Hertford and at the boys' school **Coleridge** and **Charles Lamb** entered in 1782 and **Leigh Hunt** in 1791. Lamb in his **Essays** recounts his impressions of Coleridge at Christ's Hospital. He urged Coleridge to "Cultivate simplicity" and warned him repeatedly about his opium taking and his health and said of the 54 year old poet:

"His face when he repeats his verse hath its ancient glory, an Archangel a little damaged."

Coleridge (1772-1834) the son of a Devon vicar had a most turbulent life and became the leading figure with **Wordsworth** of the Romantic Movement. His main source of income for most of his life was lecturing and journalism. A young revolutionary based in Bristol he inspired **Hazlitt** by his preaching at a Unitarian chapel and was the prime influence of his adoption of the life of a man of letters. After his marriage to Sara Fricker he lived in a friend's cottage in Nether Stowey, where he became the great friend of William and Mary Wordsworth. It was from this communion of minds that a new kind of poetry appeared, which was fresher and more vibrant than the artificial verse of the day. **The Lyrical Ballads** of 1798 was almost a poetic manifesto, heralding the arrival of the English Romantic Age. It begins with Coleridge's best known poem **The Ballad of the Ancient Mariner:**

> *"Water, water, every where*
> *And all the boards did shrink;*
> *Water, water, every where*
> *Nor any drop to drink.*
>
> *The very deep did rot: O Christ!*
> *That ever this should be!*
> *Yea, slimy things did crawl with legs*
> *Upon the slimy sea.*

And in Part VII Coleridge goes on to say:

> *He prayeth well, who loveth well*
> *Both man and bird and beast*
> *He prayeth best, who loveth best*
> *All things both great and small:*
> *For the dear God who loveth us,*
> *He made and loveth all."*

The brilliant career which lay before Coleridge was never realized mainly through his addiction to opium, and he confessed his own failures in **An Ode to Dejection** (1802). He settled in London and from 1818 in Highgate with his friends, the Gillmans. He established himself as an important critic and philosopher, with his **Biographia Literaria** (1817) a major critical work. He was no longer the inspired romantic poet but the publication of the fragment of **Kubla Khan** reminded his contemporaries of what he once was:

> *"In Xanadu, did Kubla Khan*
> *A stately pleasure-dome decree:*
> *Where Alph, the sacred river, ran*
> *Through caverns measureless to man*
> *Down to a sunless sea.*
> *So twice five miles of fertile ground*
> *With walls and towers were girded round."*

Previous pupils at the Bluecoat School included **William Camden** (1551-1623) antiquarian and historian, who as headmaster of Westminster School taught **Ben Jonson**. Jonson said he owed his headmaster "All that I am in arts, all that I know". **George Dyer** (1755-1841) a poet and friend of Charles Lamb, who after a visit to the essayist's cottage in Islington walked straight into the river and had to be rescued. His rescue is the subject of Lamb's **Amicus**

Redivivus. A later pupil was **Middleton Murry** (1889-1957) an important literary figure and husband of **Katharine Mansfield**. Through her he met **D.H. Lawrence** who had a great influence on him, and the intense and tempestuous friendship between them and their wives is part of the subject matter of **Women in Love**, one of Lawrence's best novels. He is best remembered for his work as an editor for The Athenaeum and The Adelphi, publishing the work of T.S. Eliot, Virginia Woolf and Valery, and for editing Katharine Mansfield's work.

A new school for boys was built in Horsham in 1902 and Middleton Murry studied at both new and old. The buildings in London were demolished and now the General Post Office stands on the site. The school's London connection is revived each year on St Matthew's Day, 21st of September when there is a special service for the school at St Sepulchre's, Holborn, which pupils attend with the Lord Mayor and Aldermen of the City of London Corporation. The school is now a fee paying school.

Outside the General Post Office is the statue of **Sir Rowland Hill**, who introduced the postage stamp. Before the introduction of the postage stamp the receiver of the letter had to pay for it, and if the receiver could not afford or did not like the sender of the letter he would not pay for it and the Post Office lost money, causing Sir Rowland Hill to reverse the system, getting the sender to pay by buying a stamp. The world's first adhesive stamp, the Penny Black, first appeared on 6th May 1840, and Sir Rowland Hill's innovation soon spread world-wide. It can be seen in the National Postal Museum contained inside the General Post Office, opened in 1966.

The street changes its name to King Edward Street as it sweeps round the General Post Office and a large derelict building which is in the process of demolition and stands on the site of St Martin Le Grand.

ST MARTIN'S LE GRAND was originally a monastery and college founded in the 11th century. William of Wykeham, the dean of the church, had it restored and built a new chapter house. Wykeham was later Bishop of Winchester and Chancellor of England, the founder of Winchester School and New College, Oxford.

The church here had, since the 12th c, the right to hold its own court and became a famous sanctuary for thieves and debtors, although jews and traitors were turned away.

Sir Thomas More's **History of Richard III** claims that Miles Forrest, one of those accused of murdering the princes in the Tower, 'rotted away piece-meal' in the sanctuary. This right of sanctuary continued until 1697. The monastery and college were suppressed in 1540 by Henry VIII.

There used to be a coach-stand here and Mr Pickwick took the coach from here to the Golden Cross Inn in Charing Cross. We follow the road round admiring the magnificence of the dome of St Paul's Cathedral as we sweep left into Cheapside.

CHEAPSIDE

This was the widest street in medieval London and the only street in London which is narrower today than it was in the Middle Ages. It was the principal market place for London, (the name Cheapside meaning market place, from the old English work chepe-a market). The craft guilds of the City had their own area nearby: the bakers in Bread Street, the goldsmiths in Goldsmith Row, fishmongers in Friday Street (so called as fish had to be eaten on Fridays and not meat in catholic countries during the Middle Ages), shoemakers and curriers in Cordwainer Street, ironmongers in Ironmonger Lane, grocers (then called pepperers) in Sopers Lane, poulterers in Poultry, dairymen in Milk Street and so on. The merchants, the craftsmen with their assistants, apprentices and servants would work and live in the same buildings. Cheapside was a very noisy, boisterous and busy street where there was always something happening, with brawling apprentices often causing a nuisance. In Chaucer's **Canterbury Tales** we learn:

> *"There was a prentice living in our town,*
> *Worked in the victualling trade and he was brown*
> *At every wedding he would sing and hop*
> *And he preferred the tavern to the shop.*
> *Whenever any pageant or procession*
> *Came down Cheapside, goodbye to his profession.*
> *He'd leap out of the shop to see the sight*
> *And join the dance and not come back that night!*
> (**The Cook's Tale**)

It was the street as Chaucer tells us where all the great celebrations and pageants took place, and on special occasions the water conduits at each end of the street flowed with wine. Being such an important thoroughfare other major public occasions took place in the street, including executions, the maiming of offenders and putting culprits in the pillory. After the death of Edward I's queen, Eleanor, a cross was erected in the street commemorating it as one of the resting places of the queen's coffin on its journey from Nottingham to Westminster Abbey. It was three storeys high and was decorated with statues of the Pope, the Virgin and Child and the Apostles; it was built in 1290 on the corner of Wood Street. (A 19th century replica of an Eleanor Cross can be seen at Charing Cross in front of the railway station.) It suffered at the hands of the Puritans during the 16th c and was finally demolished in 1643, 'to cleanse that great street of superstition'.

After the destruction of the Great Fire the street was rebuilt and by 1720 it was "a very spacious street adorned with lofty buildings, well inhabited by goldsmiths, linen drapers, haberdashers and other great dealers". Even with the rise of the West End it could still rival it as a shopping centre by the middle of the 19th c. This century it is a commercial street distinguished by St Mary le Bow and a few other buildings.

The first turning on the left is **FOSTER LANE**. The name is a corruption of St Vedast, to whom the 17th c Wren church in the lane is dedicated. In the pre-Wren church, **Sir Robert Herrick** (1591-1674) was baptised. His father was a prosperous goldsmith and Foster Lane was the centre for goldsmiths in this period. When Herrick was only 16 months old his father fell to his death from a fourth floor window. Suicide was suspected, but being 'moved with charity' the Queen's Almoner did not confiscate the Herrick property which was usual with suicides. After 6 years as an apprentice goldsmith he entered St John's College, Cambridge, where he enjoyed a luxurious lifestyle. After his M.A. he was ordained a priest and moved in the literary circles of London where he was well known as a poet. In 1625 Richard James in **The Muses Dirge** ranks him beside **Jonson** and **Drayton**.

He was one of our finest lyric poets with a faultless ear, and he conquered his early dislike of "this dull Devonshire" to sing the praises of the countryside:

> *"I sing of brooks, of blossoms, birds, and bowers:*
> *Of April, May, of June, and July-flowers,*
> *I sing of May-poles, Hock-carts, wassails, wakes,*
> *Of bride grooms, brides, and of their bridal cakes."*
>
> **(Hesperides)**

And combines natural images with love adroitly in his verse:

> "Gather ye rosebuds while ye may,
> Old Time is still a-flying:
> And this same flower that smiles to-day,
> Tomorrow will be dying.
>
> Then be not coy, use your time;
> And while ye may, go marry:
> For having lost but once your prime,
> You may for ever tarry."
> *(To the Virgins, to Make Much of Time)*

The next street on the left is **WOOD STREET**. On the corner of the street there is the churchyard of St Peter's, a City church destroyed in the Great Fire and not replaced. The plane tree in the churchyard is mentioned in Wordsworth's, **The Reverie of Poor Susan:**

> "At the corner of Wood Street, when daylight appears,
> Hangs a Thrush that sings loud, it has sung for three years.
> Poor Susan has passed by the spot, and has heard
> In the silence of morning the song of the Bird.
>
> 'Tis a note of enchantment; what ails her? She sees
> A mountain ascending, a vision of trees;
> Bright volumes of vapour through Lothbury glide,
> And a river flows on through the vale of Cheapside."

A coaching inn stood on the street at no 128, the Cross Keys, and it was here that the 10 year old Charles Dickens arrived in London from Rochester:

> "Through all the years that have since passed, have I lost the smell of damp straw in which I was packed – like game – and forwarded, carriage paid, to the Cross Keys, Wood Street, Cheapside, London? There was no other inside passengers, and I consumed my sandwiches in solitude and dreariness, and it rained hard all the way, and I thought life sloppier than I expected to find it."
> *(Autobiographical Fragment.)*

Pip also arrives at the Cross Keys in **Great Expectations**, and has tea here with Estella.

The Mitre in Wood Street was a tavern much frequented by Ben Jonson and later by Samuel Pepys.

MILK STREET is where **Sir Thomas More** was born in 1478, the son of a judge. He was a very successful lawyer who spent his leisure studying literature, and was the friend of the great humanists of his age, **Erasmus, Colet** and **Lily**. He became an MP in 1504 and was employed as a diplomat. While abroad he wrote his **Utopia**, a Latin work which was published on the continent in 1516. The publication was supervised in More's absence by his friend Erasmus. Because of the critical references to Henry VIII the first English translation was in 1551. Influenced by the revival of classical literature which made Plato's **Republic** widely known and the discovery of the New World **Utopia** created a new genre. Other Utopias followed, Bacon's **New Atlantis**, Harrington's **Oceana** and Campanella's **City of the Sun** and the genre has stretched up till the 20th c. Today the emphasis is no longer on more perfect 'Nowhere lands' but on chilling visions of the future, such as **Brave New World, 1984,** and **We**, and are referred to as dystopias. More can be seen as the inventor of science fiction as a genre, and the long term effect of his political fantasy has been most felt in fiction.

More became a privy counsellor and greatly admired by Henry VIII he succeeded Wolsey as Lord Chancellor in 1529, a post he retired from in 1532. His unwillingness to impugn the pope's authority after Henry VIII declared himself the supreme head of the Church of England led to his execution for high treason in 1535. More's other works are mainly on religious controversies and have little interest for us today, with the exception of his **History of Richard III**, upon which Shakespeare based his play. More's version of events was probably obtained from Cardinal Morton in whose household More lived in his youth, making his account of Richard III fascinating hearsay evidence.

Across Cheapside there is **BREAD STREET** where the **Mermaid Tavern** stood from 1411 to 1666, the meeting place of Sir Walter Ralegh's Friday Club, whose members included William Shakespeare, John Donne, Ben Jonson, Beaumont and Fletcher. The club met here on the first Friday of the month. Beaumont writing to Ben Jonson enthuses:

> *"What things have we seen,*
> *Done at the Mermaid! heard words that have been*
> *So nimble, and so full of subtle flame,*
> *As if that every one from whence they came,*
> *Had meant to put his whole wit in a jest,*
> *And had resolv'd to live a fool, the rest*
> *Of his dull life."*

A later poet, **John Keats** (1795-1821) sings the tavern's praises:

> *"Soul of poets dead and gone,*
> *What Elysium have ye known,*
> *Happy fields or mossy cavern,*
> *choicer than the Mermaid Tavern?*
> *Have ye tippled drink more fine*
> *Than mine host's Canary wine?"*

Other users of the tavern have included **Christopher Marlowe** (1594-93) government spy, atheist, pederast and brilliant young playwright who was stabbed to death in mysterious circumstances in a Deptford pub. All the major writers of his age paid tribute to his genius and reflected his influence in their work. Best known for his play **Edward II** which was a major influence on Shakespeare's Richard II, and **Dr Faustus** from which Goethe produced his Faust, he was the first to exploit the power of blank verse:

> *"Was this the face that launch'd a thousand ships,*
> *And burnt the topless towers of Ilium?*
> *Sweet Helen, make me immortal with a kiss!*
> *Her lips suck forth my soul: see, where it flies!*
> *Come Helen, come give me my soul again.*
> *Here will I dwell, for heaven be in these lips,*
> *And all is dross that is not Helena."*

Marlowe is buried in the church of St Nicholas Deptford, his brilliance and unrealized potential are reflected in his epilogue:

> *"Cut is the branch that might have grown full straight,*
> *And burned is Apollo's laurel bough,*
> *That sometimes grew within the learned man."*

John Donne, the son of a wealthy Catholic merchant was born in Bread Street in 1572, and **John Milton**, a

John Donne (1572-1631)

John Milton (1608-74)

scriverner's son was born in 1608 at the sign of the Spread Eagle. As a small boy Milton must have seen the greatest writers of his day pass his house on the way to the Mermaid Tavern. So great was Milton's fame for his controversial writings that from the 1650s onwards the house where he was born was a tourist attraction. The house and most of the street were destroyed in the Great Fire. The destruction of the last piece of property Milton owned caused the poet financial problems in his last years.

Just down from Bread Street is the famous Wren Church of **St Mary le Bow**. It is said if you are born within the sound of its bells, you are a true Londoner, a Cockney. Rebuilt after the Great Fire, Wren modelled the church on the Basilica of Maxentius at Rome. The magnificent spire is 217 feet high, with a dragon for its weathercock. The church was bombed in World War II and was rebuilt to Wren's plans. There has been a church on this site since the 11th c. The curfew used to be rung by the church bells during the 14th c., and from this originated the idea that every true Cockney is born within its sounds. The church's name probably comes from the arches in the Norman crypt. For many years the church was one of the 13 peculiars in the City owned by the Archbishop of Canterbury and as such outside the jurisdiction of the Bishop of London.

In the church courtyard is the statue of Captain John Smith, the founder of Virginia, who returned to England with the Indian Princess Pocahontas. He was a member of the vestry. In the pantomime the bells that call back **Dick Whittington** to London are those of the church destroyed in the Great Fire.

At the next traffic lights, the junction of King Street and Queen Street we turn left up King Street and proceed to the Guildhall.

THE GUILDHALL

The magnificent hall dates from the 15th c., and has the largest medieval crypt in London, which is still there. It is the centre of the Guilds of London who provide the administration of the City of London Corporation, and it is where the Lord Mayor and the Sheriffs of the City are still elected. It has a long history of use for major trials. The most famous is that of **Lady Jane Grey** and her husband Guildford Dudley for treason. They were both sentenced to death for usurping the throne of Mary I, and were executed at the Tower. As Lady Jane Grey was only Queen for nine days, we have the expression, a nine day wonder. The hall was damaged but not destroyed by the Great Fire. In 1862 it was given an open roof by Horace Jones to blend in with its medieval design; it was destroyed during the war and replaced by Sir Giles Gilbert Scott. Miraculously all the medieval parts of the building survived unscathed World War II.

Dickens chose the Guildhall as the venue of Mr Pickwick's trial for breach of promise to Mrs Bardell, and it is here that Mr Pickwick is sent to prison for his refusal to pay damages after the case is decided in Mrs Bardell's favour. The Guildhall, with its giants Gog and Magog, always exercised a great fascination for Dickens dating back to when he was lost there as a small child, newly arrived in London.

The poet **Henry Howard, Earl of Surrey** (1517-47) had his trial held in the Great Hall and was sentenced to death on the charge of treasonably quartering the royal arms; that is he used the arms of his ancestor Edward the Confessor with his own. One of the early users of the sonnet form, he was also, in his translation of the **Aeneid**, the first to use blank verse. When **Tottel's Miscellany** appeared in 1557 it contained 40 of his poems. He is with **Spenser** the archetypal courtly lover as depicted in the chivalric romances.

In the **Diary** of Samuel Pepys, he talks of attending a banquet in 1663 for the French Ambassador and later that

Henry Howard, Earl of Surrey (1517-47)

The Guildhall

year being present at a trial about a ship's insurance. **Elkanah Settle,** as City poet from 1691, wrote plays and pageants for the Lord Mayor's Show.

The Guildhall has a magnificent library formed in 1423 from money left by **Richard Whittington,** who was Lord Mayor of London four times. The manuscripts were chained in their bookcases and opened to all scholars, so it can claim to be the first public library in the world to be financed by a local authority. The collection however was removed in its entirety in 1549 by the Lord Protector, Somerset, to furnish his new house in the Strand, Somerset House. In 1828 the Corporation of the City of London opened its second library, which is now the very best source of information on London, and a fertile starting point for all major works on London. With its London directories, collections of prints, maps and drawings it is a veritable treasure trove. Its collection includes John Stow's **Chronicles** and **A Survey of London** and the deed signed by **Shakespeare** in 1613 for the purchase of a house in Blackfriars. The stained-glass window depicts **Stow** and **Milton** and there are busts of **Chaucer** and **Tennyson** on the stairs. Inside the library there is the Guildhall Clock Museum, with most of the exhibits bequeathed to the City by the Clockmaker's Company.

Adjacent to the Guildhall is the Wren Church of **St Lawrence Jewry,** which since the demolition of the Guildhall Chapel in 1820, has been the Church of the City. It was bombed in 1940 and rebuilt in 1954-7. The church's windows commemorate **Sir Thomas More,** who preached here and **Sir Christopher Wren,** flanked by his master mason and master carver.

We continue down Gresham Street (named after a former Lord Mayor of the City), passing **IRONMONGER LANE,** where St Thomas Becket was born near the corner with Cheapside. **Becket** (1118-1170), friend and Lord Chancellor of Henry II, was appointed against his wishes, Archbishop of Canterbury, an office which led him to oppose his King in order to champion the rights of the church. In constant dispute with the King he was exiled on the Continent for seven years, but was allowed back in 1170. His return revived the argument between church and state and he was murdered in his own Cathedral of Canterbury on the 29th December 1170 by four knights, following out, so they believed, the command of their King. The outrage caused by this sacrilege was so great that Henry II accepted to be publicly flogged in the Cathedral as an act of atonement, and within a few years Becket was made a Saint, with his shrine one of the major pilgrim sites in Western Europe. His tomb was desecrated by the orders of Henry VIII and he was charged with treason almost 400 years after his death.

In literature he is richly commemorated. First by Chaucer's **Canterbury Tales**, an account of a pilgrimage from Southwark to Canterbury in the 14th c, and by the 20th c plays by **T.S. Eliot** and **Anouilh**.

Very nearby in Cheapside **John Keats** lived at no 76 where he shared lodgings with his brother overlooking the street. He resided here from 1816 to 1817 while working as a dresser at St Guy's Hospital in Southwark. His first collection of **Poems** (1817) were published while he was living here, containing his sonnet **On First Looking into Chapman's Homer**:

> *"Much have I travell'd in the realms of gold,*
> *And many goodly states and kingdoms seen."*

In 1817 Keats moved to Hampstead.

The next turning off Gresham Street is **OLD JEWRY** which was the Jewish ghetto in London in the 12th c, and contained the synagogue. The London Jews were subjected to great persecution before being expelled from London by Edward I in 1291. Stow said of this: "The King made a mighty mass of money of their houses, which he sold, and yet the Commons of England had granted and gave him a fifteenth of all their goods to banish them." The Jews were allowed to return in the 17th c, the negotiations were conducted by Oliver Cromwell's Latin Secretary, John Milton with Rabbi Menasseh Ben Israel. On their return a new synagogue was established in Cree Church Lane, which became one of the sights of London, with many visitors, including Samuel Pepys, flocking to hear the ancient chants in Hebrew.

Ben Jonson's **Every Man in His Humour** has several scenes in the street. When it was first performed in 1598 by the Lord Chamberlain's Men, Shakespeare was one of the cast. Originally the play was set in Florence, when he revised it in 1606 Jonson moved the play to London.

At the next junction one turns left and into Moorgate.

MOORGATE

The city was flanked by Fens, and a postern gate was added to the City wall in 1415 leading to the moors, which were drained in 1527. After the Great Fire the 200,000 London homeless were billeted in tents on the fields, and Charles II came here to talk to them and create hope for the future. The fields were used for artillery practice for the City's militia.

The gate was demolished in 1762 and the stones were used to prevent old London Bridge being washed away by the tide. The street was laid out in the 1840s to give easier access to London Bridge. Today the street is full of banks, with many foreign banks having their London offices here.

Above the Moorgate public house at no 85 (left hand side) there is a plaque commemorating the birth of **John Keats** at what was then the Swan and Hoop in 1795. His father was the manager of a livery stables on this site. He died when Keats was only eight, his mother who remarried, died of tuberculosis when he was 14. In 1810 he was apprenticed to an apothecary-surgeon but in 1815 he cancelled his fifth year of apprenticeship and became a student at Guy's Hospital in Southwark. In 1816 he was licensed to practise as an apothecary, but soon gave it up in favour of the precarious existence of a poet. His first poems were published in that year in Leigh Hunt's Examiner. He began to meet the principal poets — Shelley and Wordsworth, and other men of letters like Haydon and Hazlitt. His first volume of **Poems** in 1817 was savagely attacked by **Lockhart** in Blackwood's Magazine, labelling Keats and his associates as members of the so-called Cockney school. The attacks on Keats, Leigh Hunt and Hazlitt singled them out as Londoners of low birth, contrasting them with the great writers, all of whom "have been men of birth." They were "the vilest vermin" and of "extreme moral depravity". This abuse was kept up for several years and when Keat's **Endymion** appeared in 1818 it was rubbished by Lockhart, who described it in Blackwood's Magazine as a poem of "calm, settled, imperturbable

John Keats (1795-1821)

Leigh Hunt (1784-1859)

drivelling idiocy." He went on to add:

> "It is a better and a wiser thing to be a starved apothecary than a starved poet; so back to the shop Mr John, back to 'plasters, pills and ointment boxes'."

Keats despite these attacks wrote to his brother George, "I think I shall be among the English poets after my death." His brother Tom with whom he shared his Cheapside lodgings died in December from consumption and Keats moved to Hampstead, where he met and fell in love with Fanny Brawne. Some of his best poems were written that year, including an **Ode to a Nightingale:**

> "O, for a draught of vintage! that hath been
>   Cool'd a long age in the deep-delved earth,
> Tasting of Flora and the country green,
>   Dance, and Provençal song, and sunburnt mirth!
> O for a beaker full of the warm South,
>   Full of the true, the blushful Hippocrene,
>   With beaded bubbles winking at the brim,
>   And purple-stained mouth;
>   That I might drink, and leave the world unseen,
>   And with thee fade away into the forest dim.
>
> Fade far away, dissolve, and quite forget
>   What thou among the leaves hast never known,
> The weariness, the fever, and the fret,
>   Here, where men sit and hear each other groan."

By the close of 1819 he became increasingly ill with tuberculosis and his great creative period was now over. His second volume of poems, **Lamia, Isabella, The Eve of St Agnes, and other Poems** appeared in the summer of 1820. It was much praised and even the criticism from Blackwood's greatly muted, but sales were slow. Keats went off with his friend Severn to Italy, where they had lodgings in Rome near The Spanish Steps where Keats died the following February, not yet 26. Today Keats is ranked as one of the truly great poets of the 19th c, and his letters, first published in 1848, as "certainly the most notable and most important ever written by an English poet." (T.S. Eliot).

Shelley laments Keats in his **Adonais:**

> *I weep for Adonais – he is dead!*
> *O, weep for Adonais! though our tears*
> *Thaw not the frost which binds so dear a head!*

★ ★ ★

> *He has out-soared the shadow of our night;*
> *Envy and calumny and hate and pain,*
> *And that unrest which men miscall delight,*
> *Can touch him not and torture not again;*
> *From the contagion of the world's slow stain*
> *He is secure, and now can never mourn*
> *A heart grown cold, a head grown grey in vain."*

Keats is buried in the Protestant Cemetery in Rome, now a shrine for literary pilgrims the world over. Keats' last days in Rome are fascinatingly evoked in Anthony Burgess' **ABBA ABBA**, with the young dying English poet spewing blood and writing sonnets as he comes to terms with death and the work of Belli, the Roman writer of pornographic sonnets.

The epitomy of Keats' poetry for most readers is the **Ode on a Grecian Urn**:

> *"Thou still unravish'd bride of quietness,*
>   *Thou foster-child of silence and slow time.*
>
> *For ever warm and still to be enjoy'd*
>   *For ever panting and for ever young;*
> *All breathing human passion far above,*
>   *That leaves a heart high-sorrowful and cloy'd,*
>   *A burning forehead, and a parching tongue.*
>
> *Who are these coming to the sacrifice?*
>   *To what green altar, O mysterious priest,*
>   *Leads thou that heifer lowing at the skies,*
>   *And all her silken flanks with garlands drest?*
> *What little town by river or sea shore,*
>   *Or mountain-built with peaceful citadel,*
> *Is emptied of this folk, this pious morn?*
>
> *'Beauty is truth, truth beauty', – that is all*
>   *Ye know on earth, and all ye need to know."*

Proceeding down Moorgate we pass on the left **ROPEMAKER STREET** formerly Ropemaker's Alley where **Daniel Defoe** died in his lodgings in 1738 'from lethargy'. He once wrote, "the best of men cannot suspend their fate:

The good die early, and the bad die late".

Further down Moorgate changes its name to City Road and we come to the large **Finsbury Square** on the right. The square was created in 1777-92 by George Dance the Younger to give the City an elegant West End Square. It is now dominated by a car-park and surrounded by offices. At the end of the 18th c the square possessed one of London's biggest tourist attractions, **The Temple of the Muses**. James Lackington's bookshop in the southeast corner of the square had a frontage of 140 ft, and in the middle of the shop was a huge circular counter around which a coach and six could have driven, so great was the space. On top of the building was a dome with a flagpole which flew Mr Lackington's flag when he was in residence. The shop was burned down at the beginning of the 19th c.

At the end of the square we see Tabernacle Street and Worship Street running off to the right which commemorate the old foundry that John Wesley leased as a place of worship before his chapel was built further down City Road. At no 40 **CITY ROAD**, we have the offices of the country's newest quality daily newspaper, The Independent, which was voted newspaper of the year in 1987. Although it draws its readership from most of the quality dailies its main rival must be considered to be The Guardian. The Literary Editor of the paper is Sebastian Faulks.

City Road was laid out in 1761. Shortly after on April 21st 1777 the 74 year old divine and preacher, **John Wesley** laid the foundation stone for his Chapel opposite Bunhill Fields. The former swamp was drained by the dumped soil from the excavations for St Paul's Cathedral. The Chapel was open for public worship on 1 November 1778. It needed major restoration and more than £1 million was raised to pay for the work in 1972-78, so that the Chapel could be reopened on the 200th anniversary of its opening for worship.

John Wesley is buried in a grave behind the Chapel, and his adjacent house, no 47 has been converted into a Museum of Methodism, for which there is a small entrance fee.

John Wesley (1703-91) was the 15th child of a vicar and as a fellow at Lincoln College, Oxford, he became the centre of a group of devout Christians, who were nicknamed the 'Holy Club' or 'Methodists'. He became a member of the Moravian Society at Fetter Lane and became a lay preacher in 1738. He opened his first chapel in Bristol and conducted his ministry with the utmost vigour. It is estimated that he travelled 250,000 miles in order to preach his 40,000 sermons, and despite all this feverish activity he still produced a large body of literary work, including hymns, practical treatises and educational works, edited by Thomas à Kempis (1735). He concentrated on the large working class areas, converting hundreds of thousands of illiterate poor to his brand of worship. During his lifetime Methodism remained a movement within the framework of the Church of England. His writings were so popular that he made £30,000 from them, which he distributed in charity during his lifetime. The most interesting of his writing today is his **Journal** which is full of pathos and humour. He was a friend of Dr Johnson who thought him a good conversationalist but complained that he was 'never at leisure'. He married in 1751, a widow Mary Vazeille, who deserted him in 1776.

As of yet there have not been any major literary weddings at the Chapel but in 1951 Margaret Roberts and Dennis Thatcher married in The Chapel.

Opposite lie **BUNHILL FIELDS,** which were enclosed in 1665-6 as a burial ground for victims of the Great Plague, although it seems that they were never used as such. It was an unconsecrated burial ground and as such much favoured by nonconformists as they could bury their dead without the use of the Common Prayer Book. The last burial was in 1854, after which the cemetery was closed. It has been described as "The Cemetery of Puritan England". The City of London Corporation undertook to maintain it and preserve it for public use by an Act of Parliament in 1867. There are very good maps which clearly indicate the graves of the famous inside.

Susannah Wesley (1742) the mother of 19 children including John and Charles Wesley, is buried here as are Oliver Cromwell's son-in-law, **General Fleetwood** (d 1692), **Dr Isaac Watts** (d 1748) the father of the English hymn. In the adjoining Quaker graveyard **George Fox** (d

John Bunyan (1628-88)

Elohim creating Adam by William Blake

1691), the founder of the Society of Friends is buried.

Famous literary figures buried here are John Bunyan, Daniel Defoe and William Blake.

John Bunyan (1628-88), a brazier's son in Bedford, was drafted into the parliamentary army and was stationed at Newport Pagnall in 1644-46. In 1653, now married, he became a member of the Nonconformist church, where he preached, coming into conflict with the Quakers against whom he published his first writings, **Some Gospel Truth Opened** (1656) and **A Vindication** (1657). Widowed with four children he married again in 1659. He was arrested in November 1660 for preaching without a licence and spent most of the next 12 years in Bedford goal, and wrote nine books while in prison, including **Grace Abounding to the Chief of Sinners** (1666). He was reappointed pastor of the same church on his release from prison in 1672, and again suffered imprisonment in 1676. While in prison he finished the first part of **The Pilgrim's Progress**, which was published in 1678, the second part followed in 1684. He continued his preaching, now licensed, unmolested. After riding through the pouring rain from Bedford to a friend's house in Holborn he died on August 31st 1688. Bunyan's religious outlook is a very narrow one but his prose, though plain is beautiful, and his writing is rich in psychological insight and realism. He is the proletarian writer par excellence, who "walk'd through the wilderness of this world".

Daniel Defoe (1660-1731) was born in London, the son of a butcher and changed his name from Foe to Defoe in c 1695. He made his living as a hosiery merchant, and was greatly attracted by travel and adventure. He travelled widely on the continent and the whole length and breadth of England. As a dissenter he took up Monmouth's cause against the catholic James II in 1685 and three years later joined William III's army as they marched on London to depose James II. He made a name for himself with his satirical poem, **The True-born Englishman** (1701), attacking the prejudice against the Dutch King of England and his friends:

> *"From this amphibious ill-born mob began*
> *That vain, ill-natur'd thing, an Englishman"*

And what was this Englishman but "Your Roman-Saxon-Danish-Norman English", and what was wanted was a good King whatever his nationality:

> *"When kings the sword of justice first lay down,*
> *They are no kings, though they possess the crown.*
> *Titles are shadows, crowns are empty things,*
> *The good of subjects is the end of kings."*

His business projects, multificarious and ingenious, enjoyed little success, and it was employment as a Tory secret agent from 1703-14 that brought him success. A great writer of pamphlets and beginner of journals, the works that endear his name to posterity were all written in his later years. **Robinson Crusoe** and its sequel appeared in 1719, **Moll Flanders** and a **Journal of the Plague Year** in 1720, and his wonderful guide book, the **Tour through the Whole Island of Great Britain**, published in three volumes from 1724 to 1726.

The first major novelist, almost before what we regard as the genre was established, he added the gifts of a journalist; detail and curiosity, to the imagination of a truly creative novelist, delivered in plain but powerful prose. His grave was given an impressive monument in 1870, an obelisque paid for by the young readers of a children's magazine after an appeal to honour the author of **Robinson Crusoe**, one of the eternal children's classics.

William Blake (1757-1827) was the son of a London hosier. He had no formal schooling, and after being apprenticed to an engraver enroled as a student at the Royal Society. Blake then began producing water-colours and engravings for magazines. He married Catherine Boucher in 1782. His first volume **Poetical Sketches** appeared with financial help from his friends in 1783, and he set up his own print shop at no 27 Broad Street in 1784. In 1789 he engraved and published his **Songs of Innocence** and **The Book of Thiel**, both mystical and deeply personal works. He sought to create his own poetical language and style so as not to "be enslav'd by another Man's". His works became increasingly more complex and ambiguous, as he developed a rebellious political fervour and a visionary ecstasy.

His work attracted little attention or support during his

lifetime, and at his death the critics viewed him as probably gifted but certainly insane. **Wordworth** said of Blake:

> *"There is no doubt that this poor man was mad, but there is something in the madness of this man which interests me more than the sanity of Lord Byron and Walter Scott."*

For **Ruskin** his manner was "diseased and wild" but his mind "great and wise".

Gilchrist's biography of Blake in 1863 aroused interest and fresh anthologies of his verse began to appear. **Yeats** produced a three volume edition of his work in 1893 and for the 20th c he has become one of the great geniuses of his time, with his pictures in The Tate and his lyric poetry in every poetry anthology.

He is, as **Auden** puts it, "Self-educated Blake . . . /Spoke to Isaiah in the Strand/And heard inside each mortal thing/Its holy emanation sing."

Blake tells us:

> *"A Robin Redbreast in a Cage*
> *Puts all heaven in a Rage."*
> ***(Auguries of Innocence)***

and that:

> *"He who would do good to another must do it in Minute Particulars.*
> *General Good is the plea of the scoundrel, hypocrite, and flatterer;*
> *For Art and Science cannot exist but in minutely organized Particulars."* ***(Jerusalem)***

and for children he is the poet of:

> *"Tyger! Tyger! burning bright*
> *In the forest of the night,*
> *What immortal hand or eye*
> *Could frame thy fearful symmetry."*
> ***(The Tyger)***

His most haunting artistic work came in the last year of his life, the twenty-one illustrations of the **Book of Job** and his unfinished series of illustrations of Dante's **Divine Comedy**, which contains all the vivid mystic power of his poetry with the greater directness of the visual image. He died on August 12th 1827, aged 70.

Behind Bunhill Fields lies **BUNHILL ROW** where **John Milton** lived from 1662 until his death in 1674. (The street was then known as Artillery Row). A widower with three daughters from his first marriage, Milton married his third wife, Elizabeth Minshull on February 24th 1663 at St Mary Aldermary. She was 24, Milton was 55. Milton, who got on badly with his daughters, forgot to tell them about his wedding and they heard of it from their servant, Elizabeth Fisher. Mary Milton's laconic comment was "that that was no news to hear of his wedding but if she could hear of his death that was something". Milton had been arrested at the Restoration in 1660, as a senior official of Cromwell's Commonwealth, but after a month in prison he was released. He was now safe but a much villified member of the community. Since 1651 he was totally blind. It is said that Milton, the most famous and gifted intellectual of the land, was offered Court employment by Charles II but refused saying that such behaviour would be inconsistent with his former conduct, for he had never yet employed his pen against his conscience. The Duke of York, the King's brother (later James II), expressed his wish to see the greatest controversialist of the age and went, it is said, to see Milton:

> *"In the course of their conversation, the Duke asked Milton, whether he did not think the loss of his sight was a judgement upon him for what he had written against the late King his father? Milton's reply was to this effect: 'If your Highness thinks that the calamities which befall us here are indications of the wrath of Heaven, in what manner are we to account for the fate of the King your father? The displeasure of Heaven, must, upon this supposition, have been much greater against him, than against me: for I have lost only my eyes, but he lost his head'."*
>
> (The Life Records of John Milton, compiled by J. Milton French — Rutgers University)

It is a wonderful anecdote, which if not literally true is certainly true in spirit. By 1665 and The Plague, Milton had finished Paradise Lost. He left London for Chalfont St Giles in Buckinghamshire, where he wrote most of **Samson Agonistes**, which clearly dramatizes his life, and is the nearest we have to an autobiography of Milton. We can imagine Milton, with his young wife and three hostile daughters crammed into a small temporary country home, an exile from his glory and the London of The Plague:

> "O loss of sight, of thee I most complain!
> Blind among enemies, O worse than chains,
> Dungeon, or beggary, or decrepit age!
> Light the prime work of God to me is extinct,
> And all her various objects of delight
> Annulled, which might in part my grief have eased,
> Inferior to the vilest now become
> Of man or worm; the vilest here excel me,
> They creep, yet see, I dark in light exposed
> To daily fraud, contempt, abuse and wrong,
> Within doors, or without, still as a fool,
> In power of others, never in my own."

But still, however dejected Milton became, he never lost sight of his power as a poet of genius:

> "But he though blind of sight,
> Despised and thought extinguished quite,
> With inward eye illuminated
> His fiery virtue roused
> From under ashes into sudden flame."

With the plague over Milton returned to London, but the London he knew was destroyed the following year in the Great Fire, including his former home in Bread Street, the last piece of property that he owned. But his life improved, the publication of **Paradise Lost** in 1667 brought him fame, at long last, as a poet in England. This reputation was increased by the publication of **Samson Agonistes** and **Paradise Regained** in the same volume in 1671. His last years were serene, his three daughters out of the house, he was well cared for by his young wife. He died on 9th November 1674, a month before his 66th birthday.

A few steps further takes us to Old Street Tube Station, where the foot-sore might choose to take a tube home, leaving the intrepid to walk through the streets of the East End back into the City and to the Tower.

It is **OLD STREET** where Mrs Guppy has "a little property at three hundred and two", a fact we learn when the young clerk proposes to Esther Summerson in Dickens' **Bleak House**. Unfortunately for Mr Guppy it is not sufficient for Esther to say yes to this up-and-coming man.

Having turned right at City Road we follow Old Street towards Shoreditch. A few streets up on the right we pass **CURTAIN ROAD**, where London's first ever theatre was started in 1577 by James Burbage, who had leased the site the year before. It was called simply, The Theatre.

THE THEATRE

In England theatre developed out of the drama inherent in the church's own ritual, and at Christmas and Easter scenes from the Bible were enacted in the church. Complete biblical plays were later written, which proved so popular that they were too large to be performed in church, and were performed in the churchyard and eventually in the town or village square. The guilds became responsible for producing the plays which became a focal part of community life. The Mystery and Miracle plays, although drawn from the Bible and the lives of saints, always contained moments of comic relief and bawdiness. Secular drama was always present waiting to get out. The Reformation and the Renaissance brought a revival of interest in Classical Literature and a greater secularization of society. Roman (and later) Greek tragedies and comedies became the models for new plays in English or Latin. These plays were mainly read in the houses of the rich and cultured, who would often perform them en famille.

It became possible to make a living as a performer, with troupes of actors going round the Great Houses and the galleried inn yards and the Halls of the Guilds up and down the country. Their arrival would be a major event and attract large crowds. The theatre's impact in Elizabethan England can be compared with that of television in our own age, and plays had to reflect the requirements of the whole of society. James Burbage, a member of the Earl of Leicester's Men (each actors' troupe was required to have a patron) had the idea of having a permanent building for the performance of his plays. It had to be outside of the City, as the City authorities considered secular plays immoral and feared so many people congregated together in the same building would create a public health risk, causing the plague to spread easily. Burbage sited his theatre near, but outside, the City in Shoreditch at what is now no 88 Curtain Road. There is a warehouse on the site which has a plaque commemorating

The Theatre.

The second theatre was built nearby in Holywell Lane and opened shortly after The Theatre. **Dr Johnson** tells of a young man who was employed to hold the horses outside The Theatre, before getting bit parts in the plays and writing the occasional scene, called **William Shakespeare**.

We know very little about the life of Shakespeare. By 1592 he was in London and making a name for himself as a dramatist which is born out by an attack on him in Greene's **Groat-Worth of Witte**, in which he warns his fellow university wits, of that "upstart Crow, beautified with our feather the Johannes fac totum, who supposes he is as well able to bombast out a blanke verse as the best of vou and in his owne conceit the onely Shake-scene in a countrey."

Born in Stratford-upon-Avon in 1564, the son of a glover John Shakespeare and the daughter of a local landowner Mary Arden, he was the eldest surviving child of the family. His father became an important municipal figure, becoming a bailiff and justice of the peace in 1568, and prosperous as the purchase of property locally shows. At some stage there was a decline in his fortunes shown by the sale of land and property. It is assumed William attended the local grammar school (still there) as he had knowledge of Latin and some Greek. What is certain is that the 18 year old William Shakespeare had to marry the 26 year old Anne Hathaway in November 1582, the first child, Susanna, coming six months later. In those days a spinster of 26 was considered an old maid with little or no expectations of marriage. With this late reprieve, Anne was able to leave the farm at Shottery where she was an unwanted member of her brother's household to live with her young husband's family in Stratford. **James Joyce** summed up matters in his **Ulysses** with the unforgettable line:

"*Where there's a Will, Anne Hath-a-way.*"

Twins were born in February 1585, Hamneth and Judith. The next reference to Shakespeare is Greene's in 1592, so at some time, Shakespeare left his family in Stratford and came to London. For most of his married life Shakespeare

William Shakespeare (1564-1616)

Ben Jonson (1572-1637)

lived apart from Anne Hathaway in London, seeing her and his children infrequently. Because of the plague the theatres were closed in 1592 and it was probably during this time that he wrote his narrative poems **Venus and Adonis** and **The Rape of Lucrece**. These, along with the short poem **The Phoenix and The Turtle**, are the only works of Shakespeare to be published by him during his lifetime, appearing in 1593 and 1594 and are dedicated to his patron, the Earl of Southampton, Henry Wriothesley. Scripts of some of his plays were printed in his lifetime, and give a very inadequate rendering when compared with **The First Folio** of 1623, and are often described as "bad quartos".

In 1594 he became a member of the Lord Chamberlain's Company, which was managed by Burbage. As an actor he performed at both The Theatre and The Curtain. After the death of James Burbage in 1597, his actor-manager son Richard dismantled The Theatre and re-erected it in Southwark, with Shakespeare, Hemmings and Condell amongst others now partners in the company. The Curtain Theatre fell in to disuse in 1625 and was destroyed in the Great Fire.

Another actor-playwright was **Ben Jonson** (1572-1637), the posthumous son of a clergyman. He worked as a bricklayer (his step-father's trade) before fighting in the wars in Flanders and embracing the life of a strolling player. By 1597 he was a member of Philip Henslowe's Company and was imprisoned that year for his part in the writing of the Satire the **Isle of Dogs** (now lost) which contained "very seditious and slandrous matter". The fiery Ben, a brave and skilful swordsman fought a duel across the road from The Curtain in Hoxton Fields (where Hoxton Square now stands across Old Street) and killed a fellow actor Gabriel Spencer. Jonson escaped being hung by pleading the benefit of clergy, a little Latin going a long way in those days. Instead his left thumb was branded, showing him to be a felon. While in prison he became a Roman Catholic, not the safest thing to do in Elizabethan England, but returned to the Anglican Church twelve years later, during a period of greater tolerance of the Catholic faith in England. His first major play, **Every Man in his Humour** was performed by the Lord

Chamberlain's Men at The Curtain in 1598, the cast including William Shakespeare. He was the first dramatist to have all his plays published together as a collected work, his **Folio** of 1616 giving literary respectability to drama, reflected by his honorary M.A. from Oxford and his appointment as a lecturer in rhetoric at Gresham College in London. It was Jonson who provided **The Preface to the First Folio** of Shakespeare's plays in 1623, singing the praises in verse of the "Sweet Swan of Avon!" and "though thou hadst small Latin, and less Greek" Shakespeare "was not of an age, but for all time!". Few major artists have ever praised so lavishly one of their contemporaries as Ben did William:

> "While I confess thy writings to be such,
> As neither man, nor muse, can praise too much."

and:

> "Soul of the Age!
> The applause! delight! the wonder of our stage!
> My Shakespeare, rise; I will not lodge thee by
> Chaucer or Spenser, or bid Beaumont lie
> A little further, to make thee a room:
> Thou art a monument, without a tomb,
> And art alive still, while thy book doth live,
> And we have wits to read, and praise to give."

Jonson's dedication of the **First Folio** (1623) shows how ridiculous the 19th c theory was that Sir Francis Bacon wrote Shakespeare's plays. A grotesque insult conjured up by Victorian snobbery and the desire for self-advertisement. Any analysis of the writing styles of Bacon and Shakespeare would have disproved it, and the existing documentation on Shakespeare makes it laughable. Bacon had superior education and learning, but not the wit or the intellect of the glover's son. It is precisely because Shakespeare avoided the rules of classical drama and relied on his own genius that his work is so alive and fresh today as it was 300 years ago. Jonson's adoption of the rules of classical tragedy and comedy put serious obstacles in the way of our enjoyment of his plays today, although his later work, **Volpone** (1605) and **The Alchemist** (1610) still holds a modern audience in their grip. One can still read his **Bartholomew Fair** (1614) with great pleasure, a play which is an account of the London of its time is an invaluable record. A lyric poet of exceptional talent we still sing in unison:

> "Drink to me only with thine eyes,
> And I will pledge with mine;
> Or leave a kiss but in the cup,
> And I'll not look for wine,
> The thirst that from the soul doth rise
> Doth ask a drink divine;
> But might I of Jove's nectar sup,
> I would not change for thine."
>
> *(To Celia)*

During the reign of James I, Jonson was the most important and feted English writer. He was made poet laureate and was given a pension. Jonson wrote and produced elaborate masques to be peformed in court with the scenery designed by Inigo Jones. The collaboration ended in 1631 with a famous quarrel about what was more important, the visual or the verbal in staging a masque, with Jonson pouring scorn on Jones in verse.

Jonson held court at the Mermaid Tavern and later at the Devil's Tavern in Fleet Street where the young writers flocked to be numbered as members of "the tribe of Ben". Jonson's standing did not hold in Charles I's reign (1625) and after a stroke in 1628 he was permanently bedridden until his death in 1637 in a house in the precincts of Westminster Abbey. He was buried in the Abbey, at his own request, standing up, to reduce the cost of his burial, under the inscription, "O rare Ben Jonson". He was one of the most colourful characters of his times, arrogant, quarrelsome and of a violent disposition, but affectionate and loving to his friends and intellectually honest.

At the end of Old Street we turn right into **Shoreditch High Street.** Across the road is the church of **St Leonard's**, where both James Burbage and his son Richard are buried. The actor Ben Jonson killed in a duel, Gabriel Spencer is also buried here, as is the jester of Henry VIII, Will Somers. Somers was perhaps the only person who could talk freely to Henry VIII in his last years as he became increasingly tyrannical and irascible, and endured great discomfort especially from his leg. Somers was buried here in 1560. Three of John Keats' brothers were baptised in the church in 1801, Keats being baptised at St Botolph's Bishopsgate. **Charles Bradlaugh** (1833-91) the social reformer, lecturer and pamphleteer was baptised in the church. He was elected MP for Northamton in 1880, but was unseated as he refused to take the parliamentary oath as an atheist. He was re-elected three times but was not allowed to affirm his allegiance, and took up his seat in 1886 when he finally took the oath. He engaged in several lawsuits to maintain the freedom of the press, and is best known for his pamphlet advocating birth control, **The Fruits of Philosophy**, which he produced with Annie Besant. It led to a six month prison sentence and a £200 fine, the prison sentence was quashed on appeal.

The church was rebuilt by George Dance the Elder in 1736-40, and has been repaired after bomb damage in World War II. It is at present being renovated. There has been a church dedicated to St Leonard on this site since the 12th c. If you go into the church garden you will find Shoreditch's old whipping post and stocks on display.

A few streets past the church there is **OLD NICHOL STREET** on the left, which is the setting for Arthur Morrison's realist novel **A Child of the Jago** (1896). Set amongst the criminal classes of the East End it tells "the story of a boy who, but for his environment, would have been a good citizen". It follows on from the work of George Moore and George Gissing to produce the most realistic novel published in the 19th c, and still reads well, although it drifts in and out of print. When published it highlighted the problems of the East End, and led to a slum clearance project and a new housing estate opened by the Prince of Wales in 1900.

THE EAST END has been for centuries the traditional area for immigrants settling in London, from the country bumpkins coming to the big City in search of work, called derisively cockneys (some reverse the origin of cockney as an insult used by the new arrivals to the City dwellers). Then the Spanish and Portuguese Jews and French Huguenots in the 17th c, the 19th c influx of Jews from Russia and Poland, followed by Jews from Hitler's Germany, and more recently people from the Indian subcontinent, especially from Bangladesh.

From being semi-rural at the beginning of the 19th c the

East End was by the end of the century London's solidly urbanised, over-populated slum district. The City had depopulated, pushing out its poor inhabitants as it developed as a financial and commodities centre. The large new Victorian thoroughfares, the railways and the tram lines were put through the London slums, and the dispossessed slum dwellers flocked to the East End. The vast docks in the East End, built to take advantage of ever-increasing trade, turned the waterfront into a dormitory area for tens of thousands of dockers and labourers. This great new prosperity which the docks should have opened for the East End failed to materialise, with the coming of steam and industrialisation transferring trade northwards to Liverpool and Hull, and shipbuilding to the Wear and the Clyde. As the City grew richer and the West End more opulent the East End became poorer. The statistics of infant mortality, disease, crime, prostitution and homelessness were frightening and the East End attracted the social scientists like Mayhew, the philanthropic Burdett-Coutts and her adviser Charles Dickens, the Salvation Army and the nonconformist preachers, while remaining largely ignored by the government until the end of the century.

Morrison's **Tales of Mean Street** (1894) highlighted the East End problems, while **The Day of the Jago** brought about much needed action. There was at last a major novel about the East End, depicting its problems artistically but also realistically. Dickens had written about the poverty of the City, of a London which was fast disappearing in his own lifetime, and it was only Morrison and later writers who took up the East End as their subject. The American writer **Jack London** (1876-1916) came to London to immerse himself in the East End slums to write his **The People of the Abyss** (1903). London already a well-known writer begins by going to a second-hand clothes shop in a poor area to buy some ragged clothes:

> *"No sooner was I out in the streets than I was impressed by the difference in status effected by my clothes. All civility vanished from the demeanour of the common people with whom I came into contact. Presto! in the twinkling of an eye, so to say, I had become one of them. My frayed and out-at-elbow jacket was the badge and advertisement of my class,*

which was their class. It made me of a like kind, in place of the fawning and too-respectful attention I had hitherto received, I now shared with them a comradeship. The man in corduroy and dirty neckchief no longer addressed me as 'sir' or 'governor'. It was 'mate' now – and a fine and hearty word with a tingle to it, and a warmth and gladness which the other term does not possess."

London's book impressed a young schoolboy at Eton, Eric Blair who was later to submerge into the East End poor to write a more real and intense and sustained narrative, published as **Down and Out in Paris and London**, the first published work of George Orwell in 1933.

The hopelessness and despair of the East End is best summed up in **A Child of the Jago**, where the young hero Dick Perrott, whose father is hanged for murder, is told by an old lag the only way out of the slums is to emulate the mobsters who rule the district:

"There it is – that's your aim in life – there's your pattern. Learn to read and write, learn all you can; but learn cunning, spare nobody and stop at nothing. It's the best this world has for you. For the Jago's got you, and it's the only way out, except the goal and the gallows."

The bull-dozers and the bombings of World War II cleared away the worst of the slums. Many of the area's inhabitants were rehoused in the outer London boroughs, creating a strong nostalgia and the myth of the East End, of a close community which stuck together, which had its moments of happiness despite the awful poverty. The East End however is still an area of appalling housing conditions, with many slums and soulless high rise council flats, with high unemployment and social deprivation. The Jews have gone and their place has been taken by the latest immigrants, the Asians. But there are major changes taking place, the derelict docklands are being re-developed for high-tech industries, with most of the newspapers relocating there. The waterfront is being re-colonized by the middle classes and house prices are rocketing as the so-called yuppies are moving in to be near the City and the new commercial enterprises of the Docklands. The social and economic forces which created the East End are now working in reverse and the working classes are being dispossessed as the East End becomes fashionable, that is in certain parts, for the middle class to live.

We leave the traffic congestion of Shoreditch High Street to turn left into the even busier Commercial Street, chock-a-block with heavy traffic which we take to the pleasant environments of Spitalfields Market.

SPITALFIELDS were the open fields adjacent to a medieval priory and hospital (a spital) of St Mary, which according to Daniel Defoe became 'all town' towards the end of the 17th c. The Flemish weavers fleeing from religious persecution in France settled in this area after the Revocation of the Edict of Nantes in 1685, around the fruit and vegetable market established by the charter of Charles II in 1682. With the Huguenot weavers, Spitalfields became famous for its silk industry. The hardworking daughters of the weavers who spent all day spinning at their loom were such a family asset that they were encouraged not to marry, and from this we have the word spinster for an unmarried woman. Some of the silk merchants became rich and there are some fine Georgian houses surviving in the area, especially in Fournier Street and Elder Street.

Opposite the market there is the impressive church by Hawksmoor, a pupil and later an assistant of Sir Christopher Wren, the 18th c **Christ Church**. It was one of the churches commissioned to be built under the Fifty New Churches Act of 1711. It is a superb example of the English baroque but always seems to be in the process of being restored. The crypt is used as a rehabilitation centre for alcoholics while next door in the church garden unreformed alcoholics use the facilities, of what is now called locally 'itchy park' after the vagrants who sleep out there at night.

It is impossible now to think of Christ Church or Hawksmoor without Peter Ackroyd's macabre but magical psychic thriller, **Hawksmoor** (1985) coming to mind. It paints the London of the day in unforgettable colour and subtlety, with Peter Ackroyd's gift for period prose bringing the novel vividly to life. Not since Charles Dickens has London possessed a novelist with such a feeling for it and its history.

In **Hawskmoor** Ackroyd tells us the area's history:

"My Church now rises above a populous Conjunction of Alleys, Courts and Passages, Places full of poor people but in those Years before the Fire the lanes by Spittle-Fields were dirty and unfrequented: that part now called Spittle-Fields Market or Flesh-Market, was a Field of Grass with the Cows feeding on it. And there where my Church is where three roads meet, viz Mermaid Lane, Tabernacle Alley and Balls Alley, was open ground until the Plague turned it into a vast Mound of Corrupcion. Brick Lane which is now a long well-paved street, was a deep dirty Road, frequented by Carts fetching Bricks that way into White-chappel from Brick-kilns in the Fields. Here I rambled as a Boy, and yet also was often walking abroad into that great and monstrous Pile of London."

Next to the church is the Jack the Ripper pub, full of period pictures and prints, and the details of the Jack the Ripper murders which took place in this area. It was the failure of Scotland Yard to find the murderer of six women, most of whom were prostitutes which led to **Conan Doyle** inventing a super-detective who could solve the crimes which were beyond Scotland Yard. The fog-ridden alleyways and dens of Spitalfields and the adjacent Whitechapel are the background for many of the **Sherlock Holmes** stories. The murders which began in August 1888 ended by the time Montague Druitt, a crazy laywer-cum-schoolmaster, was found dead in the Thames in December 1888, and he is the most likely culprit. He was a frequent visitor to the area where his brother was a doctor. Another suspect was the Duke of Clarence, a son of the Prince of Wales (later Edward VII) a noted eccentric, who was fond of deerstalker hats and capes, and spent his nights prowling the streets of London. Conan Doyle modelled Sherlock Holmes' appearance on the Duke of Clarence. Whoever the murderer was his murders engendered great terror and added to the East End's reputation for violence and crime. Today there is a flourishing tourist industry which goes in search of Jack the Ripper round the streets of the East End.

After wandering round the streets of Spitalfield Market we leave it by either Lamb Street or Folgate Street which will bring us down into **NORTON FOLGATE**, where **William Shakespeare** had lodgings when he was employed at Burbage's The Theatre. We turn left to enter **BISHOPSGATE** the road that will take us back to the

City from the East End. The street is named after one of the six original Roman gates in the City Wall, which was the exit out of London to the Bishop of London's manor house at Bethnal Green, a rural hamlet in the Middle Ages. The Bishops of London became charged with the upkeep of the gate, which stood opposite Camomile Street, and is commemorated by the Bishop's Mitre on the buildings. In the 15th and 16th centuries there were large mansions here, including Crosby Place, built in 1466-75 for a wealthy grocer, Sir John Crosby. In 1483 Richard, Duke of Gloucester, was living here when he heard of the murder of his nephews, the two little princes in the Tower. **Sir Thomas More** owned it in 1532-4, and **Sir Walter Ralegh** had lodgings here in 1601. The Great Hall, the only surviving part of Crosby Place, was bought in 1908 by the University of London and re-erected in Chelsea on what was once the site of Sir Thomas More's country garden at Beaufort House. It is now used as a hostel for women students at London University. The hall's hammerbeam roof and oriel windows have been preserved, and one of the three Holbein portraits of Sir Thomas More with his family hangs behind the high table. Nearby on the Chelsea Embankment there is a statue of the seated More in bronze by Cubitt Bevis (1969) a few yards from Chelsea Old Church where More used to worship.

On the right we pass the large redbrick complex of Liverpool Street Railway Station built on the site of Bethlehem Royal Hospital (Bedlam), which became, in the 16th c, a lunatic asylum. It was one of the sights of London with visitors eager to look at the chained patients in their gallery cells, like caged animals in a menagerie. This proved a very good way of raising money until it was stopped in 1770 as the visitors tended to disturb the tranquillity of the patients by making sport and diversion of the miserable inhabitants. The station was opened in 1874 and over 157,000 passengers a day use the terminal to travel to Eastern England, and a former poet laureate, **John Betjeman** described it as 'the most picturesque and interesting of the London termini'.

To the left is Middlesex Street where on Sunday mornings we have the famous London street market of Petticoat Lane. The market got its name as the street traders used to boast that when a women entered the market they could steal her petticoat from her on the way in and sell it back to her before she left.

Next to the railway station we proceed to **ST BOTOLPH WITHOUT BISHOPSGATE**, which dates back to the beginning of the 13th c. The medieval church was demolished in 1724 and rebuilt by George Dance the Elder in 1725-8. His building has been much altered during the seven subsequent restorations. **Edward Alleyn** (1566-1626) was christened here. He was a famous Elizabethan actor and partner with Henslowe in the Fortune Theatre in Cripplegate, and the great rival of Richard Burbage. For the Lord Admiral's Company he had the leading roles in Marlowe's **Tamburlaine, Jew of Malta** and **Dr Faustus**. He became extremely rich and bought the manor of Dulwich where he built and endowed a public school, Dulwich College. He married his partner Henslowe's stepdaughter and after her death one of John Donne's daughters. Dulwich in 1605 cost Alleyne £5,000, which was in his opinion £1,000 more than it was worth.

In the Dance church **John Keats** was christened in 1795.

Across the road is Houndsditch, which was the moat that bounded the City Wall, where there was the habit of casting dead dogs and the rubbish of the City, giving the area its name.

On the left there is **DIRTY DICKS** at no 202-4 Bishopsgate. A pub full of synthetic cobwebs and dead cats which is on the site of Nathaniel Bentley's house, a well known dandy whose fiancée died on the eve of the wedding. He locked up the dining room, complete with wedding breakfast, and spent the rest of his life in increasing squalor, saying it is said, "If I wash my hands today, they will be dirty again tomorrow". When he died in 1809, though exceedingly rich, his house was falling apart. His cellars are now part of the tavern. Dickens lifts this story and uses it for Miss Havisham in **Great Expectations** (1860-1).

We are back inside the one square mile of the City and visit the City's smallest church, **St Ethelburga-the-Virgin within Bishopsgate**, dedicated to the 7th c Abbess of Barking. The church dates back to the 13th c and before the Dissolution of the Monasteries it was under the patronage of the nearby convent of St Helen's. It was rebuilt in the 15th c and survived unscathed the Great Fire which stopped to the the north of it. The church has a ragstone facade, with a 14th c doorway and 15th c windows above, and has a charming though tiny interior. The church's size must have been typical of many of the City's churches destroyed in the Great Fire and not rebuilt. In 1607 Henry Hudson and his crew took communion in the church before setting off to look for the North West Passage. They are commemorated by Leonard Walker's three windows erected in 1928-30.

A short distance away, tucked in behind Bishopsgate, we come to **ST HELEN'S BISHOPSGATE**. The church dedicated to the mother of the Roman Emperor Constantine, a 4th c Christian, began as a Benedictine nunnery in the 12th c, although there has been a church on this site since Saxon times. The church was used by both the parish and the nuns, and this is why it was divided into two to keep the nuns away from the parishioners. At the Reformation the church reverted to being a parish church. It has 15th c choir-stalls, with a 17th c font, pulpit and doorways. **William Shakespeare** was once a parishioner of St Helen's so he is commemorated by a memorial window. There are some fine brasses and many monuments in the church and St Helen's has been called the Westminster Abbey of the City.

We branch off to the right down **Threadneedle Street**, whose unusual name probably comes from the three needles in the arms of the Needlemakers Company and would have been the sign hanging over a shop in the street. Up until the 16th c the street was called Three Needles Street. **Sir Thomas More** went to St Anthony's grammar school in this street, which was destroyed and not rebuilt after the Great Fire. We pass the modern buildings of the Stock Exchange, and what **Sheridan**, in a parliamentary speech in 1797, termed the Old Lady of Threadneedle Street, the Bank of England, easily recognised by its large white windowless wall. It has been on this site since 1734, and was rebuilt by Sir John Soane in 1788 in a neo-classical style, of which the outside walls survive, with nearly all of the interiors being rebuilt in the 1920s and 30s by Herbert Baker.

Kenneth Grahame (1859-1932) entered the service of the Bank of England after leaving Oxford and became Secretary to the Bank in 1898. He published **Pagan Papers** (1893), six of which describe the life of a family of five orphans, whose deeds are the subject matter of **The Golden Age** (1895) and its sequel **Dream Days** (1898). Narrated by a child the authentic vision of childhood was much praised, and they were successful both in England and in America. The bedtime stories Grahame told his son became **The Wind in the Willows** (1908) with little initial interest for the adventures of Rat, Mole, Badger and Toad. It was dramatised by **A.A. Milne** in 1919 and is firmly established as a children's classic.

Opposite the Bank of England are the 19th c buildings of the Royal Exchange built in the style of a Roman Temple. It is the third Royal Exchange on this site, the first erected by Sir Thomas Gresham in 1567, sought to emulate the Antwerp Bourse in its design and purpose. After a visit by Queen Elizabeth I in 1570 it became not just the Exchange but the Royal Exchange. Lloyds and the Stock Exchange used to be inside but since 1939 it has housed the Guardian Royal Assurance Company, and more recently the Futures Market.

We swing to the left to go round the Royal Exchange passing the equestrian statue of the **Duke of Wellington** (1769-1852). The Duke of Wellington is one of the protagonists in Harriette Wilson's **Memoirs**, published in instalments from 1825. The Memoirs' publisher Stockdale wrote giving Madame Wilson's clients the opportunity not to be in the book after the payment of a small consideration. When the Duke received his letter he wrote across it, "Publish and be damned" and posted the letter back to Stockdale. The Duke of Wellington found himself in good company in the courtesan's lively if libellous **Memoirs**, with many of his brother peers sharing Harriette's favours. It is not surprising that the Duke acquired a low opinion of writers and said of them:

> *"I hate the whole race. There is no believing a word they say – your professional poets, I mean – there never existed a more worthless set than Byron and his friends for example."*

Byron however paid homage to the Duke, depicting the

battle of Waterloo in **Childe Harold's Pilgrimage:**

> *"There was a sound of revelry by night,*
> *And Belgium's capital had gather'd then*
> *Her beauty and her chivalry, and bright*
> *The lamps shone o'er fair women and brave men;*
> *A thousand hearts beat happily; and when*
> *Music arose with its voluptuous swell,*
> *Soft eyes look'd love to eyes which spake again,*
> *And all went merry as a marriage bell;*
> *But hush! hark! a deep sound strikes like a rising*
> *knell! (Canto III)."*

Byron follows Wellington into battle as does Thackeray in his novel, **Vanity Fair**. Wellington features in the historical novels of **Sir Arthur Conan Doyle** (1859-1930) and **George Henty** (1832-1902).

The Duke got the most lavish funeral ever given to a subject and the pomp and ceremony of the occasion is recorded in Tennyson's **Ode on the Death of the Duke of Wellington** (1854):

> *"Speak no more of his renown,*
> *Lay your earthly fancies down,*
> *And in the vast cathedral leave him,*
> *God accept him, Christ receive him."*

As we turn we see the 18th c Mansion House in front of us, the home of the Lord Mayor of the City. He is elected annually and takes up his office on the second Saturday in November, a day of great pageantry and festivity in the City, with the livery companies out in their regalia, bands, orchestras, funfairs and fireworks.

Before we enter Cornhill we make a little foray into **LOMBARD STREET**, named after the Italian merchants from Lombardy who settled here in the 12th c, and who after the expulsion of the Jews by Edward I in 1291 replaced them as London's bankers.

At no 2 lived Maria Beadnell, the 18 year old girl that the 17 year old **Charles Dickens** fell violently in love with in 1829. They lived at no 2, next door to the Bank of Smith, Payne and Smith, where first her uncle and then her father were the managers. Dickens was not seen as sufficiently eligible and her family put an end to their romance by sending Maria off to Paris, to finish her education. This was perhaps the great love of Dickens' life, and in middle age he met Maria again who was by then a portly matron, and charmed the woman who once rejected him.

Alexander Pope (1688-1744) was born in this street where his father had a drapery shop. Shortly after his birth his father retired to Windsor. As a catholic, Pope was denied a formal education and made up for it by voracious reading at home, and had lessons in Italian and French. At 12 he had some kind of infection of the spine which ruined his health and stunted his growth. The playwright Wycherley befriended Pope introducing him to the major figures of the day. His translation of Homer brought him financial independence. In 1718 he moved with his mother to Twickenham where he spent the rest of his life, devoting much of his time to his grotto and garden. Once a member of Addison's little senate he ended by satirizing him in his **Epistle to Dr Arbuthnot** as he took up with the Scriblerus Club, whose members included Swift and Gay. It is as a satirist that we mainly think of Pope, whose poetic talents seem to be almost permanently engaged in rivalry with his critics and foes.

We take a brief glance inside the Wren church of **St Edmund the King**, rebuilt by him after the Great Fire in 1670-9. In 1716 **Addison** married Charlotte, the Countess of Warwick and Holland in the church. The marriage, it was said, was not a happy one. **Addison** died in 1719 in Holland Park leaving the countess a widow. Addison's prose **Dr Johnson** wrote in his **Life** (1781) was "the model of the middle style; on grave subjects not formal, on light occasions not grovelling". As an essayist **Addison** succeeded in his aim of bringing "philosophy out of closets and libraries, schools and colleges, to dwell in clubs, assemblies, at tea-tables and coffee-houses".

Retracing our steps we enter the parallel street of **CORNHILL**. On the corner with Lombard Street a plaque commemorates **Thomas Guy** (1644-1724) who had a bookshop on this site, and made a fortune of £500,000 by printing and selling bibles and selling his South Sea shares before the bubble burst. He built and furnished three wards of St Thomas' Hospital in 1707 and in 1722 founded the hospital which bears his name in Southwark.

Alexander Pope (1688-1744)

The Brontë sisters painted by their brother
Patrick Branwell Brontë.
From left to right Anne Brontë (1820-49), Emily Brontë
(1818-48), Charlotte Brontë (1816-55)

Daniel Defoe had a draper's shop off Cornhill when he was arrested for his pamphlet **The Shortest Way with Dissenters** (1702) which led to him being put in the pillory in Cornhill before being imprisoned in Newgate Prison. **Thomas Gray** (1716-71) was born on the site of no 39, the son of a scrivener who spent most of his life at Cambridge. His poems were immensely popular especially **Elegy written in a Country Church-Yard** (1751) and on the death of Cibber in 1757 he was offered the position of poet laureate which he declined. His poems were the first works to be printed on his friend Horace Walpole's Strawberry Hill Press. For most readers today Gray is only the author of the **Elegy**:

> *"Let not ambition mock their useful toil,*
> *Their homely joys, and destiny obscure;*
> *Nor grandeur hear with a disdainful smile,*
> *The short and simple annals of the poor.*
>
> *The boast of heraldry, the pomp of pow'r,*
> *And all that beauty, all that wealth e'er gave,*
> *Awaits alike th'inevitable hour,*
> *The paths of glory lead but to the grave."*

In a panel at no 32, the offices of the Cornhill Assurance Co., Garraway's Coffee-House is commemorated, it was in Exchange Alley off Cornhill. Founded at the end of the 17th c, by England's first ever tea dealer, it sold tea, coffee, sherry, cherry wine, punch and pale ale with its sandwiches, and operated as the chief auction house in the City. The Tatler speaks of Garraway's auction room, and it is mentioned in the works of Addison, Pope, Swift and Gay. Dickens knew it well and referred to it in **Pickwick Papers**, **Martin Chuzzlewit**, **Little Dorrit** and **The Uncommercial Traveller**, and a scene in Thackeray's **Vanity Fair** is set here. It ceased trading in 1872 and was demolished to make way for a bank.

The publishers Smith and Elder were at no 65 from 1816 until c 1868. Their authors included Thackeray, Leigh Hunt, Mrs Gaskell, the Brontes and Ruskin. There is also a panel on the door of no 32 (formerly 65) commemorating the visit of **Charlotte** and **Anne Bronte** to their publishers in 1848, and shows them meeting **Thackeray**. "We found 65 Cornhill to be a large bookseller's shop, in a street almost as bustling as the Strand", wrote Charlotte in a letter home. She tells of asking to see Mr Smith, by now the sole proprietor, and when he approached to meet Currer Bell he showed great surprise to find it was a woman. She had come to give him "ocular proof" that Currer and Acton Bell were different people, to refute the rumour that it was a pseudonym for only one writer. Charlotte Bronte modelled Mrs Bretton and Dr John on her publisher and his mother in **Villette**.

Smith and Elder began the Cornhill magazine in 1859, with Thackeray as its first editor. It serialised his last two novels, **The Adventures of Philip** and **Denis Duval**. A later editor was **Sir Leslie Stephen,** Thackeray's son-in-law, and father of Virginia Woolf. He liked the style of a rural prose idyll published in 1872 and commissioned the author's next book for the Cornhill magazine, and Thomas Hardy's **Far from the Madding Crowd** appeared brilliantly illustrated, at the end of 1873.

Set slightly back off Cornhill on the right side of the street is the Wren church of **St Michael's** where the poet **Thomas Gray** was christened in 1716. If one continues past the church St Michael's Alley leads to the George and Vulture pub where Mr Pickwick and his faithful servant, Sam Weller, had lodgings during Mr Pickwick's trial at the Guildhall for breach of promise to Mrs Bardell. It is an 18th c tavern. Back in Cornhill there is another 18th c tavern, Simpson's which was founded in 1757.

Slightly up from St Michael's is another Wren church, **St Peter's upon Cornhill,** which has a fine Father Smith organ on which Mendelssohn had played in 1840 and 1842. The church often has organ recitals and concerts.

After the junction with Gracechurch Street (where **Charles Dickens** as a boy used to watch the departing coaches from the Spread Eagle Inn, the site of no 84, and where opposite at the Swan-with-Two-Necks Estella met Pip in his **Great Expectations**) Cornhill changes its name to **LEADENHALL STREET,** one of London's most interesting streets.

At the corner of St Mary Axe stands the church of **ST ANDREW UNDERSHAFT,** the word undershaft referring to the maypole which was erected every May day on the corner of the church. The use of the maypole was for-

The monument in St Andrew Undershaft church of John Stow

Geoffrey Chaucer (1340-1400)

bidden after the May day riots of 1517. The church is now united with St Katharine Cree further up the street. There has been a church dedicated to St Andrew on this site since the 12th c. A Gothic church was built here in 1520-32, which has been restored several times. There is a fine font by Nicholas Stone installed in 1634, communion rails by Jean Tijou and interesting windows. There is a statue of **John Stow** on the historian's grave. Each year there is a memorial service for him at the Church and the Lord Mayor replaces the quill pen in Stow's hand with a new one, presenting the old one and a copy of John Stow's **Survey of London** to the child who has written the best essay on London that year.

John Stow (1525-1605) the son of a tailor gave up this trade to follow a career as an antiquarian and historian. He was the first historian to base his research on public records, and would spend the extremely large sum of £200 a year on books and manuscripts. His main publications are **The Workes of Geoffrey Chaucer** (1561), **Summarie of English Chronicles** (1565), **The Annales of England** (1580) the second edition of **Holinshed's Chronicles** (1585-7) on which Shakespeare got a lot of the materials for his plays, and **A Survey of London** (1598-1603). One cannot stress too strongly the importance of Stow's **Survey**, London's first history. Nearly any book written on London would be immeasurably the poorer without reference to Stow, who has preserved for us London's history and is the rock upon which our knowledge of London is based. He included in his **Survey** William Fitzstephen's 12th c account in Latin of the London of the day, the earliest picture we have of London as a complete entity.

Hans Holbein the painter lived in the parish and on his death in 1543 was either buried at St Andrew's or up the road at St Katharine Cree.

On the corner of Lime Street once stood East India House, where **Charles Lamb** worked as a clerk from 1792 until 1825 and the philosopher **John Stuart Mill** worked from 1823 to 1858. **Thomas Love Peacock** (1785-1866) also worked here from 1819 and succeeded to Mill's position of examiner in 1836. He published several volumes of verse, essays and prose satires, which survey the contemporary political and cultural scene from a Radical viewpoint. He was a friend of Shelley and his favourite daughter Mary Ellen married the novelist George Meredith and features in Meredith's sonnet sequence **Modern Love**. Already a widow Mary Ellen left Meredith six years after their marriage for the painter Henry Wallis, who painted Meredith as Chatterton the year before.

Peacock is best known for his satirical novels such as **Gryll Granage** (1861) and **Crotchet Castle** (1831) which normally take the form of a group of theorists assembled at a country house where they discuss the burning issues of the day, with a romantic love plot enlivening the proceedings. The format enabled Peacock to pronounce on any subject he wished:

> *"Ancient sculpture is the true school of modesty. But where the Greeks had modesty, we have cant; where they had poetry, we have cant; where they had patriotism, we have cant; where they had anything that exalts, delights, or adorns humanity, we have nothing but cant, cant, cant."*
> *(**Crotchet Castle. Ch. 7**)*

In the same work he pronounces for the edification of his fellow writers:

> *"A book that furnishes no quotations is, me judice, no book – it is a plaything." (Ch. 9)*

While you stand in Leadenhall Street your eyes can not possibly avoid being drawn to Richard Rogers' new **Lloyd's** building finished in 1986, which won its architect, who also had a hand in the Pompidou Centre in Paris, a prize. Lloyds is like a large grey gas station rising towards the heavens with its metal tubing and blue cranes, and its staircases and elevators outside as part of the design. It is a most impressive building, if not universally liked. It can and should be visited, there is a coffee house (Lloyd's originally began in a coffee house) open to the public and one can go up to the top and stare out from the viewing platform.

What is universally admired is London's finest surviving market just off Leadenhall Street on the right, the delightful Victorian enclave of **Leadenhall Market**.

There has been a market here since the 14th c, specializing in poultry. Its name came from the lead roof of Neville Hall which was acquired by the City Corporation as a market building in 1411. **Samuel Pepys** bought 'a leg of beef, a good one, for sixpence' here in 1663. The present building was erected by Horace Jones in 1881 (his other market building we saw earlier at Smithfield) and is a general market, but with poultry and fish very much in evidence. It is a joy to stroll or stop for a meal or a drink in the market, which is like stepping back into Victorian England.

Nathaniel Bentley, the notorious Dirty Dick (see the pub in Bishopsgate) kept a hardware shop at no 46, the first glazed hardware shop in England. In Dickens' **Dombey and Son**, the shop of the nautical instrument maker Solomon Gill was at no 157. The shop was advertised by the Little Wooden Midshipman, which is now in the Dickens Museum in Doughty Street. Nearby to the shop were the offices of Dombey and Son:

> *"Anywhere in the vicinity there might be seen . . . little timber midshipmen in obselete naval uniform, eternally employed outside the shop doors of nautical instrument-makers in taking observations of hackney coaches."* (Ch. IV)

Towards the end of the street on the left is **St Katharine Cree**, built in 1280 by the prior of Holy Trinity Aldgate for his parishioners so that they would not use the priory church and disturb his canons with their noise. It was rebuilt in 1504, and again in 1628-30 when it was consecrated by **Bishop Laud**. The popish manner of the services here was brought against him at his trial, and Laud who had become the Archbishop of Canterbury in 1633, and one of Charles I's triumvirate, was found guilty by the House of Lords of "endeavouring to subvert the laws, to overthrow the Protestant religion, and to act as an enemy to Parliament". The judges also maintained that this was not treason; but by an unconstitutional ordinance of attainder, he was beheaded on Tower Hill in 1645. The church survived virtually unscathed the Great Fire and World War II, and is well worth visiting to see the spectacular plaster ceiling decorated with the arms of seventeen City Livery Companies. At the east end there is a rose window symbolic of the toothed wheel upon which St Katharine was tortured for her faith in 307. The font is 17th c as is the Father Smith organ, although this has been remade several times. A good time to visit the church is on the 16th October so that one can listen to the annual **Lion Sermon**, which was endowed in the 17th c by the Lord Mayor, John Gayer, after surviving a face-to-face encounter with a lion. He also presented the font. The word cree is probably a corruption of Christ Church.

At the end of the street Leadenhall Street and Fenchurch Street meet and become **Aldgate High Street**, named after one of the six original Roman Gates in the City Wall. It was in Saxon the Ealdgate, meaning the old gate, hence its name. **Geoffrey Chaucer** rented the room above the gate between 1374 and 1385. His residency is commemorated by a plaque on the Post Office. Aldgate with the rest of the City gates was demolished in 1761. While Chaucer lived here he wrote **Troilus and Cryseyde**.

In front is the church of **ST BOTOLPH'S ALDGATE**, once the priory church of Holy Trinity, Aldgate. The first St Botolph's church on this site dates back to Saxon times. A new church was built in the 16th c, which at the Reformation became the property of the Crown, and a parish church. It was replaced in 1744 by the present church by George Dance. **Jeremy Bentham** was christened in this church in 1747. In the previous church **Daniel Defoe** married Mary Tuffley in 1683.

We turn to the right and take the Minories to the Tower.

THE TOWER OF LONDON

The last foreign prince to conquer England, William Duke of Normandy built the Tower. The White Tower was finished in 1087 and other monarchs added other buildings until Edward I's outer wall completed the development of the 18 acre site. The Tower was built to be a fortress and a palace although in its long history it has served many other functions including those of a treasury, the Royal Mint, the Royal Observatory, the Armouries, a zoo and a prison. It can be visited daily from 9.30 (and in the summer only on Sunday afternoons from 2 p.m.) for an admission price in 1988 of £4.50. The guards, the so-called Beefeaters do regular tours of the Tower precincts, and it is only on these tours that one can visit the chapel of St Peter Advincula. It is possible to write for tickets to the resident governor (no charge) to attend the **Ceremony of the Keys**, which takes place daily at 10 to 10 at night. The guards, usually led by the Chief Yeoman Warder, go round locking the towers one by one and at the Bloody Tower they are challenged.

"Halt, who goes there?
The Keys.
Whose Keys?
Queen Elizabeth's Keys."

At 10 the Tower is locked and to enter or leave the Tower one needs to know the password, which changes daily, the new password being telephoned from St James Palace.

Entering the Tower the most interesting building to visit is the original tower, made of Kentish ragstone with edging in Caen stone, called the White Tower. This contains the finest collection of armour in the world, and London's oldest church, the Norman barrel-vaulted **St John's Chapel**, which is no longer used for worship. It was here in March 1554 that Mary I and Philip of Spain were married by proxy. Behind the White Tower there is a traditional village green around which are houses, including the Queen's House. Officially a royal residence it is used by the resident governor. Next to the green there is the site of the six executions which have taken place inside the Tower precincts. Normally executions would have taken place outside the Tower on the nearby Tower Hill. By tradition the first person executed on this spot was Lord Hastings in 1483. In Shakespeare's **Richard III**, it is the noble Hastings who will not "bar my master's heirs in true descent" which was what the usurping Richard, Duke of Gloucester, wanted. Hastings meets his end in Act III:

> "*Re-enter Gloucester and Buckingham*
> *Glouc.*
> *I pray you all, tell me what they deserve*
> *That do conspire my death with devilish plots*
> *Of damned witchcraft, and that have prevail'd*
> *Upon my body with their hellish charms?*
>
> *Hast.*
> *The tender love I bear your grace, my lord,*
> *Makes me most forward in this princely presence*
> *To doom the offenders, whoso'er they be:*
> *I say, my lord, they have deserved death.*
>
> *Glouc.*
> *Then be your eyes the witness of their evil.*
> *Look how I am bewitch'd; behold mine arm*
> *Is, like a blasted sapling, wither'd up:*
> *And this is Edward's wife, that monstrous witch,*
> *Consorted with that harlot strumpet Shore,*
> *That by their witchcraft thus have marked me.*
>
> *Hast.*
> *If they have done this deed, my noble lord, –*
>
> *Glouc.*
> *If! thou protector of this damned strumpet,*
> *Talkst thou to me of 'ifs'? Thou art a traitor:*
> *Off with his head! now, by Saint Paul I swear,*
> *I will not dine until I see the same.*
> *Lovell and Ratcliffe, look it be done:*
> *The rest, that love me, rise and follow me.*
>
> (*Exeunt all but Hastings, Ratcliffe, and Lovel*)
>
> *Hast.*
> *Woe, woe for England! not a whit for me;*
> *For I, too fond, might have prevented this.*
> *Stanley did dream the boar did raze his helm;*

And I did scorn it, and disdain'd to fly.
Three times to-day my foot-cloth horse did stumble,
And started when he look'd upon the Tower,
As loth to bear me to the slaughter-house.
O! now I need the priest that spake to me:
I now repent I told the pursuivant,
As too triumphing, how mine enemies
To-day at Pomfret bloodily were butcher'd,
And I myself secure in grace and favour.
O Margaret, Margaret! now thy heavy curse
Is lighted on poor Hastings' wretched head.

Rat.
Come, come, dispatch; the duke would be at dinner:
Make a short shrift, he longs to see your head."

With Hastings' death Richard is free to usurp the throne, bastardize his nephews, and then have them killed in the Garden Tower, for ever after called the Bloody Tower.

On the spot where Hastings was killed, two wives of Henry VIII were executed, Anne Boleyn in 1536 and Catherine Howard in 1542, both charged with treason, that is, infidelity to their husband, the King. Margaret, Countess of Salisbury was executed here, as Henry VIII could not execute her son Cardinal Pole who was abroad, he executed instead the mother in 1541, for treason. The 68 year old countess did not submit willingly, and was almost hacked to pieces as she fled the executioner, screaming that she was no traitor. During the reign of Mary I, Lady Jane Grey, the young girl the Protestants tried to replace her with was executed here, and in the reign of her sister, Elizabeth I, the young Earl of Essex, who led a rebellion against the ageing Queen, was beheaded in 1601.

All the victims were buried in the nearby chapel of St Peter Advincula, which was built in the 14th c. Across from it is the Jewel House, where the State Regalia and the rest of the Crown Jewels are on display when the Tower is open to the public, with the exception of February when they are cleaned by Garrard & Company, of Regent Street, the Crown Jewellers. The Crown Jewels have been kept in the Tower since 1303, ever since some of the jewels disappeared from Westminster Abbey. There has only been one attempt to steal them from the Tower and that was by

Colonel Blood during the reign of Charles II. The Irish adventurer's attempt failed in 1671, but Charles II who visited him in prison pardoned him and gave him a pension. Blood, Charles II, the Duke of Buckingham, Titus Oates and the dwarf Sir Geoffrey Hudson are all characters in Sir Walter Scott's novel, **Peveril of the Peak** (1823) where a lot of action takes place at the Tower. It is the only novel by Sir Walter Scott to be set primarily in London.

Just past the entrance to the Crown Jewels is the Bowyer Tower which has an exhibition of instruments of torture, although the sight of the 4ft square cell in the basement of the White Tower where Guy Fawkes was imprisoned in 1605 is far more horrific.

At the other end of the green is the **Bloody Tower** where the little princes were murdered in 1483. It is now done out as it would have appeared in the days when Sir Walter Ralegh was imprisoned here. **Ralegh** (1554-1618) the Elizabethan explorer and courtier was imprisoned briefly in the Tower in 1592 for his dalliance and then marriage with one of Queen Elizabeth I's maids of honour, Elizabeth Throckmorton. He enjoyed great favour during the Queen's reign, especially the grant of a large estate in Ireland. At her death he was arrested by the new King, James I, for treason, and spent the next 13 years in the Tower on the most flimsy of pretexts. He had been convicted on charges of treason, despite the lack of evidence, and was liable to execution whenever it suited the King. His wife and his children shared his quarters in the Bloody Tower. To pass the time he wrote **The History of the World** (1614) the work was never finished as James I disapproved of his prisoner passing his time in such a way. Ralegh also taught James I's eldest son, Prince Henry, chemistry and natural sciences. In the Bloody Tower they have a copy of Ralegh's history on display, which contains the famous passage:

> *"O eloquent, just and mightie Death! whom none could advise, thou hast perswaded; what none hath dared, thou has done; and whom all the world hath flattered, thou only hast cast out of the world and despised; who hast drawne together all the farre stretched greatnesse, all the pride, crueltie, and*

ambition of man, and covered it all over with those two narrow words, Hic iacet."

Ralegh was let out of the Tower to lead the ill-fated expedition in search of gold to Guiana in 1616. On his return he was executed on the old charge of treason in Palace Yard, Westminster in 1618. He is buried in St Margaret's Westminster.

Next to Ralegh's book is a copy of James I's book, **A Counterblast to Tobacco** (1604), in which he said of the plant which Ralegh introduced with the potato into England that it was "A branch of the sin of drunkenness, which is the root of all sins". Furthermore it was:

> *"A custom loathsome to the eye, hateful to the nose, harmful to the brain, dangerous to the lungs, and in the black, stinking fume thereof, nearest resembling the horrible Stygian smoke of the pit that is bottomless.*
>
> *Herein is not only a great vanity, but a great contempt of God's good gifts, that the sweetness of man's breath, being a good gift of God, should be wilfully corrupted by this stinking smoke."*

In the Bell Tower **Sir Thomas More**, and the Bishop of Rochester, John Fisher, were imprisoned by Henry VIII for refusing to take the Oath of Supremacy and were both executed on Tower Hill in 1535. Fisher was so weak that he had to be carried to the scaffold. Two weeks later More was executed. When he was told that the traitor's punishment of being drawn and quartered was commuted to merely being beheaded he said wryly, "God forbid the King shall use any more such mercy on any of my friends". He asked for assistance to mount the scaffold, "I pray you, Mr Lieutenant to see me safe up and for my coming down let me make shift for myself". As he prepared to meet his end, he carefully moved his beard from the block, saying, "Pity that should be cut that has not committed treason". Very few people indeed can have a kind word to spare for their executioner as they await their death, but More is reputed to have said:

> *"Pluck up thy spirits, man, and be not afraid to do thine office; my neck is very short; take heed therefore thou strike not awry, for saving of thine honesty."*

More's head was put on display on London Bridge, as was the custom with the severed heads of traitors, from where his daughter obtained it by bribing a boatman. She had it interred in the Roper vault in St Dunstan's Canterbury.

Queen Elizabeth I was also imprisoned in the Bell Tower during the reign of her sister Mary I. On her return to the Tower, to spend the traditional night before her coronation, she kissed the ground in front of the Bell Tower and never returned to the Tower again.

The deposed king, Henry VI was murdered while at his prayers in the Wakefield Tower by the orders of Edward IV. In Shakespeare's **Henry VI** it is the Duke of Gloucester who does the murder, during a face to face confrontation:

> *Glouc.*
> *Think'st thou I am an executioner?*
>
> *K. Henry*
> *A persecutor, I am sure, thou art:*
> *If murdering innocents be executing,*
> *Why, then thou art an executioner.*
>
> *Glouc.*
> *Thy son I kill'd for his presumption.*
>
> *K. Henry*
> *Hadst thou been kill'd when first thou didst presume,*
> *Thou hadst not lived to kill a son of mine.*
> *And thus I prophesy: that many a thousand,*
> *Which now mistrusts no parcel of my fear,*
> *And many an old man's sigh, and many a widow's,*
> *And many an orphan's water-standing eye,*
> *Men for their sons', wives for their husbands'*
> *And orphans for their parents' timeless death,*
> *Shall rue the hour that ever thou wast born.*
> *The owl shriek'd at thy birth, an evil sign;*
> *That night-crow cried, aboding luckless time;*
> *Dogs howl'd, and hideous tempest shook down trees;*
> *The raven rook'd her on the chimney's top,*
> *And chattering pies in dismal discords sung.*
> *Thy mother felt more than a mother's pain,*
> *And yet brought forth less than a mother's hope;*
> *To wit an undigest deformed lump,*
> *Not like the fruits of such a goodly tree.*

Teeth hadst thou in thy head when thou wast born,
To signify thou camest to bite the world:
And, if the rest be true which I have heard,
Thou camest –

Glouc.
I'll hear no more: die, prophet, in thy speech: (Stabs him).
For this, amongst the rest, was I ordain'd.

Samuel Pepys in his **Diary** tells of visiting his friend Sir William Coventry while he was a prisoner in the Tower in 1669. During the visit of 9 March Pepys confided in Coventry that he was keeping a diary "and I am sorry almost that I told it him — it not being necessary, nor may be convenient to have it known". Later Pepys himself was one of the many to end up in the Tower where he spent six weeks during the hysteria of the Popish Plot, and the fears of a Catholic coup d'etat. Arrested in 1679, accused by Titus Oates of giving naval secrets to the French, he was later released on bail, and in 1681 he cleared his name.

There can be few places within the British Isles where so much of the nation's history has taken place than the Tower of London and it is surprising that it has featured so rarely in our literature. The only novelist to tackle The Tower and its history as the subject for a major novel was **Harrison Ainsworth** in 1840, a book with its marvellous Cruikshank illustrations which is happily back in print.

We leave the Tower and proceed to Tower Hill, where next to the memorial for the dead of the merchant navy in the World Wars, there is a plaque in the little garden marking the spot where the scaffold stood. It is here that the traitors from the Tower were executed in public, with the exception of the six granted the privilege of losing their heads within the Tower precincts. The last execution here was of Lord Lovatt in 1747. Lovatt had the consolation of seeing some of the audience die before him, when a scaffolding collapsed killing some of the too numerous spectators. The last prisoner kept in the Tower was Rudolph Hesse in May 1941. He was kept in the Yeoman Goaler's House, the second doorway at the beginning of the green, the house where Lady Jane Grey was imprisoned in the 16th c. Just past the Tower on the left we come to the church of **All Hallows by the Tower**, one of the few City churches to escape the Great Fire, which stopped a short distance in front of it. During the Great Fire **Pepys** climbed to the top of the church tower to watch the fire's progress, having taken the precaution first of sending his wife and his gold to Woolwich by boat. He records on the 5 of September 1666:

> *"Home, and whereas I expected to have seen our house on fire, it being now about 7 a-clock, it was not. But to the fire, and there find greater hopes than I expected; for my confidence of finding our office on fire was such, that I durst not ask anybody how it was with us, till I came and saw it not burned. But going to the fire, I find, by the blowing up of houses and the great help given by the workmen out of the King's yards sent by Sir W. Penn, there is a good stop given to it, as well as Marke Lane end as ours – it having only burned the dyall of Barkeing Church (All Hallows by the Tower), and part of the porch, and was there quenched. I up to the top of Barkeing steeple, and there saw the saddest sight of desolation that I ever saw. Everywhere great fires. Oyle cellars and brimstone and other things burning. I became afeared to stay there long; and therefore down again as fast as I could, the fire being spread as far as I could see it, and to Sir W. Penn's and there eat a piece of cold meat, having eaten nothing since Sunday but the remains of Sunday's dinner."*

Pepys lived across from the church in **Seething Lane** where he was given a house when he was appointed Clerk of the Acts of the Navy in 1660. The Navy Office was also here and where it stood there is now a small garden commemorating Pepys with a bust of the diarist. Nearby is St Olave's, Hart Street, where Pepys worshipped and where both he and his wife were buried.

ALL HALLOWS BY THE TOWER was founded by Ethelburga, Abbess of Barking in the 7th c, and is often called All Hallows Barking. Traces of the various churches on this site remain from Saxon through Norman to Gothic. The church was rebuilt in 1643-5 with a new spire added during the Commonwealth in 1658-9. The church was bombed in the war and restored in 1949-58. It has strong American connections, with William Penn being christened here in 1644 and John Quincy Adams, sixth President of the United States, marrying here in 1797. The notorious hanging judge and James II's Lord Chancellor, **Judge Jeffreys** was married here in 1667. The judge after the deposition of James II was arrested and sent to the Tower where he died of delirium tremens. Bishop Fisher was buried here in 1535, the poet **Henry Howard, Earl of Surrey** in 1547, and Archbishop Laud in 1645, all three men executed on Tower Hill and all later reburied elsewhere.

We pass the church and descend down **Lower Thames Street.** We pass the Custom House to where a new blue office block now stands on what was the site of Billingsgate Fish Market until it closed on 16th January 1982, replaced by a new building on the Isle of Dogs. The fish market dates back to the 11th c and it got fine new buildings by Horace Jones in 1877. These grade II listed buildings were pulled down to make way for the office block. In 1931 **George Orwell** down and out in London, earned a few shillings by helping the porters at the market, an experience he shared with the hero of his novel **Keep the Aspidistra Flying**, Gordon Comstock:

> *"Three mornings, on the advice of another man he met on the Embankment, he spent in Billingsgate, helping to shove fish-barrows up the twisty little hills from Billingsgate to Eastcheap. After three days of it Gordon gave up."*

Proceeding up the left hand side of the road we come to the church of **St Magnus the Martyr**. The church dates back to the 11th c. In 1563-5 **Miles Coverdale** (1488-1568) was the parish vicar. He translated while in Antwerp the **Bible and Apocrypha** from German and Latin versions with the aid of Tyndale's **New Testament** (1525). His translation appeared in Germany in 1535. It is the first complete translation of the Bible into English and a lot of its sonorous language found its way into the **Authorized Version** of 1611. Coverdale was buried in the church, which was destroyed in the Great Fire and rebuilt by Wren in 1671-6. The church is mentioned in Eliot's poem **The Waste Land** (1922) which describes the interior as "inexplicable splendour of Ionian white and gold". **The Waste Land** is the poem of a City man, Eliot being employed by Lloyds Bank at no 17 Cornhill from March 1917 until he left in 1925 to become Faber's Poetry Director. It voices all the frustrations of the young poet in its jazz rhythms with his urban and suburban life. The poem struck a chord with the young and achieved a kind of cult status. In Evelyn Waugh's **Brideshead Revisited**, Anthony Blanche reads it from the window of his college rooms. The poem is crammed with references to the City and the life of the army of commuters:

> *"Unreal City,*
> *Under the brown fog of a winter dawn,*
> *A crowd flowed over London Bridge, so many,*
> *I had not thought death had undone so many."*

We pass under London Bridge past the Guildhall of the Fishmongers and continue up to the entrance of **Southwark Bridge** where the road changes its name to Upper Thames Street. When Dickens as a small boy, working at Warren's Blacking Factory, was taken ill and Bob Fagin was detailed to take him home, Dickens had recourse to an elaborate subterfuge to conceal from him that his family's home was the Marshalsea Prison, where his father was in prison for debt:

> *"I was too proud to let him know about the prison; after making several efforts to get rid of him, to all of which Bob Fagin in his goodness was deaf, shook hands with him on the steps of a house near Southwark Bridge, on the Surrey side, making believe that I lived there. As a finishing piece of reality, in case of him looking back, I knocked at the door, I recollect, and asked when the woman opened it if that was Mr Robert Fagin's house?"* (Autobiographical fragment)

This bridge, built by Sir John Rennie in 1815-19, was replaced by the present one in 1912-21.

UPPER THAMES STREET is where **Geoffrey Chaucer** was born in c 1340. His father was a wine merchant, a vinter and this was the area of the wine trade in the Middle Ages. The street would have been full of warehouses and wharves for the unloading and storage of wine from Bordeaux. The Guildhall of the Vintners is at no $68^1/_2$. **Geoffrey Chaucer** (1340-1400) spent his life as a royal civil servant, taking part in the 100 Year War as a young man and later travelling abroad on diplomatic missions. His various appointments include being Clerk of the Works of Westminster Abbey, and it was for this reason that he was buried in the Abbey on his death. His marriage to the sister of Katharine Swynford, John of

Gaunt's mistress and later third wife, helped him find royal patronage and for most of his life he received Gaunt's patronage. From translations from old French and Latin into English he produced in his latter years his masterpieces **Troilus and Criseyde** (1385) and **The Canterbury Tales**, giving the English Language its first great works of art.

Passing the Vintner's Hall we can stop off further down the street at the Samuel Pepys pub which overlooks the river and enjoy views of the Thames. Nearby is Stew Alley where the prostitutes would take the boat across to Southwark with their clients to the brothels, which were called stews. Suitably refreshed we cross over to the other side of Upper Thames Street and retrace our steps, admiring the Wren churches. Just before the Underpass is the tower of **St Mary Somerset**, the rest of the church was demolished by an Act of Parliament in 1872 to widen the road. The magnificent tower of the Wren church of 1686-95, looks just like a chess set in stone sitting on its square base. Further up the street is **St James Garlickhythe** by Wren and a short distance away **St Michael Paternoster Royale**, rebuilt by Wren after the Great Fire in 1689-94. There was a church on this site by the beginning of the 13th c. In 1409 **Richard Whittington** (1358-1423), four times Lord Mayor of London, paid for the church to be rebuilt, and was buried in the church in 1423. We return to Lower Thames Street and turn left and proceed up Monument Street to view, and for the energetic to visit, the Monument to the Great Fire of London.

THE GREAT FIRE

It started on the night of 2 September 1666 in a baker's house in Pudding Lane. The baker and his family escaped over the roof tops to safety, only the maid who was too timid to follow failed to escape, becoming the first of the Fire's nine victims. The strong wind spread the fire quickly. The Lord Mayor was alerted but on viewing the fire he commented, "A woman might piss it out" and went back to his bed. It was **Samuel Pepys** who was sent later that day to see the Lord Mayor, Sir Thomas Bloodworth, with the King's command to destroy the houses in the fire's path to prevent its growth. He found him "in Canninge Street like a man spent, with a hankercher about his neck. To the King's message, he cried like a fainting woman, 'Lord, what can I do? I am spent! People will not obey me. I have been pulling down houses, but the fire overtakes us faster that we can do it' ". By the end of 4 September the worst was over, and the fire-fighters led by the Duke of York (later James II) had subdued the fire. Within the City Walls almost 400 acres had been burned, and 63 acres outside them; 87 churchs, 44 guildhalls, 13,200 houses had been destroyed, but amazingly only 9 people killed. Plans were submitted for the rebuilding of the City. The more imaginative and creative ones by Wren and Evelyn were rejected and the City was rebuilt very much as it had been before, but of stone. It was laid down that private houses must be "two storeys for bylanes, three storeys along the river and for street and lanes of note, four storeys for high streets and mansion houses for citizens of extraordinary quality".

   Sir Christopher Wren was given the task of rebuilding the City churches. The 87 destroyed churches were replaced by 51 new churches all designed by Wren, an Oxford professor of Astronomy, whom Evelyn had called a genius of a youth. It was Wren who designed the **MONUMENT** to the Great Fire, which is a column 320 feet high which would, if laid on its side to the left, stretch all the way to the baker's oven where the fire started. If you pay 50p you can walk to the top, it has 311 steps and no elevator. In his historical novel **Barnaby Rudge** Charles Dickens puts the following advice in Mr Willet's words to his son Joe:

> *"sixpence is to spend in the diversions of London; and the diversion I recommend is going to the top of the Monument, and sitting there. There's no temptation there, sir – no drink – no young women – no bad characters of any sort – nothing but imagination. That's the way I enjoyed myself when I was your age, sir."*

Joe unfortunately did not follow his father's advice and runs away from home instead, enlising as a soldier.

Leaving the Monument behind us it is a short walk to the end of the street where we turn left and onto the approach of London Bridge.

LONDON BRIDGE

The Romans founded their city of Londinium near where they first forded the Thames and where they created London's first bridge, which was probably built of wood sometime after 100 AD. London's bridge was burnt down by the City's allies, the Norwegians, to save London from the invading Danes in 1014. We commemorate this Norwegian help by two Norwegian churches either end of London Bridge, St Olave and St Magnus, and the children's song, London Bridge is Falling Down. The nursery rhyme, as it became in the 17th c, does not recount so clearly the epic victory over the Danes which earlier versions did:

> "London Bridge is broken down
> Gold is won and bright renown.
> Shields resounding
> War horns sounding
> Hildur shouting in the din
> Arrows singing
> Mailcoats ringing
> Odin makes our Olaf win". (Otter Svarte)

The first stone bridge was begun in 1176 by Peter of Colechurch. It had houses on both sides and a chapel dedicated to Saint Thomas Becket. The custom of putting traitor's heads on display on the bridge goes back to 1305 when the Scottish leader Sir William Wallace, executed at Smithfield, had his head parboiled, then dipped in tar to preserve it, before being put above the gatehouse of the bridge.

Thomas More's head was rescued from London Bridge by his daughter Margaret in 1535. At any one time there would be thirty heads on display on the bridge. Peter of Colechurch's bridge was one of the sites of London along with the splendour of Old St Paul's Cathedral until it was replaced by a new bridge by Rennie in 1823-31. For nearly all of its existence London Bridge was London's only bridge until Westminster Bridge was built in 1750. Today central London has seventeen bridges and the City four. Rennie's bridge, replaced by a new bridge in 1967-72, was sold to an American corporation as a tourist attraction and was re-erected over an artificial lake at Lake Havasu City, Arizona. It is often said that the Americans paid £1 million pounds for the bridge, believing they were buying Tower Bridge, which is often referred to in America as London Bridge.

Walking onto the bridge and looking to the left one has a superb view of Tower Bridge built in 1894 in a Gothic style to blend in with the Tower of London. In front of Tower Bridge there is the large grey cruiser the Belfast, a floating naval museum.

As we come over the bridge we see the symbol of the City, the dragon on either side, as we leave the City and proceed to Southwark. The first street we pass on the left is **Tooley Street** which was until recently a street of Victorian warehouses and heavy traffic on the banks of the Thames. It was here in 1931 that **George Orwell** stayed in Lew Levy's kip on his way back from hop picking in Kent. His eighteen days of hop picking in September earned Orwell twenty-six shillings. This area is still patronised by tramps, who are very much in evidence with their bottles of cider and cans of beer but it is also part of the changing face of the Docklands with the new London Bridge City. Smart shops, offices, wine bars, restaurants and studios are the modern face of the road with a very pleasant walkway along the whole length of the Thames in front of the complex. The far end of the street has a redbrick school where a blue plaque commemorates St Olave's Grammar School where John Harvard, founder of Harvard University in America went to school. His father was one of the school governors. A street which leads off Tooley Street is **Dean Street** where **John Keats** had lodgings at no 8 when he was a student at Guys Hospital. The little that is left of Dean Street is now called Stainer Street and is under the railway arch at the beginning of Tooley Street. In October 1816 John Keats walked to Clerkenwell to see his friend Charles Cowden Clarke, and it was at his lodgings that Keats saw for the first time his folio edition of Chapman's translation of Homer. After a night spent reading and discussing Homer, Keats walked back to Dean Street where he immediately wrote his sonnet:

> *"Much have I travell'd in the realms of gold*
> *And many goodly states and kingdoms seen"*

We enter into **BOROUGH HIGH STREET** and embark upon our visit to historic Southwark.

SOUTHWARK

A Roman settlement on the southern side of the wooden bridge built to span the Thames at Londinium it developed as a market town outside of the City. Most of Southwark was owned by religious houses, and contained the town houses of the Bishops of Winchester and Rochester amongst others. During the Middle Ages it was famous for its prelate houses, its taverns, brothels, prisons and breweries. By the end of the 16th c it had become London's theatre land, with the Globe, the Rose, the Swan and the Hope amongst others, and also possessed the largest bear-baiting pit in London and its surrounding villages. Contrary to what one would imagine today the prelates went well with the lowlife entertainment. It was because so much of Southwark was owned by the church that the officers of the law had no jurisdiction, and thieves, prostitutes and debtors could reside here in safety. It was on the land of the Bishops of Winchester, called Bankside, where most of the brothels stood, which were regulated by the ordinances of the Bishops. As the prostitutes contributed to the coffers of the Bishops of Winchester they acquired the nickname of Winchester Geese. The brothels, or stews as they were called, were closed down by Henry VIII but were soon re-opened and kept company with the newly founded theatres and the bear-baiting pit.

Southwark was the route out of London to the south, to Kent and the Continent and the coaching inns stood side by side along Borough High Street until the 19th c and the loss of their paying customers to the railway. As the London Bridge of Peter of Colechurch was narrow and difficult for coaches to pass, and London's one and only bridge's gate was locked at 9 p.m. the coaching terminals were all in Southwark for destinations to the South. The playwright **Thomas Dekker** described Borough High Street as "a continued ale house with not a shop to be seen between". The most famous were the George, the Bear, the Queen's Head, the White Hart and the Inn immortalised by Chaucer, the Tabard. It is from the

Tabard that Chaucer's pilgrims began their journey to Canterbury in **The Canterbury Tales:**

> *"In Southwerk at the Tabard as I lay*
> *Ready to wende on my pilgrimage*
> *To Caunterbury with ful devout corage*
> *At night was come in-to that hostelrye*
> *Well nyne and twenty in companye,*
> *Of sondry folk, by aventure y-falle*
> *In felawshipe, and pilgrims were they alle,*
> *That toward Canterbury Wolden ryde;*
> *The chambres and the stables weren wyde,*
> *And well we weren esed atte beste."*

The Inn was demolished in 1873 and the Talbot Yard is now on the site. Nearby stood the White Hart Inn which was in existence in the 15th c. It is mentioned in the letters of a well-to-do Norfolk family the Pastons. Three volumes of family correspondence dealing with three generations of the family and the turbulence of the reigns of Henry VI, Edward IV and Richard III were published. **The Paston Letters** begin in 1420 and end in 1504 and present an invaluable picture of the England of the times, its violent anarchy and how the well-to-do fared in these conditions. The Inn is also mentioned in Shakespeare's **Henry VI, Pt.2** where it becomes the headquarters of Jack Cade and his rebels. Buckingham and Clifford come here to woo the rebels from their leader's cause, making Jack Cade protest:

> *"Hath my sword therefore broke through London gates, that you should leave me at the White Hart in Southwark?"*

It is also where we meet Sam Weller for the first time in **Pickwick Papers**, cleaning boots. Dickens takes the opportunity to regret the passing of the coaching inns as he sings the praises of The White Hart:

> *"There still remain some half dozen old inns, which have preserved their external features unchanged, and which have escaped alike the rage for public improvement, and the encroachment of private speculation. Great, rambling, queer, old places they are, with galleries and passages, and staircases, wide enough and antiquated enough to furnish material for a hundred ghost stories."*

The same half dozen coaching inns left in Southwark in Dickens' day have now become one, The George which we shall see on the left hand side as we proceed down the High Street. All that remains of the White Hart is its name in White Hart Yard.

A great event which used to take place in Borough High Street and its adjacent courtyards and alleys was Southwark Fair which vied with the Fairs at Smithfield and Stourbridge (Cambridgeshire) as the most important in England. The right to hold a fair was given by charter in 1402 by Edward IV and from lasting three days it grew to two weeks. This September Fair of Our Lady, as it was called, attracted both **Evelyn** and **Pepys**. In his **Diary** Pepys records his visit in 1668:

> *"To Southwark Fair, very dirty, and there saw the puppet show of Whittington which was pretty to see; and how the idle things do work upon people that see it, and even myself, too! And thence to Jacob Hall's dancing on the ropes, where I saw such action as I never saw before and mightily worth seeing."*

Many people will know Hogarth's celebrated picture of Southwark Fair, with its booth proprietors and performers. In Lee and Harper's acting booth the City poet, Elkanah Settle's **Siege of Troy** was being performed. The picture captures the vivacity and the vulgarity of the Fair which was suppressed in 1763 by the City of London Corporation who controlled it, because of the rowdiness and danger to public order caused by the pickpockets, the prostitutes and the drunks.

Proceeding down Borough High Street on the left we pass **ST THOMAS' STREET**, which leads to Guy's Hospital, founded in 1721 by the bookseller and publisher Thomas Guy. **Keats** was a student at the hospital from 1814 to 1816. The Street is named after St Thomas's Hospital which was in the street until 1865 when it moved to Lambeth Palace Road. Its buildings were demolished to make way for an extension to the nearby railway station with the exception of a fine early 18th c chapel which now serves as the Chapter House of Southwark Cathedral. In the tower of the chapel was the operating theatre of the hospital where operations on women were performed. It has now been restored to its original form and is well worth visiting. St Thomas's Hospital was founded in the 12th c as part of the priory of St Mary Overie and was dedicated to

St Thomas Becket. At the Dissolution of the Monasteries the hospital was closed but later re-opened in 1551 dedicated to St Thomas the Apostle (Thomas Becket was decanonised by Henry VIII for having opposed the authority of the King, Henry II). Thomas Guy the bookseller and publisher was also a benefactor of St Thomas's, and Florence Nightingale founded her revolutionary Nightingale Training School of Nursing at the hospital.

Passing the yards of the once numerous coaching Inns we arrive at London's only coaching inn, the truly splendid **George**. The inn was probably founded during the Middle Ages but the first reference to it that we have is 1542. That building, like most of Southwark, was destroyed in the Great Southwark Fire of 1676, ten years after the Great Fire in the City which failed to reach Southwark. The wooden galleried structure now standing is only a third of the 1676 building, with two wings having to be demolished to make way for the railway in 1899. Dickens mentions The George in **Little Dorrit** (1855-57).

A little further on we pass Mermaid Court the site of the **MARSHALSEA PRISON** commemorated by a plaque in the High Street. The prison was founded during the Middle Ages before the end of the 14th c. Wat Tyler and his rebels attacked it during the Peasants Revolt of 1381. By the end of the 16th c it had become London's most important prison after the Tower. Its inmates were mainly debtors or men who had incurred the authorities displeasure by their actions, so many writers have been imprisoned at the Marshalsea. In 1605 the comedy **Eastward Hoe** led to its three authors, **Ben Jonson, George Chapman** and **John Marston** being imprisoned here. The play contained derogatory comments about people from Scotland, not a very politic thing to do with a Scottish King of England James I (1603). Influence at court got the playwrights released. **Christopher Brooke**, the poet who had met John Donne when they had shared chambers at Lincoln's Inn as young law students was imprisoned here in 1601 for having witnessed the secret marriage of the 17 year old Anne More with John Donne, which was illegal as Anne was under age.

In 1614 **George Wither** was fined and imprisoned for his seditious **Abuses Stript and Whipt** (1613), and wrote in the Marshalsea his pastoral collection **Shepherd's Hunting** and his sonnet, **Shall I, wasting in despair/ Die because a woman's fair**". Wither was again imprisoned here in 1621 when his **Motto** was published. His self-eulogy aroused the suspicion of the authorities that they were being satirised so Wither was sent to the Marshalsea.

In 1738 an anonymous pamphlet was published called **Hell in Epitome**, which described the Marshalsea as:

> "*An old pile most dreadful to the view,*
> *Dismal as wormwood or repenting rue.*"

The buildings were in such a poor state of repair that a new building was erected on the former site of the King's Bench Prison a little further down the High Street in 1811. It was here that Charles Dickens' father, John Dickens, was imprisoned for debt in 1824. Charles Dickens while his parents were in the Marshalsea had lodgings with Mrs Roylance in Bayham Street, Camden Town and would come and see his parents on Sunday with his sister Fanny. As the 12 year old Dickens was unhappy at being away from his family, lodgings were found for him near the Marshalsea in Lant Street. It was the death of John Dickens' mother (who had been in service at Lord Blandford's house as a maid and later as the Marquis of Crewe's housekeeper) in 1824 which freed her profligate son from prison. The £450 he inherited was sufficent to get John Dickens out of prison but not quite enough to totally discharge his debts.

Dickens used his father's experiences in the Marshalsea for **David Copperfield** (1845-50) and sets **Little Dorrit** in and around the prison. In his **Preface** to the novel Dickens wrote:

> "*Whoever goes into Marshalsea Place turning out of Angel Court (now Angel Place) leading to Bermondsey will find his feet on the very stones of the extinct Marshalsea Jail.*"

Little Dorrit was born in the Marshalsea where her father, William Dorrit, served sufficient time to earn the accolade "The Father of the Marshalsea". The prison is described in Chapter 6 as:

> "*an oblong pile of barrack buildings, partitioned into squalid houses standing back to back, so that there were no back rooms; environed by a narrow paved yard, hemmed in by high walls duly spiked at the top.*"

The Marshalsea Prison was closed in 1842.

The King's Bench Prison was on the site of the Marshalsea until 1758. It too was mainly a debtor's prison. In 1613-19 Thomas Dekker, the playwright was confined here for debt. **Dekker** (1570-1632) was imprisoned on several occasions for debt and was always poor. He was employed by Henslowe from 1598 to write plays, many of which are now lost, and collaborated with Jonson, Marston, Webster and Ford and other playwrights. His work gives a vivid and realistic picture of the domestic and commercial life of London at the beginning of the 17th c, and shows great sympathy for the poor and oppressed, and a remarkably cheerful disposition. His description of a London plague in 1603, **The Wonderfull Yeare**, is used by Daniel Defoe for his **Journal of the Plague Year**. **Dekker his Dreame** (1620) recounts his experiences in prison.

Richard Baxter (1615-91) imprisoned and fined by Judge Jeffreys in 1675 for his **Paraphrase of the New Testament** which was deemed to have libelled the Church, was joined by his wife in the King's Bench Prison and said that they "kept house contentedly as at home, though in a narrower room". He was a Puritan divine whose book **The Saint's Everlasting Rest** (1650) was favoured by Mrs Glegg in **The Mill on the Floss** at times of crisis.

In 1759 **Tobias Smollet** (1721-71) was tried for defaming the character of Admiral Sir Charles Knowles in his piece for the Critical Review, and was fined £100 and given 3 months imprisonment. By that time the King's Bench Prison was in a new building further down Borough High Street (close to where it meets Newington Causeway). Smollet's picaresque novels, **The Adventures of Roderick Random** (1748), **The Adventures of Peregrine Pickle** (1751) and **The Expedition of Humphrey Clinker** (1771) are still widely read today, especially Humphrey Clinker. A Scottish surgeon he also wrote many articles, reviews and completed several histories and travel books. His epistolary **Travels through France and England** (1766) caused Sterne to nickname him Smelfungus in his **A Sentimental Journey** (1768). Smollet's translation of **Don Quixote** appeared in 1755. He was the editor of various journals including the Critical Review and the Tory periodical, The Briton, which lost its battle with Wilkes' The North Briton. Another magazine Smollet founded was the monthly British Magazine, which published his short novel, **The Life and Adventure of Sir Launcelot Greaves** (1762) a lot of which was written while Smollet was in the King's Bench Prison. He described it as "an agreeable medley of mirth and madness" and contains the famous lines, "I think for my part one half of the nation is mad — and the other half not very sound".

It was Smollet in a letter to Wilkes who said of Samuel Johnson, "The great cham of literature".

John Wilkes (1727-97) the politician and journalist was imprisoned in the King's Bench Prison in 1768 and fined £1,000 for his **Essay on Woman** which was found to be libellous. The St George's Field Massacre occurred in 1770 when a mob assembled in the nearby fields with the intention of escorting Wilkes to the House of Commons. Wilkes was a popular hero, expelled from Parliament because of his libel. He was returned by the electors of Middlesex but declared ineligible to take up his seat by the House of Commons, until in 1774 he was re-elected by Middlesex and this time allowed to take his seat. His status as a folk hero, the darling of the mob disappeared after 1780 when he helped the militia fight the Gordon Rioters. It was Wilkes' arrest under a general warrant for libel in 1762 which led to the ruling that it was unlawful to arrest anyone on a general warrant, and that all warrants must contain the name and the crime of the person being arrested. An important civil liberty. Wilkes was a political adversary of the very Tory Samuel Johnson and Boswell tells in his **Life of Johnson** how he engineered a friendly dinner for these colossuses of the 18th c. Burke's treatise **Present Discontents** (1770) is a discussion on Wilkes' exclusion from Parliament, and argues in favour of the people's right to elect their representative, and making it clear that a cabal led Parliament has no right to reject the people's choice.

Christopher Smart (1722-71) a poet who spent several years incarcerated in a hospital for the insane in Bethnal Green was imprisoned here for debt from 1769 until his death. Smart's illness expressed itself in a compulsion to public prayer, leading his friend Dr Johnson to comment: "I'd as lief pray with Kit Smart as anyone else". Smart's reputation as an original and highly creative poet has been established in the last 50 years, based very heavily on his unfinished work, **Jubilato Agno**, which was largely written while he was incarcerated in Bethnal Green. It contains the charming lines on his cat:

> *"For I will consider my Cat Jeoffrey,*
> *For he is the servant of the Living God, duly and daily serving Him.*
>
> *For he counteracts the powers of darkness by his electrical skin and glaring eyes,*
> *For he counteracts the Devil, who is death, by brisking about Life."*

The novelist and poet **Charlotte Smith** (1748-1806) spent some months with her family in the prison when her husband was a debtor in 1784. She is best remembered for her novel **The Old Manor House** (1793) which Sir Walter Scott admired greatly. The satirist **William Combe** (1741-1823) had several spells of imprisonment here for debt. Eton educated Combe is best known today for his verses written to accompany Rowlandson's colour plates and drawings about the comic adventures of **Dr Syntax**.

The painter and writer, **Robert Haydon** (1786-1846) was imprisoned here for debt four times between 1822 and 1837. At first his large paintings on biblical and classical themes were enormously successful but because of his quarrelsome disposition he alienated all of his patrons and got himself into debt, committing suicide in 1846. It was Haydon's vigorous advocacy which helped to secure the Elgin Marbles for the British Museum. His views on state patronage of the arts, industrial design and art education were published as **Lectures on Painting and Design**

(1846) and proved to be very influential. It was his posthumously published **Autobiography** (1853) that has kept his name alive and from which we draw much of the information we possess of the major literary figures of his day: Keats, Wordsworth, Hazlitt, Leigh Hunt, Mitford and Elizabeth Barrett. It was at Haydon's house in Great Marlborough Street that John Keats was entertained and so entranced by the company that he composed the sonnet on the way home, "Great spirits now on earth are sojourning".

When imprisonment for debt was abolished in the middle of the 19th c it was used for some years as a military prison before being demolished in 1880.

Another prison was built nearby in 1791-9. **Horsemonger Lane Goal**, a so-called model prison, was used for public executions. Dickens watched the execution of Mr and Mrs Manning here in November 1849 which prompted his letter to The Times:

> *"I do not believe that any community can prosper where such a scene of horror as was enacted this morning outside Horsemonger Lane Gaol is permitted. The horrors of the gibbet and of the crime which brought the wretched murderers to it faded in my mind before the atrocious bearing, looks and language of the assembled spectators."*

Leigh Hunt (1784-1859) and his brother John were both sentenced to two years imprisonment and fined £500 in 1813 for libelling the Prince Regent as 'a fat Adonis of forty'. Leigh Hunt served his imprisonment here, where he was allowed to have his family join him, to continue to write and edit the Examiner, and to receive visits from friends. Leigh Hunt wrote of his prison room:

> *"I papered the wall with a trellis of roses . . . the barred windows I screened with Venetian blinds; I had the ceiling covered with clouds and sky and when my bookcases were set up with their busts, and flowers and a pianoforte made their appearance, perhaps there was not a handsomer room on that side of the water."*

His visitors included Charles Lamb, who compared his room to one in a fairytale, Keats, Haydon and Byron, who met Hunt for the first time here.

As an editor Leigh Hunt was very influential and he

published the early work of Keats, Shelley and the Romantic poets and continued to champion their cause. It was Hunt and his brother John who published Byron's **The Vision of Judgement** when it was turned down by Byron's publisher John Murray, and the later cantos of **Don Juan**. Hazlitt and Tennyson were others of their authors. As an author Leigh Hunt wrote poetry, essays, plays and a lively **Autobiography**. Most of his work is no longer read, although his poem **Abou Ben Adhem and the Angel** was until recently learnt by heart in British Schools:

> *"Abou Bed Adhem (may his tribe increase!)*
> *Awoke one night from a deep dream of peace,*
> *And saw, within the moonlight in his room,*
> *Making it rich, and like a lily in bloom,*
> *An angel writing in a book of gold:-*
> *Exceeding peace had made Ben Adhem bold,*
> *And to the presence in the room he said,*
> *'What writest thou?' - The vision raised its head,*
> *And with a look made of all sweet accord,*
> *Answered, 'The names of those who love the Lord'*
> *I pray thee then,*
> *Write me as one that loves his fellow-men'.*
> *And lo! Ben Adhem's name led all the rest."*

Hunt however remains important as a figure who championed the very best literature of his time and who stood up for free speech and the freedom of the press.

Horsemonger Lane Goal was closed in 1878 and demolished in 1880. On its site today is Newington Recreation Ground.

Between Southwark's prisons stood, and still stands, the church of **St George the Martyr**. The first record of the church is 1122 when it was given to the nearby Bermondsey Abbey. The present buildings date from 1734-6, with a splendid plaster ceiling of cherubs added in 1897. The church is often called the Little Dorrit church and many scenes from Dickens' novel are set here. Little Dorrit who was born in the nearby Marshalsea Prison, was christened in the church, rescued from sleeping on the steps of the church by a kindly verger and ends up by marrying Arthur Clennam in St George's. She is depicted in a modern stained-glass window in the East end at prayer.

Still in the footsteps of Charles Dickens we cross over Borough High Street and walk down a few streets to **LANT STREET**. The 12 year old Charles Dickens had lodgings in the street when his father was a debtor at the Marshalsea. He introduced his landlord and landlady into literature as Mr and Mrs Garland in **The Old Curiosity Shop** (1841). On the site of their former house now stands the Charles Dickens Primary School. Dickens made use of his lodgings for **David Copperfield** when Mr Micawber was in the King's Bench Prison (**David Copperfield. Chapter II**). It is clear from the description of Lant Street in **Pickwick Papers** that Dickens had unhappy memories of the area. He uses it for Bob Sawyer's lodgings, conveniently close to Guy's Hospital where Sawyer is a medical student. He entertains Mr Pickwick to dinner here. The street is described in Chapter XXXII of **Pickwick Papers:**

> "There is a repose about Lant Street, in the Borough which sheds a gentle melancholy upon the soul. There are always a good many houses to let in the street; it is a by-street too and its dullness is soothing. The majority of the inhabitants either direct their energies to the letting of furnished apartments or devote themselves to the healthful and invigorating pursuit of mangling. The chief features in the still life of the street are green shutters, lodging bills, brass doorplates and bell handles; the principal specimens of animated nature the pot boy, the muffin youth and the baked potato man. The population is migratory, usually disappearing on the verge of quarterday and generally by night. Her Majesty's revenue are seldom collected in this happy valley; the rents are dubious, and the water communication is very frequently cut off."

We return along Borough High Street in the direction of London Bridge. We pass **Southwark Street** on the left which leads to **BANKSIDE** (a street facing onto the Thames the other side of Southwark Bridge) where the theatres of Southwark used to stand. The first theatre erected here was Philip Henslowe's Rose Theatre in 1586-7. It was an octagonal building of wood and plaster with a partly thatched roof. Amongst the dramatists employed by Henslowe here were George Chapman, John Webster, Thomas Dekker, Thomas Kyd and Michael Drayton.

Henslowe's **Diary** records the life at the Rose. Shakespeare acted at the Rose and it was here that Edward Alleyn made his name as one of the greatest actors of the time. Rose Alley commemorates the theatre which was demolished shortly after 1605 when the lease ran out.

The Globe Theatre was built here in 1598-9 from materials from the dismantled theatre owned by Richard Burbage in Curtain Road, Shoreditch. The theatre was in the shape of a wooden O and had a partly thatched roof. As the theatre was open to the elements it was only used in the summer, in the winter Burbage's Lord Chamberlain Company used the Blackfriars Theatre which was fully roofed. Shakespeare was one of Burbage's partners at the Globe and many of Shakespeare's plays had their first performances here with Richard Burbage in the lead role. Shakespeare often had small supporting parts in his own plays. The theatre's name came from its sign, which showed Hercules carrying the world on his shoulders. It was burnt down in 1613 when two cannons fired during Shakespeare's **Henry VIII** set the thatch alight. The audience and the actors escaped unhurt except for one man who had "his breeches on fire that would perhaps have broyled him if he had not with the benefit of a provident wit put it out with bottle ale". The theatre was rebuilt and re-opened in 1614 and can be seen on Visscher's famous map of 1616. The theatre was closed by the Puritans in 1642 and demolished in 1644. It stood to the south of Park Street and is commemorated by a plaque on the Park Street brewery. Shakespeare was believed to have lived within the vicinity close to the Bear Garden, with Beaumont and Fletcher with whom he collaborated as near neighbours.

The Hope Theatre was built in 1613 by Henslowe and Jacob Meade out of a former bear-baiting arena to take advantage of the Globe Theatre's destruction by fire. It was here that Ben Jonson's **Bartholomew Fair**, was first performed in 1614. Later the theatre alternated between bear-baiting and plays being performed. It was dismantled in 1656 and was where Bear Gardens Alley is today.

The Swan Theatre built in 1594-6 was the largest of the Southwark theatres with a capacity of three thousand. It did not have its own resident theatre company and would stage all manner of events, including displays of fencing. It fell into disuse in 1632 and was demolished. It stood to the west of Hepton Street.

Bankside also possessed a famous bear-garden and there are accounts of a visit to the gardens in both Pepys' and Evelyn's Diaries. **Pepys** thought it a "very rude and nasty pleasure" and **Evelyn** found himself "most heartily weary of the rude and dirty pastime". The sport in the garden comprised bull and bear-baiting, cock and dog fighting.

At no 1 Bear Gardens there is the Bear Garden Museum and Art Centre which was opened in 1972. It provides an interesting picture of Elizabethan theatre and the development of the theatre in England and contains a replica of a small early 17th c theatre with seating for 120. At Bankside a replica of the Globe Theatre as it must have been in Shakespeare's day is currently being constructed so by the end of the decade we can be once again watching Shakespeare's plays at the Globe Theatre.

The brewery at Park Street is a successor to the one owned by Henry Thrales, Dr Johnson's great patron, and Johnson was a frequent visitor to the Thrales house in Park Street where he had his own room. Mrs Thrales wrote her account of Johnson at his death: **Anecdotes of the Late Samuel Johnson** (1786). No one knew Johnson more intimately than **Hester Thrales** from 1756 until 1781. It is in her anecdotes we see the informal and domestic Johnson, which must be added to Fanny Burney's picture of Johnson as playful and teasingly flirtatious, before with Boswell's **Life** we have the total portrait of Samuel Johnson. When Henry Thrales died in 1781 Dr Johnson was one of his executors and had a hand in the selling of the brewery to Barclay and Perkins. Lord Lucan tells the story that:

> "Johnson appeared bustling about with an ink-horn and pen in his buttonhole, like an exciseman; on being asked what he really considered to be the value of the property, answered, 'We are not here to sell a parcel of boilers and vats, but the potentiality of growing rich beyond the dreams of avarice'."

Mrs Thrales it was rumoured was about to remarry with Samuel Johnson, a suggestion Boswell found ridiculous and made the subject of a mocking ode. She did remarry however, and after her marriage to Piozzi her friendship with Samuel Johnson came to an end and he was full of scorn for Mrs Piozzi. The brewery is now a bottling plant for Courage.

Bankside today is dominated by the large power station. From Southwark Street we proceed up the High Street until we reach **SOUTHWARK CATHEDRAL**.

The Cathedral Church of St Saviour and St Mary Overie is the fourth church to be built on this site, the previous churches have all been destroyed by fire. In the 12th c it was part of an Augustinian priory, and parts of their Norman church survived the fire of 1206. The church was rebuilt in 1220 in the new Gothic style, and is the earliest Gothic church left in London and is Southwark's most impressive building. It was surrendered to Henry VIII at the Dissolution of the Monasteries and became the parish church of St Mary Overie (St Mary over the water). It became by the end of the 16th c the actors' church with nearly all London's theatres situated in its parish. This was something which did not please the parish chaplain, Sutton, and in 1616 he preached a sermon denouncing those "who dishonour God by penning and acting of plays". A tower was added to the church in 1689 and the church was extensively restored in the 19th c, with a new nave built in 1890 by Arthur Blomfield. The great expansion of South London in the 19th c caused by the creation of several new bridges across the Thames led to St Mary Overie being made a Cathedral Church in 1897 and in 1905 Edward Talbot was enthroned as the first Bishop of Southwark.

The most impressive monument in the church is the highly painted effigy of **John Gower** (1330-1408) whose head rests on his three main works, **Speculum Meditantis, Confessio Amantis** and **Vox Clamantis**, and his gilded tomb has the inscription: Angl. poeta celeberrimus.

A member of the gentry he devoted the latter part of his life to his writing and lived at the priory of St Marie Overie from 1377. He married twice, the second time in 1398 when he was approaching 70. He went blind in 1400. A good friend of Geoffrey Chaucer he is with Strode the dedicatee of **Troilus and Criseyde**. Gower was a man of great learning, and wrote in French, Latin and English. His first major work **Mirour de l'Omme** (Speculum Meditantis) is an allegory concerned with fallen man, his virtues and his vices. There are 32,000 lines of octosyllabics in twelve line stanzas written in French in about 1376. His second major work is in Latin, **Vox Clamantis**. It is an apocalyptic poem of seven books in 10,265 lines of elegiac couplets, dealing with politics and kingship, with reflections on the Peasant Revolt and the early troubled years of Richard II's reign.

Gower's principal work is in English, the **Confessio Amantis**, and three manuscript versions of the poem from the 1390s survive. It is over 33,000 lines long and its 141 stories in octosyllabic couplets are related in a metrical skill unsurpassed in English. The lover's confession to Venus's priest is the framework for an encyclopedic account of the philosophy and the courtly love ethos of the times. It introduced into English Literature the chivalric romances of Italy and France, and Ovid and the major authors of classical antiquity. Gower's reputation would stand far higher if it was not for the achievements of his friend and fellow English author, Chaucer. The **Confessio Amantis** is still read with readers taking great delight especially in its Prologue which tells us:

> *"It hath and schal ben evermor*
> *That love is maister wher he wile."*

John Gower's effigy is to be found in the North aisle. Across the church from Gower is an alabaster monument of **Shakespeare**, above which there are stained-glass windows showing characters from his plays. Each year the Cathedral has a memorial birthday service for Shakespeare who used to worship in the church, and his younger brother, Edmund, also an actor, was buried here in 1607.

John Fletcher (1579-1625) the dramatist was buried in the church after his death from the plague. He collaborated very successfully with Beaumont in the writing of 15 plays and also wrote plays with Chapman, Jonson, Massinger, Rowley and Middleton. It is believed that he wrote some 16 plays of which he was the sole author, and wrote part of Shakespeare's **Henry VIII**. It is Fletcher who said, "Charity and beating begins at home".

Philip Massinger (1583-1640) who collaborated with John Fletcher after the withdrawal of Beaumont was buried at St Mary's in 1640 in the same grave as John Fletcher. One of the major dramatists of the post-Shakespearean era his plays are currently out of favour, the plays of Webster and Tourneur being preferred. His best works are the tragedies **Duke of Milan, The Roman Actor** and **Believe as you List**, although his most performed plays were the comedies **A New Way to Pay Old Debts** and **City Madam**. His creation of Sir Giles Overreach in **A New Way to Pay Old Debts** allowed Kean and Kemble, amongst many other actors, to show their talent. He and Fletcher are commemorated by inscriptions on the flagstones in the choir.

Having paused in the tranquillity of the churchyard we make our way round the church into the back streets to **CLINK STREET**, where the Clink Prison used to be. It was a small prison in the Bishop of Winchester's park. John Stow said it was used for the people who broke the peace on Bankside and in the brothels. It is the origin of the expression 'in the clink'. It was burnt down in the Gordon Riots. In this area stood the magnificent town house of the Bishops of Winchester. The Bishop's Palace had a long river frontage and a 70 acre park. The last Bishop to live here was **Lancelot Andrewes** (1555-1626) one of the clergymen appointed to translate the **Authorised Version of the Bible**. He was a highly popular preacher, and as a writer is remembered for his sermons, which 'rank with the finest English prose of their time' (T.S. Eliot). He is buried in Southwark Cathedral in the South ambulatory. In 1642 when the episcopacy was suppressed by order of Parliament, the palace was converted into a prison for royalists. **Sir Kenelm Digby** (1603-65) while imprisoned here wrote his **Critical Remarks on Sir Thomas Brown's Religio Medici** (1643). His most readable work is his **Private Memoirs** (published in 1827) which tell of his secret marriage to Venetia Stanley, one of the greatest beauties of the period, whose early death, aged only 33, is lamented by Jonson and others in verse. At the Restoration the Bishop's estates were returned but were so delapidated that they were leased out for building. Today it is a street of warehouses.

We return to Borough High Street, cross over London Bridge and turn left into **CANNON STREET**, and back into the City. The name is an abbreviation of Candlewick Street after the many candle makers living in and around the street during the Middle Ages. Where Cannon Street Railway Station stands was the site of the Roman Governors' Palace, and the centre of Roman Britain. The London stone from which the Romans measured the distances in Britain was, and still is, here. It was embedded in the wall of St Swithin's Church opposite the station but when the church, like most of the street, was destroyed in World War II, it was put in the wall of the Overseas-Chinese Banking Corporation at no 111, a vivid green building built on the site of St Swithin's. The piece of sandstone is covered by a black grill, but it is clearly visible. It is mentioned in Shakespeare's **Henry VI. Pt. 2, Act IV:**

> *Scene VI. Cannon-Street.*
>
> *Enter Jack Cade and his followers. He strikes his staff on the London stone.*
>
> Cade
> *Now is Mortimer lord of this city. And here, sitting upon London-stone, I charge and command that, of the city's cost, the pissing-conduit run nothing but claret wine this first year of our reign. And now henceforth it shall be treason for any that calls me other than Lord Mortimer."*

We follow Cannon Street into **QUEEN VICTORIA STREET** going past the Financial Times newspaper, which like most newspapers is in the process of relocating to the Docklands. Its Literary Editor is Anthony Curtis. Next to it is the Wren church of **St Nicholas Cole Abbey**, the first of the 51 City churches he rebuilt after the Great Fire. It was gutted by fire bombs in 1941 and restored to Wren's original designs in 1962. It is now a Scottish Presbyterian church. Across the road are the splendid redbrick buildings of **St Benet** rebuilt by Wren after the Great Fire in 1677-83. The novelist **Henry Fielding** married Mary Daniels here in 1747, his second wife, who had been his first wife's maid. In the pre-Wren medieval church built in the 12th c **Inigo Jones** (1573-1652) was buried in the chancel, and has his monument in the Wren church. It was Jones who brought Palladian architecture to England and as the surveyor of the King's Works designed the harmonious classical masterpieces of the Queen's House in Greenwich and the Banqueting Hall in Whitehall. He began designing the scenery and costumes for masques from 1605 and collaborated with Ben Jonson for most of them until 1631, when they quarrelled violently about the respective merits of their work. St Benet is now a Welsh Episcopalian church and services are conducted in Welsh.

A little further down from Queen Victoria Street we arrive at the College of Arms, a fine 17th c redbrick building which houses the royal heralds. Next to the College is Peter's Hill which gives one of London's finest views of St Paul's Cathedral. We take the short walk up Peter's Hill to visit the church of the City of London, St Paul's Cathedral.

ST PAUL'S CATHEDRAL

The present Cathedral is the 5th church to be built on this site, the first was built of wood in 604, with Mellitus becoming the first Bishop of London. The largest church to be built on this site was the Norman Cathedral begun at the end of the 11th c to replace the church destroyed by fire in 1087. It was 'worthy of being numbered amongst the most famous of buildings', and was enclosed by a wall with six gates, and a complex of buildings associated with the Cathedral developed in this close including **St Paul's School** and **Paul's Cross**. Until the beginning of the 14th c there was a thrice yearly folk moot at Paul's Cross, where it was compulsory for all the citizens of London to attend. Papal Bulls, announcement of royal weddings and proclamations, victories and ex-communictions were issued here. Political speeches and sermons were preached from it. Jane Shore, the mistress of Edward IV at his death, was forced by the Bishop of London on the orders of Richard III, to do penance before the Cross, dressed only in her kirtle and carrying a taper. Her plight became the subject of Rowe's tragedy **Jane Shore** (1714). **Carlyle** called Paul's Cross the 'Times newspaper of the Middle Ages'. It was destroyed in 1643 on the orders of the Puritan Parliament. A memorial Cross was erected almost on the same site in 1910.

Old St Paul's saw one royal wedding, when Arthur, Prince of Wales married Catherine of Aragon here in 1501. The young Prince died within five months of the wedding, and Catherine, with a dispensation from the pope was betrothed to the 11 year old younger brother, their wedding taking place in June 1509, seven weeks after Henry VIII's accession to the throne. When Henry VIII brought about the English Reformation St Paul's suffered greatly, with not enough money being forthcoming to maintain the church adequately. The loss of respect to London's Cathedral, led to the nave becoming 'a common thoroughfare between Carter's Lane and Paternoster Row for people with vessels of ale and beer, baskets of bread, fish, flesh and fruit, men leading mules, horses and other beasts' and was now referred to as Paul's Walk. Servants were hired and shops set up on the tombs and fonts and by 1560 the nave was described by Bishop Pilkington as, "The south side for Popery and Usury; the north for Simony; and the horse-fair in the middle for all kinds of bargains, meetings, brawlings, murders, conspiracies; and the font for ordinary payments of money." Elizabeth I gave money for makeshift repairs to the Cathedral, but when the 500 ft spire was destroyed in the fire of 1561 it was not replaced. It was only in 1628 with Inigo Jones as the King's Surveyor and with money from Charles I's own purse that the Cathedral fabric was properly restored, with a new classical portico, making St Paul's 'the envy of all Christendom for a piece of Architecture not to be parallelled in these last ages of the World'. The English Civil War interrupted the work of restoration. The church was used as a cavalry barracks and the roof collapsed when the supporting scaffolding was sold off with St Paul's soon reverting to its former state of decay. Charles II employed the young Oxford professor of Astronomy, Christopher Wren to draw up plans to restore the church. His plan was accepted six days before the Cathedral was destroyed by the Great Fire. The Cathedral ruins were past restoration, and Wren with explosives and battering rams razed them to the ground and began work on the present church.

In Old St Paul's **Sir Philip Sidney** was buried with great pomp in 1586 after his death overseas fighting the Spanish. The most illustrious of all the Cathedral deans **John Donne** was buried here in 1631. His monument by Nicholas Stone is the only monument to survive unscathed the Great Fire and can be seen today in the ambulatory. The history of Old St Pauls was the subject matter of one of Harrison Ainsworth's best historical novels, **Old St Pauls** (1841) whose admirers stretch from Dickens to Thomas Hardy. In fact on Hardy's first visit to London as a young boy he traced the action of Ainsworth's novel round the streets surrounding the Cathedral, and borrowed heavily from Ainsworth's style in his first published novel, **Desperate Remedies** (1871).

The Wren church was built in 35 years and was the first church in England to have a dome. The church Wren built was very different from the plan commissioned by the royal warrant. Wren relied on a clause giving him 'liberty to make some variations rather ornamental than essential, as from time to time he should see proper' to build, not the traditional English Gothic church, but one in the new baroque manner of St Peter's in Rome. Built in Portland stone from Dorset and paid for by a tax on coal arriving in London by sea it was finished in 1710. The cross on the dome is 365 ft from the ground, one foot for each day of the year. Wren was one of the first people to be buried in the crypt, and next to his tomb is the inscription composed by his son, "Lector, si monumentum requiris, circumspice" (those who seek a monument, look around), and few architects could boast such a superb monument to their glory as St Paul's Cathedral.

Also buried in the crypt are **Walter de la Mare** (1873-1956) novelist and poet, who is perhaps best remembered for his anthologies of verse for children. As a boy he attended St Paul's Choir School. **Max Beerbolm** (1872-1956) critic, essayist and caricaturist, best known for his Oxford novel, **Zuleika Dobson** (1911) was cremated and his ashes are in the crypt.

There are memorials in the crypt to **William Blake, Charles Reade** and **Walter Besant** (1836-1901) novelist, critic and philanthropist, who wrote several history books and produced several works on London, including **A Survey of London** (1902-1912) and an autobiography. Today he is best remembered as the founder of the Society of Authors in 1884, and as a vigorous campaigner for proper remuneration for writers.

T.E. Lawrence (1888-1935), better known as Lawrence of Arabia is also commemorated in the crypt. His **The Seven Pillars of Wisdom** (1935) achieved the status of a bestseller, and has recently been re-issued. It is just as compulsive reading today as when it was first published. Lawrence lost most of the first draft of the book when changing trains in Reading in 1919, and re-wrote the whole work after that. It was originally printed in 1926 for private circulation in a limited edition. Churchill declared it, "the greatest book ever written in the English language". To help with his writing style Lawrence sought and received the advice of E.M. Forster and G.B. Shaw.

His life has inspired many biographies, a film, **The Ascent of F6** by Auden, the character of Private Meek in Shaw's **Too True to be Good** and Ratigan's play, **Ross** (1960).

Sydney Smith (1771-1845) was a canon at St Paul's and is honoured in the crypt. Another canon honoured in the crypt was **R.H. Barham** (1788-1845) who had great success with his **The Ingoldsby Legends** (1840) a poetic rendering of medieval legends, full of the comic and the grotesque, which are now referred to but never read.

There is a monument for **W.E. Henley** (1849-1903) a minor poet and a very influential editor of the National Observer and the New Review, publishing the work of Hardy, Kipling, Stevenson, Yeats, Henry James and H.G. Wells. His main claim to fame is as the inspiration of Long John Silver in Stevenson's **Treasure Island**.

In the main part of the church there are memorials and monuments to **Samuel Johnson**, who is buried in Westminster Abbey, and his friend **Joshua Reynolds**, who painted his portrait. Also to the artist **Lord Leighton** (1830-96) whose habit of educating his models inspired Shaw's **Pygmalion** (1913) and appears as Clive Newcome 'the cock of the whole painting school, the favourite of all' in Thackeray's **The Newcomes**, and as Gaston Phoebus in Disraeli's **Lothair**. In Henry James' story **The Private Life**, he is unflatteringly drawn as Lord Mellifont, the public artist.

The most impressive monument in the Cathedral is Nicholas Stone's effigy of **John Donne** copied from the picture which Donne posed for wrapped in his shroud. Donne, a man of great talent and even greater ambition tried every avenue for advancement, from the law, the armed forces, the court and the patronage of the important persons of the day to rise in the world. It was only his acceptance of becoming a Protestant at the instigation of James I that led to his eventual preferment. He acquired rich livings as a Church of England divine and in 1621, through the influence of James I's favourite, the Duke of Buckingham, was made Dean of St Pauls. A careerist undoubtedly Donne was, who knew how to flatter the great, but his poetry and his prose show a greater depth of feeling and sensitivity than almost any other writer of his day. In Donne we have great learning in metaphysical conceits, combined with excitement and eroticism in his love poems, and an obsessive pre-occupation with death in most of his work. It is he who can turn **Going to Bed** into the exploration of the New World:

> *"Licence my roving hands, and let them go,*
> *Before, behind, between, above, below,*
> *O my America! my new-found-land,*
> *My kingdom, safliest when with one man mann'd."*

Standing on his urn Donne stares out at the Cathedral in his final resting place just a short walk away from the bottom of Ludgate Hill, where he was imprisoned in the Fleet Goal in Seacoal Lane, for his illegal marriage to the 17 year old Anne More.

To enter the ambulatory to see Donne's statue there is a small fee, and on the way to John Donne there are the photos of Prince Charles's marriage to Lady Diana Spencer in 1981, the first royal wedding in Wren's St Paul's. There is also a small fee for visiting the crypt and going upstairs to the Whispering Gallery. There is no charge for visiting the church, and if you go about 4.00 in the afternoon you will be able to hear St Paul's truly splendid choir sing Evensong.

Sir Winston Churchill's funeral was at St Paul's and he is commemorated by an inscription on the floor as you enter the church. Two times Prime Minister, Churchill also won the Nobel Prize for Literature in 1953. Before leaving the church one can view Holman Hunt's The Light of the World and the wartime photo showing St Paul's surrounded by flames, reminding us that without the volunteers, like Sir John Betjeman, putting out the fires in and around the Cathedral in the last World War we would not have Wren's Church to admire.

We leave St Paul's and enjoy a walk around the churchyard. In front of the church is the statue of Queen Anne, who was affectionately known as Brandy Nan for her habit of drinking a bottle of gin every day. She was so fat that she could not walk and had seventeen children, all of whom died in infancy, the oldest getting to be 11. Anne was Queen when the church was finished. There is also a statue of Becket, the Archbishop of Canterbury murdered in his own Cathedral in 1170. It is to be found close to the coach park.

ST PAUL'S CHURCHYARD was the principal centre of the London book trade and up to the bombings of World War II, an important area for publishers. The first book to contain the imprint "sold by the booksellers of St Paul's Churchyard" was in 1500. **Wynkyn de Worde,** Fleet Street's first printer had a bookshop by the Cathedral with the sign of 'Our Lady of Pity'. Other foreign booksellers set up in the 16th c in the Churchyard (which was outside the control of the City Guilds) and their competition led to booksellers elsewhere setting up their shop in St Paul's Churchyard. The bookseller and publisher John Newberry traded from here in 1744. He employed both Johnson and Goldsmith as writers, and in this great age of periodicals of every description began the first children's magazine the Lilliputian Magazine. In Goldsmith's novel, **The Vicar of Wakefield** he is portrayed as "the philanthropic publisher of Saint Paul's Churchyard, a red-faced good-natured little man who was always in a hurry". In Johnson's the Idler he is gently satirised as Jack Whirler. He set up his nephew Francis Newberry in the publishing trade up at the Crown, Paternoster Row, and it was to him that Samuel Johnson sold Goldsmith's novel, **The Vicar of Wakefield** for £60 to relieve his friend's destitution.

St Paul's Coffee House stood in the churchyard from c 1702 and **Boswell** was a member of a club of clergymen, physicians and professional men which met here on a Thursday for conversation. It is also mentioned in Dickens. It moved to Ludgate Hill in 1772 under the name of the London Coffee House.

ST. PAUL'S SCHOOL founded by Dean Colet in 1509 with William Lily as the first High Master stood in the Churchyard until its removal to Hammersmith in 1884. It has been in Barnes since 1968. Famous literary Old Paulines include William Camden, John Milton, Reynolds, Barham, L. Binyon and **G.K. Chesterton** (1874-1936) the creator of the detective Father Brown and the poet **Edward Thomas** (1878-1917). Other pupils include the great general, the Duke of Marlborough, the hanging judge, Judge Jeffreys and briefly, Lord Montgomery.

While the school was in the Churchyard the boys had to

attend the services in the Cathedral, and the young John Milton must have sat in the choir listening to the Dean John Donne preaching, wondering whether or not he would ever emulate the Dean as a poet or as a divine.

Sir Philip Sidney (1554-86)

BIBLIOGRAPHY

Books on London

The London Encyclopedia — Ben Weinreb and Christopher Hibbert, Macmillan 1983.
This is the best general reference book on London for almost every topic.
A Survey of London — 48 vols. prepared by the CLC.
The most detailed reference book available.

London Guides
Blue Guide to London
Penguin Guide to London
Companion Guide to London — David Piper (Collins 1978) the most readable of the guides but very out of date.
Streets of London — S. Fairfield (Papermac 1983) — a history of street names.

History and Development of London
A Survey of London — John Stow (1598) — London's first guide book. Available in an Everyman paperback.
Trivia, or the Art of Walking the Streets of London — John Gay (1716)
Georgian London — John Summerson (Penguin 1978) — very readable and enjoyable.
The Biography of a City — Christopher Hibbert (Penguin 1980) — recommended.
The Making of Modern London — Gavin Weightman & Steve Humphries (Sidgwick & Jackson, 3 vols.)
London Labour and the London Poor — Henry Mayhew (1861)
London 1808-1870 The Infernal Wen — Francis Sheppard (Secker & Warburg 1971)

Books on Specific London Places
City of London Churches — John Betjeman (Pitkin)
London Wall Walks — Museum of London publication.
St Paul and the City — Frank Atkinson (Park Lane Press 1985).
Illustrated Geological Walks — Eric Robinson (Scottish Academic Press 1984, 2 vols.)
The Streets of East London — Bill Fishman (Duckworth 1979)

Literary London
Guide to Literary London — Williams (Batsford 1971) — somewhat laconic.
Oxford Literary Guide to the British Isles — Dorothy Eagle and Hilary Carnell (O.U.P. 1980)

Blue Guide to Literary Great Britain and Ireland — Ian Ousby (A.C. Black 1985)
— both recomended. Oxford does it place by place, the Blue Guide does it writer by writer.
Blue Plaques on houses of Historic interest — GLC pamphlet.
The Pink Plaque Guide to London — Michael Elliman and Frederick Roll (GMP 1986)

Architecture
Buildings of England: London — Pevsner Vols. 1 & 2 (Penguin)
A Guide to the Architecture of London — Edward and Christopher Woodward (Weidenfeld and Nicholson)

General Books on English Literature
The Oxford Companion to English Literature — editor Margaret Drabble (O.U.P. 1985 5th edition)
— invaluable work of reference.
A Short History of English Literature — Harry Blamires (Methuen 1984)
The Concise Oxford Dictionary of Proverbs — J.A. Simpson (O.U.P. 1982)
Oxford Dictionary of Nursery Rhymes — Iona and Peter Opie (O.U.P. 1951)
The Oxford Dictionary of Quotations — 3rd edition 1979
The Dictionary of National Biography — O.U.P.
Chambers Biographical Dictionary

Books on specific authors

James Boswell
London Journal — James Boswell (1950)
James Boswell and his World — David Daiches (Thames & Hudson 1976)

Anthony Burgess
Little Wilson and Big God — A. Burgess (Heinemann 1987)
This Man and Music — A. Burgess (Hutchinson 1982)

Geoffrey Chaucer
Geoffrey Chaucer — L.D. Benson (1974)

Charles Dickens
Life of Dickens — John Forster (1872-4)
The Making of Charles Dickens – Christopher Hibbert (Penguin)
The World of Charles Dickens — Angus Wilson (Panther 1978)
Dickens' London — Peter Ackroyd (Headline 1987) — the photos of London are worth the price of the book.
The London of Charles Dickens — Midas Publications 1979.

John Dryden
John Dryden and his World — James Winn (1987 Yale University)

John Donne
Life and Letters — E. Gosse (2 vols. 1899)
Life of John Donne — Izaak Walton (1640)

T.S. Eliot
T.S. Eliot — Peter Ackroyd (Abacus 1985)

Thomas Hardy
Thomas Hardy's England — John Fowles & Jo Draper (Cape 1984)
Young Thomas Hardy — Robert Gittings (Penguin 1978)
The Older Hardy — Robert Gittings (Penguin 1980)

Samuel Johnson
The Life of Samuel Johnson — James Boswell (unabridged O.U.P., abridged Penguin)
Samuel Johnson — John Wain (1974)
The Personal History of Samuel Johnson — Christopher Hibbert (1971)
Anecdotes of the Late Samuel Johnson — H.L. Piozzi

John Keats
John Keats — Robert Gittings (1968)
ABBA ABBA — A. Burgess (Faber 1987)

John Milton
Milton: A Biography — W.R. Parker (2 vols. Clarendon 1968)
The Life of John Milton — A.N. Wilson (O.U.P. 1984)

John Mortimer
Clinging to the Wreckage — John Mortimer (Penguin 1983)

George Orwell
George Orwell: A Life — Bernard Crick (Penguin 1982) — excellent
Orwell's London — John Thompson (Fourth Estate 1984)

Samuel Pepys
Diary of Samuel Pepys — edited by Robert Lathan & William Mathews (Bell & Hyman 1978)
Shorter Pepys — the abridged version by the same editors is now available as a Penguin paperback
Illustrated Pepys — illustrated edition by the same editors (Bell & Hyman 1978)

Alexander Pope
Alexander Pope — Maynard Mack (Yale 1988)

Ezra Pound
Ezra Pound — Peter Ackroyd (Thames & Hudson 1981)

William Shakespeare
Samuel Johnson's Preface to the 1765 edition of Shakespeare's Complete Works.
Also Samuel Johnson's Lives of the Poets
Brief Lives — Aubrey (1813)
Shakespeare — Anthony Burgess (Penguin)
Nothing Like the Sun — Anthony Burgess (Penguin) — interesting attempt to write a novel on Shakespeare using Shakespearean English.
Enderby's Dark Lady — Anthony Burgess (Abacus)
Ulysses — James Joyce (Bodley Head) — Joyce puts forward an interesting and lively theory on Shakespeare at the beginning of the book.

Lytton Strachey
Lytton Stracey — Michael Holroyd (2 vol. Penguin) — good for all the Bloomsbury group.

Dylan Thomas
Dylan Thomas — Paul Ferris (Penguin 1978)

Oscar Wilde
Oscar Wilde — Richard Ellman (Hamish Hamilton 1987)
Selected Letters of Oscar Wilde — edited by Rupert Hart-Davis (1964 O.U.P.)
Letters to Reggie Turner — Max Beerbohm edited by Rupert Hart-Davis (1964 O.U.P.)
Last Testament of Oscar Wilde — Peter Ackroyd (Abacus 1984) — a short novel which captures the atmosphere of Wilde's life and is highly recommended for those who have not the time to read Ellman's definitive study.

W.B. Yeats
Yeats: The Man and the Masks — Richard Ellman (1948)

Sir John Soane's Museum

INDEX OF AUTHORS

Ackroyd, Peter 52, 139, 233, 234
Addison, Joseph 162, 165, 240
Ainsworth, Harrison 68, 104, 137, 180, 257, 286
Akenside, Mark 15
Andrewes, Lancelot 282
Aubrey, John 89, 126
Auden, W.H. 219

Bacon, Francis 42, 43, 46
Barham, R.H. 143, 288, 290
Baxter, Richard 272
Beaumont, Francis 98, 197, 198
Becket, St Thomas 205, 206, 270
Beerbohm, Max 166, 287
Bentham, Jeremy 1, 250
Besant, Walter 287
Binyon, Laurence 13, 290
Blake, William 218, 219, 287
Blackstone, William 65, 83
Boswell, James 70, 75, 97, 122, 290
Bradlaugh, Charles 230
Bronte, Anne 243, 244
Bronte, Charlotte 243, 244
Brooke, Christopher 131, 270
Browne, William 98
Buchan, John 84
Bunyan, John 123, 217
Burgess, Anthony, 19, 20, 33, 68, 212
Burke, Edmund 92, 123
Burne-Jones 48, 61, 62
Byron, Lord, 39, 48, 93, 103, 276

Camden, William 47, 191, 290
Campbell, Thomas 65
Campion, Thomas 47
Carew, Thomas 86
Cavendish, George 124

Chapman, George 270
Chatterton, Thomas 52, 138, 139
Chaucer, Geoffrey 76, 194, 250, 260, 261, 268, 286
Chesterton, G.K. 290
Churchill, Charles 178
Cobbet, William 118
Coke, Edward 95
Coleridge, Samuel Taylor 102, 118, 190
Collins, Wilkie 31, 65
Combe, William 274
Congreve, William 91
Coverdale, Miles 259
Cowper, William 21, 92, 93, 97, 121
Crabbe, George 180
Crashaw, Richard 162
Cumberland, Richard 16

Darwin, Charles 2
Davies, John 85
Davies, W.H. 14
Defoe, Daniel 179, 180, 212, 217, 218, 243, 250
Dekker, Thomas 94, 267, 272
de la Mare 287
Denham, John 131
Denning, Lord 78
de Worde, 101, 111, 290
Dickens, Charles 28, 31, 32, 35, 36, 37, 38, 41, 46, 65, 66, 93, 103, 105, 114, 117, 126, 133, 134, 137, 142, 143, 144, 170, 180, 181, 196, 202, 238, 239, 240, 244, 260, 263, 268, 270, 271, 272, 275, 276, 277
Digby, Kenelm 282

Disraeli, Benjamin 15, 38, 39, 132, 140
Disraeli, Isaac 15, 39, 140
Donne, John 69, 119, 120, 122, 129, 131, 197, 198, 286, 288, 289, 291
Doyle, Conan 234, 239
Dryden, John 90, 109, 112, 148, 166, 179
du Maurier, George 7
Dyer, George 191

Edwards, Richard 130
Eliot, T.S. 7, 16, 19, 20, 54, 259, 260
Evelyn, John 89, 112, 143, 168, 170, 269, 279

Fielding, Henry 77, 78, 85, 109, 283
Fletcher, John 197, 281
Ford, John 88
Forster, E.M. 25, 26, 27, 34
Forster, John 65, 98
Fox, George 214, 217
Foxe, John 154, 159
Frobisher, John 159
Fry, Roger 25, 33

Galsworthy, John 97
Garnett, Richard 13
Gascoigne, George 47
Gay, John 64
Gissing, George 9
Goldsmith, Oliver 82, 83, 85, 95, 96, 110, 114, 154, 290
Gower, John 280, 281
Grahame, Kenneth 238
Gray, Thomas 21
Greene, Graham 5, 6, 68
Greville, Fulke 137, 138
Guy, Thomas 240

Haggard, Rider 96
Hanway, Jonas 57
Hardy, Thomas 9, 52, 117, 153, 170, 244
Haydon, Robert 274, 275
Hayley, William 92, 93
Hazlitt, William, 104, 105, 140, 190, 208
Henley, W.E. 288
Henty, George 239
Herrick, Robert 195
Hobbes, Thomas 119
Hogarth, William 66, 173, 174, 269
Hope, Anthony 6, 84
Hunt, Holman 160
Hunt, Leigh 208, 275, 276

Jeffreys, Judge 181, 258, 272, 290
Johnson, Samuel Dr 55, 68, 70, 73, 75, 78, 82, 83, 103, 104, 110, 114, 115, 116, 117, 118, 122, 123, 126, 133, 134, 150, 151, 152, 153, 168, 177, 189, 223, 240, 273, 279, 280, 290
Jones, Inigo 283, 284, 288
Jonson, Ben, 94, 101, 126, 196, 197, 206, 207, 227, 228, 278

Keats, John 139, 198, 206, 208, 211, 212, 236, 265, 266, 269, 275
Kipling, Rudyard, 62

Lamb, Charles, 62, 63, 95, 97, 121, 122, 140, 169, 178, 190, 247, 275
Lawrence, D.H. 7, 186, 192
Lawrence, T.E. 5, 287, 288
Leighton, Lord 288
Lockhart, John 39, 208
Lodge, David 1, 10
Lodge, Thomas 130, 131
London, Jack 231

Lovelace, Richard 111, 112, 156, 162
Lyly, John 69, 177

Malory, Thomas 178, 190
Macaulay, Lord 48
Mackenzie, Compton 98
Mansfield, Katharine 192
Marlowe, Christopher 174, 177, 198
Marston, John 94, 270
Massinger, Philip 282
Mayhew, Henry 125, 145
Meredith, George 57, 139
Middleton, Thomas 47
Mill, John Stuart 1, 247
Milton, John 89, 112, 123, 124, 154, 155, 156, 157, 159, 160, 186, 189, 198, 201, 220, 221, 290, 291
Mitford, Mary Russell 20
Moore, George 96
Moore, Thomas, 93, 103
More, Thomas 130, 134, 161, 193, 197, 235, 237, 255, 256
Morrell, Ottoline 7
Morris, William 48, 61, 62, 149
Morrison, Arthur 230, 231, 234
Mortimer, John 98, 99
Murphy, Arthur 126
Murray, John, 39, 103
Murry, Middleton 192

Needham, Marchamont 69
Newbolt, Henry 132
Nicholson, Harold 96

Oates, Titus, 179, 254
Orwell, George 2, 5, 6, 19, 54, 78, 232, 259, 265
Otway, Thomas 179, 254

Paine, Tom 119, 154
Peacock, Thomas Love 247, 248
Penn, William 179, 258
Pepys, Samuel 79, 95, 103, 106, 107, 112, 120, 121, 154, 168, 196, 202, 249, 257, 258, 262, 269, 279
Pitt, William the younger 129
Pound, Ezra 28
Pope, Alexander 131, 165, 240
Pynson, Richard 101

Ralegh, Walter 85, 89, 95, 197, 254, 255
Randolph, Thomas 101
Reade, Charles 132, 287
Richardson, Dorothy 27
Richardson, Samuel, 109, 110, 112
Robinson, Henry Crabb 20, 96
Rochester, earl of 67, 69
Rogers, Samuel 37, 97
Roget, Dr 22, 33
Rossetti, Christina 61
Rossetti, Dante Gabriel 48, 57, 58, 61
Rowe, Nicholas 92, 285
Rowley, William 86, 281
Ruskin, John 219
Russell, Bertrand 7, 54

Sackville, Thomas 111
Sackville-West 27, 96, 111
Savage, Richard 140, 152, 180
Sayers, Dorothy 52
Sedley, Charles, 15, 69
Selden, John 95
Settle, Elkanah 166, 168, 205
Shadwell, Thomas 89
Shakespeare, William, 14, 85, 123, 140, 141, 142, 168, 197, 223, 224, 227, 228, 229, 237, 252, 253, 256, 268, 278, 283

Shelley, Percy Bysshe 123, 202, 259
Sheppard, Jack 180
Shirley, James, 47, 177
Sidney, Philip 46, 75, 138, 286
Smart, Christopher 274
Smith, Charlotte 274
Smith, Sydney 36, 288
Smollet, Tobias 272, 273
Southerne, Thomas 90
Southey, Robert 47
Speed, John 159
Spenser, Edmund 75, 76, 77
Steele, Richard 14, 162
Stephen, Leslie 25, 32, 244
Stow, John 205, 206, 247
Strachey, Giles Lytton 25, 27, 38
Strachey, John St Loe 38
Surrey, earl of 103, 202, 259
Swinburne, Algernon Charles 48, 49

Tawney, R.H. 35
Tennyson, Lord 37, 103
Thackeray, William Makepeace 16, 32, 33, 35, 83, 97, 166, 243
Thomas, Dylan 22, 173
Thomas, Edward 290
Tonson, Jacob 123
Tottel, Richard 103
Trollope, Anthony 5, 130

Waller, Edmund 64
Walton, Izaak 119, 120, 122, 124
Ward, Mrs Humphry 21
Watkins, Vernon 173
Watson, Thomas 177
Watts, Isaac 214
Webster, John 86
Webster, Lyn 113
Wellington, duke of 238, 239
Wesley, John 156, 166, 213
Whittington, Richard 201, 105, 261
Wild, Jonathan 180
Wilde, Oscar 22, 28, 182, 183, 184, 185
Wilkes, John 273, 274
Wilson, A.N. 38
Wilson, Angus 10, 11
Wilson, Colin 10
Wilson, Harriette 238
Wither, George 178, 271
Woolf, Virginia 20, 22, 25, 26, 27, 32, 34, 35, 96
Wordsworth, William 102, 169, 190, 196, 219
Wyatt, Thomas 103
Wycherley, William 90, 91, 144

Yeats, W.B. 28, 114